PSYCHOANALYTIC DISAGREEMENTS IN CONTEXT

PSYCHOANALYTIC DISAGREEMENTS IN CONTEXT

Dale Boesky

JASON ARONSON

Lanham • Boulder • New York • Toronto • Plymouth, UK

Published in the United States of America
by Jason Aronson
An imprint of Rowman & Littlefield Publishers, Inc.

A wholly owned subsidiary of
The Rowman & Littlefield Publishing Group, Inc.
4501 Forbes Boulevard, Suite 200, Lanham, Maryland 20706
www.rowmanlittlefield.com

Estover Road
Plymouth PL6 7PY
United Kingdom

British Library Cataloguing in Publication Information Available

Library of Congress Cataloging-in-Publication Data

Boesky, Dale.
   Psychoanalytic disagreements in context / Dale Boesky.
     p. ; cm.
   Includes bibliographical references.
   ISBN-13: 978-0-7657-0555-6 (cloth : alk. paper)
   ISBN-10: 0-7657-0555-9 (cloth : alk. paper)
   ISBN-13: 978-0-7657-0556-3 (pbk. : alk. paper)
   ISBN-10: 0-7657-0556-7 (pbk. : alk. paper)
   1. Psychoanalysis. I. Title.
   [DNLM: 1. Psychoanalytic Theory. 2. Dissent and Disputes. WM 460 B6725p 2007]

   RC506.B58 2008
   616.89'17–dc22   2007024942

Printed in the United States of America

♾️™ The paper used in this publication meets the minimum requirements of American
National Standard for Information Sciences—Permanence of Paper for Printed Library
Materials, ANSI/NISO Z39.48-1992.

For
Judy, Elaine
Sara, Amy, and Julie
Jennifer, Rachel, Sacha, Elisabeth, Madeline, and Ben

Contents

Acknowledgments

I WISH TO EXPRESS MY APPRECIATION to colleagues whose work informed my preparations for this book: first, to honor the memory of Dr. Rubovitz-Seitz, for his monumental book *Depth Psychological Understanding: The Methodologic Grounding of Clinical Interpretation*; to Dr. Warren Poland for his unswerving support and wise counsel; and for illumination in the dark corridors of epistemology, ontology, and the philosophy of science, my gratitude to Dr. J. Ahumada, Dr. Marcia Cavell, Dr. Lawrence Friedman, and Dr. Charles Hanly.

Chapter 2 is a modified version of a paper entitled "Analytic Controversies Contextualized" (D. Boesky, 2005; *J Am Psychoanal Assoc;* 53, 835–863). The original version of this article was published in the *Journal of the American Psychoanalytic Association*. It is used with permission © 2005 American Psychoanalytic Association. All rights reserved. Portions of chapter 3 were excerpted from the article entitled "The Something More Than Interpretation," (2005, Boston Change Process Study Group; *J Am Psychoanal Assoc;* 53(3), 693–730). Used with permission. © 2005 American Psychoanalytic Association. All rights reserved.

I thank the *Psychoanalytic Quarterly*, for permission to reprint portions of Ilany Kogan's paper (2003) "On Being a Dead Beloved Child" and portions of its commentary by Charles Brenner, *72*, 727–776.

Excerpts from *The Cambridge Dictionary of Philosophy*, edited by R. Audi (2nd ed., 1999) are reprinted here with the permission of the Cambridge University Press. Copyright 1998. From *Depth-Psychological Understanding: The Methodological Grounding of Clinical Interpretations* by Philip Rubovits-Seitz. Reproduced by permission of Lawrence Erlbaum Associates Inc., a division of Taylor & Francis Group.

Preface

Psychoanalytic Disagreements in Context

A poem is a triumph of association.

—Robert Frost

THIS BOOK REFLECTS THE VIEW that our numerous competing theoretic models deserve careful consideration because they have originated to account for various problems, that each of them succeeds in doing so with varying degrees of success, and that they are all imperfect—but not equally imperfect—and we have no consensual agreement about three interrelated questions: Which models are better? Why are they better? and What methods shall we use to decide those questions? There is, of course, a vast literature about the first two questions, but the literature about our primitive methodology for comparing our diverse theoretic models remains relatively small.

How shall we evaluate our clinical truth claims? Just as our civilization has devised destructive weapons that far surpass our available methods for conflict resolution, so we psychoanalysts have devised multiple theories that far surpass our available methods for evaluation or even comparisons of them. I suggest that one of the reasons for this problem is that we have never codified a methodology of contextualization that could reliably demonstrate the inferential processes by which the analyst arrives at conjectures about the disguised meaning of the patient's associations. This is the location of many of our incoherent disagreements.

Like many other candidates in the sixties, I became an analyst in a climate of certainty and in the era of the hegemony of structural theory. And like those of many other analysts, my views of theory and technique have gradually changed. The collapse of the Soviet empire was greeted by many in a new generation of analysts as a metaphor for the relational manifestos proclaiming the defeat of the hegemony of ego psychology. The revolutionary proposals of the relational turn were also intended to solve the defects of the one-person model. The intersubjective field, a system of interacting subjective worlds that constituted the constructed narratives co-created by the patient and analyst, replaced the authoritarian, depriving, inadvertently subjective "observations" of a non-participating analyst in the one-person model. It is well known that criticisms of the basic therapeutic investigative method of psychoanalysis actually date back to Ferenczi, Balint, Winnicott, and Kohut.

There was much accuracy about the criticisms of ego psychology regarding the omission of the constitutive role of the participating analyst, abstinence, authority, neutrality, and countertransference, but as in every revolution, some of the new relational solutions brought problems of their own. Enough time has passed now for us to consider some of the problems that face us in our efforts to sort out what we have gained but also what we are in danger of losing as a consequence of our continuing science wars in which constructivist epistemology and critical–realism–science have been proclaimed as antinomian opposites.

Freud published the Dora case in 1905, the very year that Albert Einstein announced his special theory of relativity. This revolutionary advance in physics, which changed our perception of the universe so profoundly, held that all measurable motion is relative to some other object and that no universal coordinates exist (Updike, 2007). Analogously, all meaning is relative to some context, and no universal meanings exist outside of context. Although most analysts would agree with that statement, there has been a remarkable dearth of attention to what we might call the special theory of relativity of meaning in the psychoanalytic literature. The central role of context in our understanding of meaning in the psychoanalytic treatment situation will be one of the major topics of this book. All of our understandings of our patients are preceded by and anchored in a contextualization in which the analyst has privileged certain communications of the patient. There can be no assumptions of meaning without contextualization, and yet our methodology of contextualization remains obscure and controversial. The neglect of this problem is all the more remarkable because it has always been, and remains, the Achilles' heel of psychoanalysis.

Whatever our numerous disagreements, all psychoanalysts would still probably agree that psychoanalysis is an investigation of meaning. But our interpretations of latent meaning from the manifest associations of the patient have always been subject to the valid criticism of infinite overdetermination. After all, anything can be said to mean anything. Fenichel called this the weakest link of psychoanalysis, and it remains so. This book calls for renewed attention to this daunting problem that has persisted to the present day. It is an instructive irony to consider that when the polemic about interpretations versus the relationship as the cardinal mutative factor in treatment was raging, there was little attention directed to our confusion about our methodology for the formulation of our interpretations. I suggest that it is precisely this confusion that has been an important source of our polemics between our psychoanalytic scientists and our hermeneuticians. I demonstrate that a good objective in addressing this problem is to clarify the manner in which we contextualize the associations of patients as a means for improving the chances of comparing interpretations within and across models.

But so much attention to context and associations will certainly arouse questions for many analysts. What about the nonverbal communications of our patients and the questions about our diverse epistemologies in recent years? If psychoanalysis is to be defined as the science of intersubjectivity, if empathy is to be our instrument of observation, if the problems with our views of neutrality and authority of the analyst are updated, and if we have no knowledge of the actual reality of the thing in itself, how are we to make valid comparisons of the interpretations of different theoretic models? It can be argued that neither observation nor inference (theory) is itself reality. Therefore, as the argument goes, we never have reality as a third term to compare the adequacy of any knowledge claims to see which is a better approximation to it. With these questions, we have entered the controversies about the various epistemologies that have been proposed for psychoanalysis in recent years. Moreover, my emphasis on the role of context and the associations of the patient presupposes the acceptance of the principle of psychic determinism, and this formerly bedrock assumption has, of course, been challenged long ago—for example, by Schafer (1980), who said,

> Psychoanalysis is an investigation of meaning; . . . once psychoanalysis is viewed as an empathic-introspective method the place of determinism in psychoanalysis is uncertain at best; . . . there must be a constant and close relation between theory, technique, and the phenomena of the psychoanalytic situation; and that psychoanalysis is a unique discipline which *creates* a reality of its own in which things can only appear in a certain way and not in others. These assumptions are at variance with the traditional metapsychological assumptions according to which a natural-science model is accepted as a pre-commitment and an objectivist stand toward data is accepted without question. *According to the objectivist (or empiricist) stand, the data are out there in the world waiting to be encountered; data are discovered rather than constituted within a framework of assumptions and methods.* (p. 83; italics added)

The plan I follow in the book is to anchor my discussion of these topics in detailed clinical material. That allows me to consider the anatomy of these disagreements by directing attention to our often unrecognized diversity of methods for contextualizing the communications of our patients. Therefore, Part I concerns clinical illustrations of the theoretic issues that occupy the second section of the book. After an introductory first chapter, chapter 2 is about the controversy concerning the widely discussed reports by Patrick Casement in his articles and books about his patient who developed a critical impasse during her analysis. Chapter 3 is devoted to a discussion of the work of Daniel Stern and his followers in the Boston Change Process Study Group. Chapter 4 is about one of my own patients as an illustration of the fallacy of the dichotomous view of one- and two-person models. Chapter 5 reports a discussion of a disagreement between two analysts from within the same theoretic model, Dr. Charles Brenner and myself, concerning a case report by Dr. Ilany Kogan. These chapters form the clinical core of the book.

Psychoanalysts would do well to devote greater research to the comparative advantages of each of our theoretic models, but to do so, we will need to clarify smaller questions on lower levels of abstraction. Parallel to the major changes that occur in successful treatment are an entire series of local and minor therapeutic changes that take place during psychoanalysis, and they are heterogeneous, composite, and multilayered. We have confused matters by speaking of change at a level too far up the scale of all the antecedent changes that have to occur. We have asked questions that are too big (Edelson, 1984) and too vague about events that are too complex for us with our present crude methodology for the evaluation of evidence. The clarification of the manner in which we psychoanalysts arrive at inferences about our raw data offers the promise of improving our ability to describe how we think we are supporting our truth claims. Ideally, our confusion of tongues can be ameliorated with the invention of a heuristic lingua franca of contextualizing criteria that will at least allow us to talk to each other rather than past each other.

In the decade or so that I have worked on the ideas for this book, I have progressively reduced the scope of the topics that I could discuss. From the Mount Everest of our problems with the methodology of clinical evidence I gradually carved out the question about the inference of latent from manifest meaning as a neglected aspect of our efforts to compare the work of various psychoanalysts. The current title "Comparative Psychoanalysis" for seminars in many of our institutes is a misnomer because truly meaningful comparisons are impossible as long as our inferential processes remain so ambiguous. It is my intent to stimulate discussion among ourselves about how we can find more rational and productive ways to agree or disagree about the comparative merits of our views about our disagreements. When such disagreements arise,

I argue for the need to anchor such disagreements in clear linkages to the original clinical material.[1]

We know that we work on many levels of abstraction. The inference of assumed meaning from the associations of the patient is the level closest to experience. This is the level where we can best view the manner in which the analyst links his theoretic assumptions to the raw data of the communications of the patient in a treatment session. We immediately encounter an objection. There is no longer a unitary mainstream of clinical theory and practice, and in a number of postpositivist models, associations are de-emphasized because some of these models attempt to correct what they have regarded (with good reason) to be the reductive errors of one-person theoretic models. The use of the inferential power of the associations of the patient has eroded or even disappeared in wide areas of the psychoanalytic community for reasons beyond the scope of this discussion. I discuss the loss to theory and practice that this has caused and argue for the value of attempting a systematic reconsideration of the contextualizing choices and strategies of the analyst at work. I discuss that topic in the first of the three theoretical chapters composing Part II.

To make the reasons for the contextualizing choices of the analyst explicit would be a preliminary step toward a future comparative psychoanalysis that would be more coherent. That is, when we disagree about unrecognized premises, we are talking past each other, and our disagreements are incoherent. It is not news that our methodology for the evaluation of evidence is crude and deficient. To reduce that tendency, I suggest in this book that we need to clarify at the level of clinical data the contextualizing strategies that underlie the far more abstract and visible differences between the competing models. Although I am, of course, influenced by my own bias, this is not a book that knowingly trumpets the superiority of any one theoretic model over another. The scientific enterprise never leads and was never intended to lead to absolute truth, merely to arrive instead at the best currently available explanation for certain phenomena. The main advantage of some day establishing a more reliable comparative psychoanalysis will be to arrive at a more rational eclecticism. Another objection is also visible. To pin so much hope on the concept of contextualization links the justification of our truth claims to hermeneutics, and some argue that this requires us to abandon the definition of psychoanalysis as a science. I strongly disagree with that view and devote a refutation of that argument to the two chapters that end the book, about contextualization and hermeneutics.

These are highly complex issues that bear on the topic of clinical evidence. They include the problems of situating psychoanalysis as a scientific enterprise, the challenges of postmodern pluralism, and the vexing confusion about the relevance of epistemology for clarification of the questions about whether and what the psychoanalyst can observe and what constitutes psychoanalytic "facts." Even if one were to consider only the narrower question of the evaluation of clinical evidence, it would be necessary to consider the question of outcome studies, empiric research, extra-psychoanalytic validation of psychoanalytic hypotheses, third-person assessment of process material, and tape-recorded samples of psychoanalytic treatment data. The relevant problems of psychoanalytic theory, the methodology of evidence, the current disagreements among philosophers about epistemology and ontology are so large and complex that even if I were competent to discuss them all (and I am not), their scope defies even an adequate summary. So, this book is a personal, therefore arbitrary and highly selective discussion of these topics based on a summary of my clinical and teaching experience. Although I am aware of the incompleteness of the ideas I present here, I have become convinced that some preliminary steps are now available that would enhance our ability to engage in more coherent comparisons of data that were generated in our numerous competing theoretic models.

The problems of presenting clinical material are famously difficult. But I am referring here to something different from the widely recognized impossibility of presenting a complete case, the problems of violating confidentiality, or the pitfalls that arise from the irreducible subjectivity of the analyst. Instead, I am referring to the neglected fact that even when a group of analysts from the same theoretic school discusses the detailed notes of a single session taken after the session is concluded, one of our most important unsolved problems emerges more visibly. There are often substantial differences in the data that these analysts who adhere to the same theoretic model will emphasize or privilege versus the information that they might ignore or de-emphasize in their inferential hunches about the meaning of the data. These different contextualizing strategies commonly appear in study groups or meetings where members of the "same" theoretic school are considering the "same" material (see Chapter 5).

The psychoanalytic literature in recent years reflects a useful theoretic pluralism. There is an emerging consensus that there is much value in every one of the competing theoretic models of psychoanalysis—for example, object relational, Kleinian, conflict theory (structural), relational, self-psychology, intersubjectivity, Lacanian, and Winnicottian. Many analysts now agree that each of these models was introduced to solve deficiencies and problems in some of the other models and that each has its own validity and value. But there is a conceptual stowaway hiding in this manifestly reasonable argument. There has been a trend toward confusing the obvious advantages of theoretic pluralism with evidential nihilism—for instance, when we compare clinical experience across models, we are commonly advised to take consolation in the fact that clinical examples never did really prove anything but have always been merely illustrative. Sad to say, that is true. We will benefit from clarifying much better than we have to date why this is true. Too many analysts have merely shrugged their shoulders about this state of affairs for a long time. In fact, this is one of the central problems in the methodology of evaluating clinical evidence, and it dates to the writings of Freud himself. As a consequence, "comparative psychoanalysis," as taught in our institutes and debated in our literature, is in a crude and nascent state.

I want to clearly distinguish between the pursuit of an unattainable canon of contextualization, or rules of evidence, from our devising a practical way to report our methodology of contextualization. This will help to clarify whether analysts in a clinical disagreement are able to define the actual constituent elements of a disagreement or an assertion. At issue is not to achieve the one true theory but to clarify the basis for knowing whether a disagreement can be adjudicated on the grounds of clinical evidence and, if so, to clarify the definition of evidence in a given disagreement. If we discover that the clinical evidence in a disagreement has been gathered in a frame of reference that renders the criteria of evidence logically incompatible with a contradictory view of the evidence, then we can at least agree that we have arrived at a disagreement that cannot be settled on the grounds of evidence. Such disagreements are familiar in religion and politics.

I agree with the view that theoretic eclecticism is necessary and logically inescapable. Yet, evidential nihilism is a fallacy rooted in a mistaken notion about the nature of science as the pursuit of absolute rather than contingent truth. The relevant philosophical and epistemological issues concerning science and truth claims are discussed in a large literature and are beyond the scope of this book. Instead, I discuss these important and difficult problems within the narrower constraints of the topics of associations, contextualization, and hermeneutics, in Part II.

In the struggle to make sense of the enormously complex information that emerges in any one psychoanalytic treatment session, the analyst of some (certainly not all) theoretic schools assumes that it is useful to view the manifest information of the patient's actual words and behavior as being defensively altered or disguised. When that is agreed, the various theoretic models differ in their explanations of what is defensively altered, how it is altered, and what would be advantageous to explain to the patient, but my views in this book rest on the assumption of this one commonality: The manifest communications of the patient disguise emotionally painful latent meanings. All of our models assume that there are emotional issues unknown to the patient that are the cause of the patient's suffering. But there are profound differences in the various views within these models of why the patient doesn't know what the analyst thinks she or he knows. I argue that we have failed to appreciate the consequences of our neglect of one of the bedrock assumptions of some but not all of our current theoretic models: that the sequential patterning of the associations of the patient is defensively determined. In the sense of the proposals of this book, those models that share this view are in this important way more similar to each other than would seem to be the case in the common descriptions of these competing models in our recent literature. And those models that do not derive inference of meaning from the associations of the patient are in a different frame of reference. Attempts to compare phenomena derived in two different frames of reference that are incommensurate, without recognizing the incongruence of this difference, are properly called *category errors*.

Within the theoretic models that share in common this belief in the paramount importance of the seminal significance of the associations of the patient—whatever differences these models might hold with regard to childhood sexuality, the nature of unconscious mental processes, the role of unconscious conflict, the nature of mental activity in early mental life, the role of the analyst in the intersubjective matrix, and so forth—there is another neglected difference that I expose: a disquieting inconsistency among analysts, no matter what their official theoretic allegiance might be, with regard to how closely they attend to the associations of the patient and to how willing the analyst is to discard, de-emphasize, or ignore certain associations. Furthermore, this confusion and disagreement about the importance of contextualizing the patient's *associations*—in contrast to the close monitoring of the psychoanalytic *process*, a la Paul Gray and his followers—is abundantly present to varying extents in every one of our major theoretic models. One of the great ironies that I pursue in this book is that the noisy disagreements in the psychoanalytic community are at the high levels of abstraction, whereas at the experience-near level, the level of what the patient actually says to the analyst, there is striking (erroneous) agreement across models that our criteria for contextualizing (privileging or ignoring) the associations of the patient can be overlooked. I argue here that this assumption is a serious threat to the advance of psychoanalytic science and psychoanalytic pedagogy. Chapters 2–5 illustrate this danger.

Even two analysts from the same theoretic school will predictably often contextualize the "same" clinical material very differently (chapter 5). I have used the protective quarantine of quotation marks to highlight that our erroneous assumption that the contextualization of the patient's associations can safely be neglected has preserved the illusion that we analysts are all listening to the same information when we are with the patient. The actual raw data of the communications of the patient and even the most experience-near conjectures about meaning are different. I propose that we can advantageously expose this problem by introducing the concept of conceptual horizons.[2] What has been insufficiently appreciated is that we have no explicit agreement about the constituent elements of our contextual horizons, even among adherents of the same theoretic model.

By the term *contextual horizon*, I mean a group of associations that are dynamically linked by the contextualizing criteria utilized by the analyst to capture the major dynamic urgency in a given session. This horizon defines the dots that the analyst has chosen to connect (contextualize) from the myriad of associational dots.[3]

To avoid misunderstanding, I clarify that there are many important pieces of information about the patient other than the actual verbal associations that are essential to constituting the contextualizing criteria utilized by the analyst. Thus, I agree that the behavior of the patient in the sense of the total transference described by Betty Joseph and others is critically important, as are the relational communications, the countertransference, the data about the history of the patient, and the entire panoply of the past clinical experience and theoretical orientation of the analyst. It is the absence of attention to the associations rather than their exclusive importance to which I draw attention here.

To my earlier definition of incoherent disagreements, I now add that incoherent psychoanalytic disagreements are the unrecognized opposition of theoretically abstract opinions that have been deracinated from actual experience-near clinical events. This disconnection between actual clinical data and far more abstract inferences "supported" by that data favors tendentious arguments at an abstract level. The disputing psychoanalysts often do not require careful clarification of the clinical events about which they are purportedly disagreeing but have instead too often assumed that their abstract disputes are based on clinical information that can be compared by each party in the dispute when in actuality their data and inferences derive from different frames of reference used to infer meanings from those clinical events. None of this is news. The novelty of my book resides in my emphasis on locating this incoherence in our failure so far to clarify our methods for inferring latent from manifest meanings. I suggest preliminary steps to reduce this ambiguity about our inferential processes by refining our understanding of our methodology for contextualizing the associations of the patient when we infer latent meanings from manifest associations. The profound contextually generative power of the associations of our patients has been obscured by a widespread confusion between technique and epistemology. I emphasize our need to distinguish the obsolete fundamental rule as a technical exhortation versus the associations of the patient as an epistemological foundation for our inferences and conjectures (Spacal, 1990).

This book does not champion any theory against others but attempts to address the neglected question in comparative psychoanalysis of finding a better way to anchor our comparisons of various rival models in a closer view of the actual "raw" clinical data that putatively instantiates the theoretic claims of that model. Part II contains relevant discussions of the epistemic status of associations, and discussions about contextualization and hermeneutics in psychoanalysis.

Notes

1. For a similar view, see Tuckett (1995).
2. Contextual horizons are discussed in chapters 2, 7, and 8.
3. This and related aspects of contextualization are discussed in chapter 8.

References

Edelson, M. (1984). *Hypothesis and evidence in psychoanalysis.* Chicago: University of Chicago Press.

Schafer, R. (1980). Action language and the psychology of the self. *Annual of Psychoanalysis, 8,* 83–92.

Spacal, S. (1990). Free association as a method of self-observation in relation to other methodological principles of psychoanalysis. *Psychoanalytic Quarterly, 59,* 420–436.

Tuckett, D. (1995). Editorial afterthought: The conceptualization and communications of clinical facts in psychoanalysis. *International Journal of Psychoanalysis, 76,* 653–662.

Updike, J. (2007, April 2). The valiant Swabian. *New Yorker Magazine,* pp. 74–78.

1

Introduction

Nothing is less real than realism. Details are confusing. It is only by selection, by elimination, by emphasis, that we get at the real meaning of things.

—Georgia O'Keefe (quoted in Crunden, 2000, p. 284)

W<small>E SHOULD BE WARY</small> about whether we are entitled to strong opinions about our agreements, as well as our disagreements, if we lack information about how an author linked his theoretic assertions and truth claims to the underlying clinical material. A major premise in this book is that we psychoanalysts have been too willing to agree or disagree with each other without knowing enough about the clinical derivation and origin of the debated assumptions. Much of the history of psychoanalytic controversies can be characterized in just that way. It is far more common in our literature to see dogmatic disputes similar to the Casement controversy described in chapter 2 than to read a discussion in which the conclusion was *non liquet* or to read a discussant who indicates that the available data do not allow one to know if the disagreement at issue is about commensurate assumptions. I argue here that after more than a century, it is time for us to demand more information before we can feel sufficiently qualified to have coherent opinions about a variety of theoretic and clinical disagreements. This is exacerbated by a tendency in our history for the authors of potentially valuable ideas to transcribe their views into a new language that has no recognizable articulation with the rest of our literature or to use old terms in different ways without clear and explicit announcements that translations would be required.

Our literature reflects extensive confusion about the links between evidence and inference at a variety of levels of abstraction. In this book, I suggest not a remedy but a preliminary and necessary early step toward an ultimate clarification. Our methodology for linking our theoretic assumptions to the original patient data from which they were derived has always been the most vulnerable point of the entire psychoanalytic enterprise.

That ambiguity arises from the "contextual dependence and inexhaustibility of meaning" (Friedman, 2000, p. 237) of our patients' communications in the psychoanalytic treatment situation. We are well aware that anything that the patient says can be said to mean practically anything. Exuberant plausibility without evidential restraint has always been one of our biggest problems and not so much because psychoanalysts have not known or cared about this problem. Quite the contrary, a vast literature is devoted to it. And although we await a methodology for resolving our theoretic disagreements, how are we to add new knowledge to our field without discarding hard-won prior experience? Not the least of the daunting problems that have kept us from resolving these issues for over a century is our inability to arrive at an agreement about exactly what constitutes "evidence" or whether it is even logically permissible to speak of such a thing as evidence.

Rubovits-Seitz (1998) put the problem as such:

> Paradoxically . . . a vast literature has accumulated on problems of interpretive "technique," that is, whether, what, when, and how to communicate depth-psychological information to patients, while relatively little attention has been paid to our methods of seeking, construing, formulating, and justifying latent meanings, and determinants . . . [i.e.] the methods clinicians employ in the process of interpretive inquiry. (pp. xi–xii)

Of the various commonalities that link our various types of psychoanalysis, there is another neglected bedrock: the shared assumption in each of our models that latent meanings can be inferred from manifest meanings. To be sure, there are profound differences in the views within models about how to translate these latent meanings from the manifest meanings and about what the important meanings are, but there is always a translation in each of our models. That is so even in the strongest relational models where it is held that the emotional experiences of the patient's interacting with the analyst is the key epistemic factor. It is about the epistemological definition of interpretation that an old controversy about meaning has been waged. Does the analyst discover meaning, or is meaning co-created by the patient and analyst? This is one of the several tendentious polarized debates I discuss in this book. And this debate has been between the so-called constructivists (subjectivists) and objectivists in our literature. Against the constructivists is Ahumada (1997a):

Is it then as held by constructivism that truth is made rather than discovered? This seems truer for advertising, politics and rhetoric than for clinical enquiry. While there is no doubt that much that is genuinely new comes forth in the course of the psychoanalytic process the analyst does not make truth. He builds a setup and a holding to frame complex unfoldings which the analysand then accesses, helped by whatever interpretive conjectures he comes to muster. Thus, *epistemic weight falls less on the interpretations as such than on the distinctions brought by the analysand's evolving ability for grasping and processing incoming disclosures.* Per *via di levare*, not *via di porre* and with the distinction between psychoanalysis and psychosynthesis Freud accords the analysand at each point of the clinical process, the role of epistemic arbiter. Our interpretations are not truth injections. (pp. 22–23; italics added)[1]

No matter how slight the mutative role of interpretation of verbalized thought might be in some of our numerous models, the analyst eventually wants to explain something to the patient that the patient had not previously understood. But there is widespread suspicion and criticism of using theory to establish these explanations.

Hirsch (2003), who is himself an adherent of the interpersonal model, stated,

The broad spectrum of interpersonal, relational, and post-modern thinking reflects the development of theories that their proponents wish were not theories. They are theories in part born out of the desire to be atheoretical, and they live in contradiction—or, at best in a dialectical tension between theory and naïve perception. (p. 218)

The same author states, "No one theory can be scientifically demonstrated to be more effective than all the others" (p. 220). That is true, but perhaps equally interesting are such questions as these: Can we scientifically demonstrate that any one theory is effective at all? Can any one theory be scientifically demonstrated to be less effective in dealing with any particular specific problems? Can any one theoretic model be adequately judged by evaluating just one of its constituent theories? If we are unable to scientifically prove that any theory is better or worse than any other about anything at all, then why do we practice in the way that we do?[2] Can there be a comparative psychoanalysis if we shrug our shoulders about these questions? For those who have a wish to contrast theory and practice as polarized opposites, the answers to these questions will appear quite different. Our differences across models occur at every level: what should be translated from one model into another, how to translate, and can a translation even be logically achieved. This is the context in which I am going to discuss the link between our methodology of inference and a proposal to relate this to comparative psychoanalysis.

Glover (1952) called the uncertainties of inferring latent meanings and determinants in clinical data the Achilles' heel of psychoanalysis. In his comments about this, Rubovits-Seitz (1998) said,

> Inferring latent contents is the "stock in trade" of psychoanalysts . . . but the literature on this process is surprisingly meager and does not convey its central role in our clinical and investigative work. Because the construal of latent meanings and determinants is crucial to depth-psychological understanding, we must know as much as possible about the nature and functioning of interpretive methods—their modes of operation, capabilities, limitation, problems, and corrective measures. We have taken these methods largely for granted, however, . . . and have assumed mistakenly that they are more reliable and accurate than they actually are. (p. ix)

Psychoanalysis is a science that has much in common with poetry. That is a view that is rejected as being oxymoronic by many analysts on the right who define science in terms of "well-behaved variables," in the felicitous phrase of Ahumada (1997b). That would be like Gill's proposal (1988) to call psychoanalysis a hermeneutic science. And the link to poetry would be embraced by many analysts on the left as a warrant for evidential nihilism. But the noted poet, translator, and essayist Charles Simic (2005) perhaps unknowingly captured the mordant link between psychoanalysis and poetry in his remarks about the task of translating poetry from one language into another (for a discussion of the role of translation in psychoanalysis, see Goldberg, 1984):

> Translation of poetry is that pigheaded effort to convey in words of another language not only the literal meaning of a poem but an alien way of seeing things. Since poetic imagination cannot fully be detached from the place of origin, no two languages share identical *associations*. Can one truly convey in English the elements that elude the translator's complete understanding and yet contribute to the character of the work for the native reader: In short, can one translate another person's view of reality, which, as it happens, is already a kind of translation. If all writing is a conversion of some subjective or objective reality into language, translation is the most philosophical of all activities. To translate is not only to experience what makes each language distinct, but to draw close to the mystery of the relationship between word and thing, letter and spirit, self and world. To work with fragments of ancient lyric poems, is to return to these questions again and again. As if that were not enough, it's not only the meaning of words that she has to worry about, but also the gaps where the words that once were are no more. The translator in these circumstances is an archaeologist of the invisible whose tools are her learning and her imagination. (p. 28; italics added)

We psychoanalysts have always been vexed by our paradoxical tasks as archaeologists of the invisible. We, too, are translators of another person's view of reality whenever we make an interpretation. If translation can be viewed as another kind of interpretation, we see that we are in the heartland of the hermeneutic endeavor. Just as there are various definitions of science, so are there differing views on exactly what constitutes modern hermeneutics (Friedman, 2000). In a reductive and polarized trend in our literature, there has been a tendency by some to insist on two separate epistemologies in our own culture wars (Snow, 1993). In these disputes, or *science wars,* those who view themselves as scientists adhere to a correspondence theory of truth, and those analysts who view themselves as hermeneuticists define truth in the contingent terms of coherence. The scientists fear that the hermeneutic–relativist–coherence–subjectivist ascendance on the left will destroy psychoanalysis, and the former group says the same about the objectivist–positivist–scientistic group. The contiguous philosophic problems of the proper definition of science and the relation between science and differing epistemologies is, of course, a daunting topic that is beyond the scope of this book. Appendix B contains a list of references concerning psychoanalytic epistemology that I have found especially helpful. There is, of course, a vast literature about these problems, and this book does not resolve these disagreements, which have defied the best minds in our civilization for at least three millennia. I discuss only some of the related issues, insofar as they are linked to the question of how best to compare the justification methods of our various theoretic models.

The problem with our efforts as psychoanalytic translators when we compare findings across theoretic models is that when we justify our translation, we cannot rely on the reliability of the interpretation in any model. There is such a thing as a bad translation (interpretation), and there are some translations that are better than others. We (i.e., in my opinion, which is by no means consensually shared) want to map a correspondence of some kind between the actuality of the suffering of our patients (suffering that existed before the analyst ever had a chance to construct it) and our interpretations. I therefore agree with the view of the epistemology called *critical realism* (Hanly & Hanly, 2001). In fact, I argue that this polarized controversy about science versus hermeneutics is one of a group of tendentious either–or arguments that express the requirements of rhetoric rather than disciplined justification.

At the present time, we work in an era of theoretic pluralism, which has been increasingly the basis for self-congratulation. We are eclectic and open-minded. What good scientist or hermeneuticist isn't? And it certainly is a healthy development for psychoanalysis. But it has been said that the mind, like the mouth, should be open at certain times and not others. The world is round and not flat. Pluralism, as I understand it, does not mean "anything goes"; it doesn't mean an equivalence of all theories. What it does mean is that each of our competing models was introduced to map a part of the psychoanalytic terrain that was imperfectly described by all the other models. Physics in this sense is also pluralistic; think of string theory and quantum mechanics. Physicists do not yet have one theory of everything. One of the advantages of pluralism of theories is the stimulus to recognize deficiencies in existing theories. There is a disquieting parallel between the recent retraction of the concept of limbo by the Vatican and the fate of the concept of the death instinct in our own literature. Would these two retractions have taken so long in groups more congenial to pluralism? Contrary to the view of some hermeneuticists, science does not and never could claim to possess absolute truth. Science aspires to clarifying methods to compare competing explanations of observable data to determine which available theory affords a better explanation of these phenomena. The advantage of theoretic pluralism is the better opportunity to compare theories. But with the increased freedom afforded by pluralism, it is essential that we develop more refined methods for evaluating the justification of the rival views. We have done a far better job of generating new theoretic models than that of validating our existing ones. This has highly consequential relevance for the present state of our views about comparative psychoanalysis. We suffer from a serious asymmetry between our profusion of theoretic models and the paucity of our critical evaluations of each model. I have stated elsewhere (Boesky, 1998) that with the progress brought to us by our theoretic pluralism, we must attend to the obligation of developing a methodology for comparing the justification claims of each of our new models. Studying the justification methodology of a theoretic model is difficult enough, but it is a more modest enterprise than that of validating the truth claims of the model.

I agree with the view that our theoretic pluralism has created a healthy ferment, but I conclude that our theoretic inventiveness has outstripped our methods for comparing the data and claims generated by each of these numerous models. I refer without exception to all of the models encompassed or informed by conflict theory and relational theory, as well as Kleinian, Lacanian, self-psychology, intersubjective, interpersonal, object relations attachment, constructivist, complexity, Winnicottian, Loewaldian views, and so on. Merely summarizing this familiar inventory does no justice to the fact that many analysts are eclectic and cannot be accurately described as belonging to any one school. Yet, in comparative psychoanalysis, we seem to speak mostly of pure culture conflict theorists, object relationists, Lacanians, or Kleinians. Comparative psychoanalysis is increasingly a feature of the curricula in many, if not most, of our institutes, and it is usually taught fairly, in a balanced manner. Efforts in these seminars are usually made to investigate in some depth the nature of the questions and problems that stimulated the formation of the particular model under discussion. But, in general, these seminars are reading seminars, and there is not much rigorous attention to how the particular model derives its abstract theory from the clinical data generated within that model. When clinical material is discussed in these seminars, it is too often merely illustrative, and the methodology of inference from data to theory is scanted. Consider the exponentially increased complexity of understanding the eclectic shifts that occur when the analyst applies more than one model in various sessions or in various portions of one session.

It has been said that it is easier to understand mankind than to understand a single man.[3] Like any scientific or poetic enterprise, psychoanalysis has always been concerned with the dialectic between the universal and the particular. Bach (1998) cited a poet to illustrate:

> We do not know the Hells and Heavens of people we pass in the street. There are two possible perspectives. According to the first, on a miniscule ball of earth, in a smudge of mold called a city, some microorganisms move around, less durable than mayflies. And the internal states of [such] beings, deprived of any reason for their existence, perfectly interchangeable, what importance can they have? According to the second perspective, that of a reversed telescope, every one of these beings grows up to the size of a cathedral and surpasses in its complexity any nature, living or inert. Only in the second case can we see that no two persons are identical and that we may at best try to guess what is going on inside our fellow men. (p. 657, quoting Milosz, 1986, p. 120)

Thus it has been easier for us to "explain" the outcome of an entire analysis than to come to agreement about the usefulness of a single interpretation. I am in strong agreement with the observation of Rubovits-Seitz (1998):

> One of the basic reasons that systematic methods of justifying interpretations are essential scientifically is because interpretations are the first-level inferences, the lowest level of theoretical statements of psychoanalysis and dynamic psychotherapy, and as such they are the only propositions that can be tested by direct empirical evidence, that is, evidence from the case being studied. Higher level theories are tested in other ways. The evidential base of clinical interpretations is a major source of controversy in debates about the scientific status of psychoanalysis. . . . *Without generally accepted criteria of evidence for interpretation, every clinical finding and scientific claim of psychoanalysis and dynamic psychotherapy must be questioned.* (p. 212; italics added)

In view of our lower-level confusion, the abstract battles at higher levels of abstraction about the claimed advantages of the various theoretic models would therefore appear to be overly ambitious. In Chekhov's correspondence with the novelist and playwright Ivan Shcheglov, there is included a letter in reply to Shcheglov's criticism (May 29, 1888) for ending his story "Lights" with the words "You can't figure anything out in this world." Chekhov replied on June 9:

> A psychologist should not pretend to understand what he does not understand.
> Moreover, a psychologist should not convey the impression that he understands
> what no one understands. We shall not play the charlatan, and we will declare
> frankly that nothing is clear in this world. Only fools and charlatans know and
> understand everything. (quoted in Malcolm, 2000, p. 244)

I think, in this sense, Chekhov would have concluded that it is something of such a fool's errand for us to be arguing about the rival truth claims of these various theoretic models at this time when we know so little about how these claims were derived. Too much of our literature is stridently and dogmatically free of negative capability or uncertainty. I refer to the common examples of authors whose truth claims rest on a dearth of clinical facts. The focus in this book is therefore not on truth claims or proof in comparative psychoanalysis. (Although it may be obvious that I have a strong bias, I try to remember in this book that I do not have a horse in this race.) Instead, I attempt to show that we are often disagreeing with each other incoherently because we do not recognize that we are arguing with each other about inferences gathered in different frames of reference.

My remarks up to this point reflect the common misconception that our important differences are mostly between the various theoretic models. Our inability to establish the reliability of the inferences of analysts from within the *same* theoretic school has been no secret, but it is insufficiently recognized. We have erred in starting our studies of comparative psychoanalysis from the top down instead of from the bottom up on the ladder of levels of abstraction.

I suggest that comparative analysis should begin with comparisons of disagreements between adherents of the same model instead of with the disagreements of analysts from different models. Instead, we have, for the most part, simply carried over all the ambiguities about our methodology of inference from the days of the alleged monolithic hegemony of mainstream theory to our brave new world of multiple theories. I argue for the advantages of carefully investigating the disagreements between analysts within each of these models to refine our understanding of the anatomy of the inferential processes of the analyst at work. It would be useful in comparing one model with another to specify what methodology exists within the model, if any, for challenging the truth claims in that model.

There is an advantage to the premise that one important commonality across many of the theoretic models is the assumption that it is helpful to explain something to the patient that the patient did not understand previously. It affords us an opportunity to see if we are agreeing or disagreeing in the same frame of reference. That is not to say that interpretations are the primary mutative factor in the theory of change in each of these models or even that interpretations should be viewed as being mutative at all—only that to explain something to a patient that the patient had not understood before (regardless of the explanation for the causes of the patient's ignorance) is common to most of our models. If a theoretic model is based on assumptions that do not call for any kind of interpretation, my suggestion is that we openly acknowledge that we are dealing with a category error when we try to compare the views of that model with the views of a model that gives epistemic weight to interpretations of latent meaning.

The reason is that a psychoanalytic theoretic system inevitably generates a domain of data and inferences. Attempts to compare views without awareness that they derive from different frames of reference is a logical error called a *category mistake*—for example, "to place the activity of showing team spirit in the same class with the activities of pitching, batting and catching is to make a category mistake" (Audi, 1999, p. 123). A second illustration of category mistake is the attribution to an entity of a property that the entity cannot have (and not merely does not happen to have), as in "this memory is violet." Category mistakes reveal a basic and unrecognized misunderstanding of the nature of the things being discussed. Incoherent disagreements are often fostered by unrecognized category errors.

I suggest here that careful attention to comparing the methodology of inference will reveal that some of our polemics about rival truth claims represent unacknowledged category mistakes. In this book, I discuss a methodology of inference that is anchored in assumptions about the basic importance of the associations of the patient and how those associations are contextualized by the analyst. A psychoanalytic model that derives from clinical data other than the associations of the patient is therefore in a different category. Much will be gained if we begin to sort out which of our models can and cannot be compared with other models—for example, models can be compared on the basis of their explanation of how to conceptualize the role of experience in childhood. To cite a different example of so many that are possible, the modern Kleinian and modern Freudian models are clearly separated by certain assumptions, such as the notion of internal objects, but these two models are in the same category with regard to their privileging the inference-generating importance of the associations of the patient, and in this sense, they certainly can be logically compared. That is not true of a radical constructivist–interactive model that derives important explanations from the spontaneous co-created flux of the interaction with the analyst in which the inferential value of the associations of the patient had not been coherently utilized. That does not make the former models better than the latter, but it does mean that we are talking past each other until we recognize this difference when we have disagreements. The battleground of our historical controversies is strewn with the corpses of straw men.

It would be misleading to speak of defining interpretation in a manner narrow enough to be accurate and broad enough to include all of the varieties of interpretation in all of our models. So, as a starting point, I speak of interpretations loosely, in the general sense of explanations about unconscious ideas and feelings offered to the patient by the analyst. And even though doing so would be but a beginning, we immediately confront our confusion of categories because *unconscious* is a word used quite differently in some of our theories—for example, the dynamic unconscious of Freud, the "dynamical" unconscious of implicit relational knowing (Boston Change Process Study Group, 2005a, 2005b), and the relational unconscious (Zeddies, 2000) are three different frames of reference. The latter two are more alike, but both are radically different than the first.

This clarification of frames of reference affords us the opportunity to reconsider the following question: Can we logically compare the defensive ignorance produced by repression with the cognitive ignorance underlying gaps in procedural memory? There is an integral link between the associations of the patient and the inferential processes of the analyst. And if we agree with that conclusion, we are forced to consider that the organization of these associations into some plausible interpretation is integrally linked to the contextualization of these associations. Here we arrive at a useful way to view the daunting complexity of these inferential processes of the analyst at work, and here we see the ambiguities that have fueled our science wars. Strong constructivists claim that the integral link between interpreting and observing is a fatal flaw because observing can only mean a carryover of all the flaws of positivism, the one-person model, and the neutral–authoritarian analyst. The scientists among us often claim that the link between interpretation and hermeneutics automatically nullifies serious consideration because hermeneutics can only mean the use of a constructivist, subjectivist pluralism and silly endless relativism in which there is no anchor in any external reality. Although I view psychoanalysis as a science, I think we would make a serious mistake if we ignored the value of the hermeneutic tradition for its heuristic vitality in clarifying our methods of contextualization. In the ensuing discussion, I try to give persuasive voice to the less extreme arguments of both sides.

For over a century, the inexhaustibility of meaning and the arbitrariness of its inferences of meaning have been the charges leveled against psychoanalysis from outside the psychoanalytic community. As I discuss at a later point, serious challenges to our methodology of interpretation have been brought to bear from within our ranks on the basis of the alleged Popperian positivism of our observations and theoretic conclusions and the fateful consequences of our ignorance of the hermeneutic tradition. Indeed, with the ascendance of postmodern pluralism, a number of epistemological arguments have been mounted in which the validity or accuracy of our interpretations has been replaced by the aspiration for coherence and internal narrative consistency.

Clearly, the inferential processes utilized by the analyst to arrive at an interpretation are complex, and we are fortunately more appreciative of this problem today than what was true in decades past. But this increased awareness of the ambiguities inherent in our interpretations has not led to much improvement in refining our understanding about how we formulate inferences. Instead, and too often, this complexity has become an argument against the pursuit of evidence.

Our inability to fill this long-standing gap in our theory is one of the major reasons that we have no consensually accepted methodology to guide us in understanding how the analyst infers meanings from the raw data of the patient's communications. To be sure, this topic is pursued in supervision of our candidates, in continuous case seminars, and it is scattered through our literature. But it is nevertheless still true that one can predict that if a group of analysts listen to an analytic session and discuss their understanding of what is going on, they will certainly agree part of the time, but it is equally true that they will often disagree even though they all officially adhere to the same theoretic model. We would gain a great deal if we could clarify better than we have why this disjunction has been such a neglected topic for so long. "Our theory is better than their theory" between theoretic models is not disconnected from "I am a better analyst than she or he" within a given model.

The link between the associations of the patient and the inferences of the analyst has been the terra incognita of our theoretic maps since the dawn of psychoanalysis. This has always been the weakest link in our theoretic systems, regardless of what model is at issue. One reason why epistemology became a prominent issue was the accelerating controversy about whether it was possible to speak logically of an observing analyst.

More analysts today no longer accept the idea of the analyst as a detached, nonparticipating observer, but I argue that omitting the observational role of the analyst for that reason reflects a misunderstanding of these tendentious views of an antinomian polarity between subjectivity and objectivity. Such was the view expressed in the now increasingly outmoded one-person model but also in some of the stronger relational models as well. If the analyst is to be viewed as a participant in the very process that she or he is observing and if we fully accept the inevitable influence of the subjectivity of the analyst in observing while participating, is it ever possible to capture the elusive essence of the actual clinical experience? This has gradually become one of the bases for a nihilistic attitude in some of our literature about the futility and even the harm of pursuing clinical evidence to support theoretic ideas.

There has been a fateful joining of the argument that observation is logically impossible with the discarding or de-emphasis of associations. This again relates to confusion about one-person and two-person theoretic models. Observation by the analyst, one-person models, and free associations have been erroneously welded together. Observation, association, and the one-versus two-person domain is actually a loosely coupled group of concepts. In this fallacious argument, it has been insisted that observing must be linked only to a one-person theoretic model. In chapter 4, I give a detailed clinical example illustrating that this is still another misleading either–or argument. In that illustration, I demonstrate the analyst's shifting back and forth from the interpersonal domain of interaction to the intrapsychic domain of observing and then contextualizing the associations of the patient.[4]

With the ascendance of postmodern pluralism, constructivism, and subjectivism, the external criticisms against psychoanalysis for being unscientific were joined by those critics within the psychoanalytic community who rejected the claim that psychoanalysis should be viewed as a science at all. What became clearer in the 1990s was that the pluralism of postmodern coherence–constructivist epistemology, at least in the minds of some of our colleagues, constituted a fatal challenge to the idea of pursuing clinical evidence. Such a pursuit was dismissed as a vestige of scientistic positivism, and the definition of knowledge—based on a coherence theory of truth rather than a correspondence theory of truth—became increasingly influential in the United States. Indeed, that is still the case. Of course, the attendant problems of supporting truth claims had been noted by the enemies of psychoanalysis from without and by constructive critics from within. But the closed, monolithic tone of our literature had changed substantially by the 1990s, and pluralistic views gained an ascendance. The convergence of attacks on the interpretive methodology of psychoanalysis from within and without psychoanalysis constituted a withering confluence of attacks against the legitimacy of the notion of psychoanalytic evidence.

Here we confront still another source of confusion. It is erroneously held by a number of analysts that if contextualization is to be viewed as a major component of the inference of meaning, then we are espousing hermeneutics as a defining feature of psychoanalysis. This is then claimed to be a fatal argument to the possibility of viewing psychoanalysis as a science. I argue against that view in chapter 8. Suffice it here to say that hermeneutics is not in itself an epistemology. Hermeneutics is an ancient, rich, and complex group of views about interpretation—originally, only the interpretation of texts. But especially in the last century, the problems of interpretation were extended into the entire realm of knowledge, as hermeneutic ideas became linked to ontological and epistemological controversies. The polemics of the culture wars between the arts and the sciences came then to gradually include a similar fault line among psychoanalysts, which illustrates the problem of reductive polarized antagonism between adversaries who misread each other and refuse to acknowledge the usefulness of objections from the other side. The hermeneutic tradition has much to teach us about the thorny problems of contextualization, and we psychoanalysts will lose a great deal if we do not deal with the challenges that hermeneutics has leveled against our epistemological assumptions. I argue that the either–or view that psychoanalysis is either a science or a branch of hermeneutics is still another example of these flaws in dichotomous thinking.

The postmodern turn followed the cultural pluralism in universities around the world as the Berlin Wall fell and epistemological considerations were invoked to support the relativistic advantages of all theories. Just as some analysts now turn to neuroscience, cognitive psychology, or attachment theory to support their views of psychoanalysis as a science, others have used philosophy to support their views that psychoanalysis should be viewed as a hermeneutic enterprise. It is one thing to be sure that we do not make assumptions that contradict established knowledge gained from other disciplines. But it is quite another to rest our justification methods on flimsy analogies across disciplines without turning to our own clinical work for our primary methods of justification. Appendix B suggests some selected readings about this topic. In that work, Hanly (1990, 1992, 1995, 1999) and Ahumada (1994a, 1994b, 1997a, 1997b) have issued a much needed clarification about the erroneous idea that there is a philosophic warrant for abandoning the notion of psychoanalysis as a science. But we cannot afford to remain ignorant about the important contributions to psychoanalysis from the hermeneutic tradition over the span of many centuries. Our institutes would benefit from including seminars about the relevance of epistemology to psychoanalysis. The major points I stress relate to the fact that the polarized view of psychoanalysis as either a science with a correspondence–realist epistemology or as a branch of hermeneutics with a coherence–idealist epistemology is a false dichotomy. Dichotomous and polarized thinking has vexed the history of psychoanalytic disagreements since the beginning of our history.[5]

We have been arguing about our truth claims and too often assuming that we need not clarify our methods of justification. That has seriously flawed our understanding. The term *justification* is borrowed from a much older philosophic tradition: "In epistemology we need to distinguish justification from truth, since either of these might apply to a belief in the absence of the other" (Audi, 1999, p. 457). (Also see Appendix A, p. 216.)

The term *justification* would be useful in improving our understanding of our methodology of evaluating clinical evidence. As I am using the term, I intend it to mean the methods used by psychoanalysts to support their theoretic assumptions with the associations of the patient—or, in the case of those models that de-emphasize the associations of the patient, to spell out how their data from the patient links to their theoretic assumptions. When we ask a psychoanalyst to justify his or her assumptions about the patient, we are saying, "Tell me clearly what the patient did or said that justifies or entitles you to assume such and such about that patient." We are not asking our colleague to prove that what he or she said was true, only to say why he or she thinks it might be. That is the difference between justification and truth. Learning more about the comparative justification of theoretic inferences and assumptions than about comparative truth claims across diverse models would be far more realistic at this still early development in our crude methodology for evaluating evidence. I return to the topic of justification in the chapter on hermeneutics. The absence of clarity about justification is a root cause of the problem in our literature and in our meetings when we disagree with colleagues at high levels of abstraction with no real information about the lower-level inferential processes in such disputes. There is a neglected irony here. Within an individual theoretic model, a number of analysts believe that they are agreeing, but their agreements are at the higher levels of abstraction and not at the lower.[6]

Clearly, it is easier to prolong debates when there is inadequate clinical information. It is my belief those the deracination of theoretic conclusions from clinical details is the cause of many of our controversies as well as a pathognomonic symptom of this disjunction of clinical facts and abstract theories. Our failure to develop a consensually accepted canon of correspondence between clinical details and theoretic assumptions has legitimized the plausibility of many erroneous ideas past and present. But it is not that if we were only provided more clinical information, we could settle our disagreements. Quite the contrary. The reason is that we have no consensus about what we need to know—for example, many contemporary clinical reports clearly indicate that there is no need to know sexual information about the patient.

This prevalence of incoherence in our controversies is not by any means due to a cavalier attitude toward the absence of relevant clinical data. In fact, since the very inception of Freud's earliest work, we have been vexed by our inability to report our clinical experiences persuasively. Over the span of a century, from Freud's first apologies for case histories that sounded more like fiction than science to our present confusion about how to even define a clinical fact, we have had no agreement on what exactly we want a psychoanalytic author to tell us for us to feel persuaded about the plausibility of the author's views.

We are immediately confronted with daunting problems. If a disagreement is deemed to be incoherent when the details of its underlying actual clinical experience cannot be logically related to its inferred theoretic assumptions, could we have a consensual understanding of the nature of any actual clinical experience if only we were told more or even if we were told everything about the clinical material? We could not. The problem of defining what else we want to know about the patient from available case reports is well known (see Michels, 2000). And as we know so well, from the side of the treating analyst, a mere recording of the raw associations of the patient in a session cannot include the essential private and subjective experience of the patient or the analyst in the dyad, whose interaction with the patient is a vitally important constituent component of the actual clinical experience.

In some instances, we are drowning in the blooming, bustling confusion of clinical details with no agreement about what to do with that information. In fact, we have no consensual agreement about what constitutes adequate clinical information—adequate for which hypotheses in relation to which data? Nor does this sketchy summary do justice to the actual complexity of the problems with our confusion about the relation between clinical detail and theory.

The disconnection between clinical data and far more abstract inferences supported by those data favors tendentious arguments at an abstract level.[7] As psychoanalysts, we do not often require careful clarification of the clinical events about which we are purportedly agreeing or disagreeing. Instead, we too often assume that our abstract assumptions are based on a clear understanding of how clinical information was contextualized by each analyst and thus eligible to be compared by each party in the dispute. In actuality our data and inferences too often derive from very different methods of contextualization, used to infer meanings from those clinical events. None of this is news. What is novel in this book resides in my proposals to reduce this ambiguity about our inferential processes by directing our attention to a better understanding of our methodology for contextualizing the associations of the patient when we infer latent meanings from manifest associations. This proposal introduces problems because there is no consensus among psychoanalysts about the role that associations should play in the treatment situation. I discuss selected aspects of these topics relating to contextualization in chapters 6, 7, and 8.

To be clear, I wish to say that my use of the term *associations* in this book includes all of the communications of the patient, not only the verbal associations.[8] I want to emphasize that nothing said here is intended to omit the vitally important significance of nonverbal, noninterpretive relational factors in evaluating clinical evidence in any model. When I refer to the inferences of the analyst from manifest content, I include every aspect of the patient's communications and behavior, including the nonverbal. I also include the effects of the verbal and nonverbal behavior of the analyst in our evaluations of the conjectures and inferences of latent meaning made by the analyst. I am using the broadest possible definition of associations of the patient as an umbrella term to provide a theoretic basis for the assumption that psychic determinism is relevant to all of the patient's communications during the treatment—behavioral, nonverbal, and verbal—and not only to the verbalized associations of the patient. I discuss this further in chapters 5 and 6. My point of difference with our literature on this issue lies in the erosion and, in some instances, the almost total disappearance of attention to the associations of the patient.

To advocate justification methods that depend on evidence and to suggest that some theories offer better explanations of certain problems than others is viewed by some strong constructivists as merely an elitist or political bias. That may be part of the reason for our current disquieting tendency to dismiss the important and gritty contradictions that are perforce introduced when we compare clinical data derived from quite different frames of reference and, therefore, from different frames of observation. It is consoling instead to emphasize our commonalities but not much more effective than it has been in the United Nations. Another argument is that the very assumption that there can be such a thing as evidence is a scientistic carryover of the fatally flawed epistemology of logical positivism. Such a view reflects a misunderstanding of the nature of science and the place of positivism in the history of philosophic disagreements in the last two centuries.

I have gained the impression that the use of philosophy to support opposing views in psychoanalytic disputes is similar to the use of information from outside psychoanalysis, from other disciplines such as neuroscience, cognitive psychology, and attachment theory. It is one thing to be sure that we do not make assumptions that contradict established knowledge gained in other disciplines, but it is quite another to rest our justification methods on flimsy analogies across disciplines without turning to our own clinical work for our primary methods of justification. My purpose in this book is to expose the incoherent nature of many of our clinical disagreements rather than to advocate for a special point of preference. I demonstrate that without information of a detailed kind about how and why theoretic claims were derived from the relevant clinical events, it is often the case that parties in a disagreement are talking past each other and thereby disagreeing incoherently. It would be vastly premature to claim that even if we could always arrive at coherent disagreements, we would be able to know who was correct in a theoretic dispute. And it is quite possible—indeed, it is more likely—that both parties in an incoherent dispute are at least partially correct but for reasons that one or both of them had not previously understood. It would be no small achievement if we could demonstrate that certain of our disagreements about theory were capable of additional support or refutation and that others could never be resolved with evidence.

An illustrative example of the latter form of controversy would be the current political–educational disagreement about the teaching of evolution in our schools. In many segments of the U.S. population, the plausibility of an intelligent designer responsible for the evolution of species is already settled in spite of the evidence, not because of it. Persons on the Kansas Board of Education with graduate degrees recently maintained that the world was created 6,500 years ago and that this belief has nothing to do with their scientific opinions, because it is a part of their faith. They say that they, too, have a pluralistic view of reality, that there are many different realities, and that it is a sign of intolerant, antireligious bias to object to the equivalence of scientific and spiritual reality. It has been said that in scientific disputes, when the facts do not fit the theory, one must change the theory. In religious disputes, the opposite is true. When the facts do not fit the theory, one changes the facts. It is in just this sense that a number of our heated and polarized psychoanalytic disputes have a religious character.

But for many analysts, such concerns about evidence seem quaint and outmoded. The use of clinical evidence to support or refute either side of a theoretic or clinical disagreement has fallen for some into the shadows of postmodern relativism and for others into pragmatism. Many of our controversies degenerate into the mere question of who is right and who is wrong. We want winners and losers. Too often, the term *evidence* has become a synonym for *truth*. A closer examination of what we are disagreeing about and a careful examination of how either side in a disagreement supports their views will often reveal surprising and misleading assumptions by both sides. In this book, I use the term *evidence* narrowly, to refer to justification for beliefs rather than as proof of any claims.

Still another supporting argument for evidential nihilism is based on the false assumption of equifinality: We "know" that all experienced practitioners get comparable results no matter what their theoretic adherence might be, and this in turn is supported by empiric outcome studies, often without information about how the outcome was attained. For many analysts, my assertion about the incoherence of many of our disagreements is itself a fatal error because, as this argument goes, there is no way to determine which clinical reality would be relevant. A paraphrased version of this argument goes like this: What you do not acknowledge is that you never have reality as a third place from which to compare the adequacy of any knowledge claims to see which is a better approximation to it; all you have are various versions of observation and inference, none of which can rely on direct access to the thing in itself to support its claims.

This statement is self-contradictory in that its strong repudiation of claims about reality is itself rooted in the assumption that this view itself is better than another.[9] After all, if the adherents of this view want us to share it, they must believe that it is not merely constructed. More important to the purposes of this book, however, is not to settle philosophic issues that have remained unresolved for millennia. My purpose is to advocate the view that if the persons engaged in a psychoanalytic disagreement were better able to demonstrate the links between their actual clinical experience and their theoretic inferences about those experiences, then we could finally say, "At least I now know more clearly what it is exactly we are disagreeing about." That is quite different from proving anything at all. It would be a useful contribution, however, to deciding whether one explanation fits the available information better than another does. It is my hope that exposing this problem and offering some suggestions about initial steps to remedy it will augment the further development of our much-needed discipline of comparative psychoanalysis.

I describe in this book some preliminary findings about a method that is amenable to comparison of some, but not all, differing theoretic models and is grounded in careful reading of process material that would allow for better intermodel clinical comparisons. This method consists of comparing the contextualizing criteria utilized by various analysts in supporting their theoretic claims based on careful examination of process material. This method is even more valuable in comparing the various inferences that are made by analysts who nominally adhere to the same theoretic model but who derive different meaning from the same clinical material. Shedding light on our intramodel disagreements is a neglected path to the vastly more complex task of evaluating intermodel disagreements.

Logic and experience suggest that our numerous theories are not all of equal value and that we need to devise better methods for comparing the strengths and weaknesses of each model. It is the central thesis of this book that clarifying our methodology of contextualization will help us to resolve our disagreements more coherently.

Notes

1. I return to this topic in chapter 8 in the discussion of hermeneutics.
2. On this basis, Fonagy (2003) goes so far as to make the following suggestion: "If theory were decoupled from practice, technique might progress on purely pragmatic grounds, on the basis of what is seen to work" (p. 13).
3. Quoted by Poland (1996) from Rochefoucauld.
4. For a discussion of the analyst's oscillating between one- and two-person models, also see Boesky (1990).

5. Dichotomous, polarized disputes are further discussed in chapter 8 (see also, Bach, 1998; Rubovits-Seitz, 1998).

6. I give detailed examples of the illusory assumption of intramodel agreement in chapter 2 about the Casement disagreements and also in chapter 5 about the disagreement between Brenner and Boesky about the Kogan case.

7. It is equally and ironically true that unquestioned agreements have turned out to have been incorrect.

8. This includes the "total situation" (Joseph, 1985).

9. In the most radical forms of perspectivism, the very idea of evidence is an epistemological fallacy. In this view, all that we can know is what we construct, and meaning is always limited to local contexts. This was the view so effectively attacked in the hoax perpetrated by the physicist Alan Sokal (2000), who published a mock essay about the cultural and constructed elements of the mathematical constant pi. But there is a powerful argument against the radical perspectivists (I distinguish radical perspectivists from disciplined eclecticists). The objections of those who reject the idea that psychoanalysis is a science because such a view depends on outmoded positivism and scientism are in turn open to a powerful criticism raised by Bernard Williams (1998) and other philosophers of science. If the more radical hermeneutic "postmodern" analysts wish to maintain that their criticisms are sufficiently powerful to discredit the view that psychoanalysis is a science, then they must admit that they believe that they have made objections that they themselves do not consider to be local in time, culture, relevance, and place. They cannot have it both ways. They want us to believe that their view of things is about things as they actually are. Why else would they bother to try to persuade us?

References

Ahumada, J. (1994a). Interpretation and creationism. *International Journal of Psycho-Analysis, 75,* 695–707.

Ahumada, J. (1994b). What is a clinical fact? Clinical psychoanalysis as inductive method. *International Journal of Psycho-Analysis, 75,* 949–962.

Ahumada, J. (1997a). Disclosures and refutations: Clinical psychoanalysis as a logic of enquiry. *International Journal of Psycho-Analysis, 78,* 1105–1118.

Ahumada, J. (1997b). Toward an epistemology of clinical psychoanalysis. *Journal of the American Psychoanalytic Association, 45,* 507–530.

Audi, R. (1999). *Cambridge dictionary of philosophy* (2nd ed.). Cambridge, England: Cambridge University Press.

Bach, S. (1998). Two ways of being. *Psychoanalytic Dialogues, 8,* 657–673.

Boesky, D. (1998). Clinical evidence and multiple models: New responsibilities. *Journal of the American Psychoanalytic Association, 46,* 1013–1020.

Boston Change Process Study Group. (2005a). Response to commentaries. *Journal of the American Psychoanalytic Association, 53,* 761–769.

Boston Change Process Study Group. (2005b). The "something more" than interpretation revisited. *Journal of the American Psychoanalytic Association, 53,* 693–730.

Crunden, R. (2000). *Body and soul: The making of American modernism.* New York: Basic Books.

Fonagy, P. (2003). Some complexities in the relationship of psychoanalytic theory to technique. *Psychoanalytic Quarterly, 72,* 13–48.

Friedman, L. (2000). Modern hermeneutics and psychoanalysis. *Psychoanalytic Quarterly, 69,* 225–264.

Gill, M. (1988). Metapsychology revisited. *Annual of Psychoanalysis, 16,* 35–48.

Glover, E. (1952). Research methods in psychoanalysis. *International Journal of Psychoanalysis, 33,* 403–409.

Goldberg, A. (1984). Translation between psychoanalytic theories. *Annual of Psychoanalysis, 12,* 121–135.

Hanly, C. (1990). The concept of truth in psychoanalysis. *International Journal of Psycho-Analysis, 71,* 375–383.

Hanly, C. (1992). Inductive reasoning in clinical psychoanalysis. *International Journal of Psycho-Analysis, 73,* 293–301.

Hanly, C. (1995). On facts and ideas in psychoanalysis. *International Journal of Psycho-Analysis, 76,* 901–908.

Hanly, C. (1999). On subjectivity and objectivity in psychoanalysis. *Journal of the American Psychoanalytic Association, 47,* 427–444.

Hanly, C., & Hanly, M. (2001). Critical realism. *Journal of the American Psychoanalytic Association, 49,* 515–532.

Hirsch, I. (2003). Analysts' observing participation with theory. *Psychoanalytic Quarterly, 72,* 217–240.

Joseph, B. (1985). Transference: The total situation. *International Journal of Psycho-Analysis, 66,* 447–454.

Malcolm, J. (2000, February 21–28). Travels with Chekhov. *New Yorker Magazine,* p. 244.

Michels, R. (2000). The case history. *Journal of the American Psychoanalytic Association, 48,* 355–375.

Milosz, C. (1986). *Unattainable earth* (C. Milosz & R. Hass, Trans.). Hopewell, NJ: Ecco Press.

Poland, W. (1996). *Melting the darkness.* Northvale, NJ: London.

Rubovits-Seitz, P. F. (1998). *Depth psychological understanding: The methodological grounding of clinical interpretation.* Hillsdale, NJ: Analytic Press.

Simic, C. (2005, November 3). The spirit of play: *Decreation: Poetry, essays, opera,* by Anne Carson Knopf. *New York Review of Books,* pp. 28–30.

Snow, C. (1993). *The two cultures.* Cambridge, England: Cambridge University Press.

Sokal, A. (2000). *The Sokal hoax.* Lincoln: University of Nebraska Press.

Williams, B. (1998, November 19). The end of explanation: Review of *The last word,* by Thomas Nagel. *New York Review of Books.* Available at https://www.nybooks.com/articles/article-preview?article_id=678

Zeddies, T. (2000). Within, outside, and in between: The relational unconscious. *Psychoanalytic Psychology, 17,* 467–487.

I
CLINICAL EXAMPLES

2

Psychoanalytic
Controversies Contextualized:
A Model of Clinical Disputes

The very idea of empirical certainty is irresistibly comical.

—C. S. Peirce (1955, p. 3)

There are the trivial truths and the great truths. The opposite of a trivial truth is plainly false. The opposite of a great truth is also true.

—N. Bohr

THE INFERENCE OF LATENT MEANING from the associations of the patient is the central task of the analyst and the patient who is on the path to therapeutic change.[1] But for many reasons, psychoanalysts have never developed a consensually accepted canon of rules of evidence for deriving inferences from these associations. We know all too well that various analysts derive different meanings from the same clinical material. But it still is not sufficiently appreciated that this defect in our methodology has obscured the fact that many of our psychoanalytic controversies have been prolonged because the adversaries were really talking past each other.

Analysts differ a great deal in the way that we organize the associations of the patient as we are listening. The artificial description of the analyst's listening with free-floating attention, innocent of memory or desire and refraining from imposing bias on the data, is a fiction that seems to persist in spite of the correctives in our abundant literature on the irreducible subjectivity of the analyst. This helpful concern about our subjectivity has, to date, primarily emphasized the emotionally constituted subjectivity of the analyst and neglected the important problem regarding our confusion about how the analyst contextualizes the communications of the patient.

The inference of latent meanings from manifest data is a bedrock concept for all forms of psychoanalysis, and future historians of our field will no doubt investigate why we were content for so long to allow our inferential processes to remain so ambiguous. Whether within one theoretic model or in comparing different theoretic models, we have learned the hard way that anything that the patient says or does can potentially mean anything. One important reason for this chaotic diversity of inferences lies in our failure to explicitly refine our methodology for defining the essential antecedent precursors of contextualization that will profoundly shape our inferences. Our various models map different explanations for the transformation from the raw data of the patient's associations into the inferred and imputed meanings. Our noisiest controversies have been at the higher levels of abstraction and too uncommonly at the lower experience levels. It is at this lower level that we have the best chance of reconstructing and comparing among ourselves the contextualizing criteria used to infer meaning during individual sessions. The neglect of this information has seriously impeded the development of a methodology for a coherent comparative psychoanalysis.

What we reductively call listening, of course, subsumes a complex array of subprocesses. It is timely to recall that our large literature about the integration of our numerous theoretic models is rather silent about the role of the associations of the patient in how the analyst listens. Certainly it is true that not all analysts in all models give epistemological weight to the associations of the patient. But even within the so-called classical or traditional mainstream U.S. model, it is by no means true that all analysts listen to their patients with their inferential assumptions firmly linked to the conviction that all of the associations of the patient are of potential significance.

What I have to say about contextualizing these associations is rooted in those above assumptions. This is a crucial point because our literature shows that we cannot assume that all analysts have ever privileged a close listening to the sequential unfolding of these associations as an organizing factor in the manner used to achieve contextualization. As the analyst listens, she or he oscillates between mere listening and trying to understand what she or he hears as that which is transformed or altered. In many but not all models, it is assumed that this alteration is defensive. The assumption of some form of alteration is in evidence whenever the analyst offers an interpretation. To be clear, I do not wish to reduce the complex question of what is mutative in the psychoanalytic process to the single factor of interpretation. Instead, I wish to raise questions about the inferential processes of the analyst who decides to explain something to himself or herself and possibly but not always to the patient. In this discussion, I emphasize only one of these processes: a complex reciprocally enhancing and dialectical interaction between trial contextualizations and contextualizing criteria.

By *contextualizing criteria*, I mean any or all of those inferential assumptions employed by the analyst to infer meaning from the raw data. These criteria derive from numerous and diverse levels of abstraction. Putting red beads together must precede deciding if there are more red beads or more blue baubles. Only then can one decide if the red beads are worth more than the blue baubles. Contextualizing criteria filter the communications of the patient and privilege some of them and de-emphasize others. The analyst has used a contextualizing criterion whenever she or he considers whether or not things said by the patient should be linked together or whether certain things said by the patient should be linked to the theoretic ideas of the analyst. Contextualizing criteria are often made preconsciously or unconsciously but not always. These contextualizing criteria represent a vastly diverse group of linking decisions made by the analyst that derive from many different frames of reference. This is another instance where the use of a noun (*criterion*) instead of a verb tends to reify the manner in which we form contextualizing hunches. It would be far closer to my intended meaning to speak of contextualizing processes and ideas because the term *criterion* promises too much certainty, as though the analyst at work had a reliable and repeatable manual of contexts or a canon of contexts.[2]

Our literature is strangely silent about the problem we have with confusion about how to compare alternative contextualizations. Given the daunting complexity of the antecedents and precursors of the inferences at which the analyst arrives, it is nonetheless quite possible to state clearly and exactly what the patient said that was the basis for the inference. But it is a rarity to find such information in our literature, and the discussion that follows illustrates the confusion and errors that arise from ignoring this problem. I am not suggesting that we can catch Niagara Falls in a small bucket or that we can reduce the extraordinary complexity of the exquisitely complex intersubjective interaction of analyst and patient to simple linear accumulations of data. What I am suggesting, instead, is that this very complexity serves too often as an excuse to avoid clearly stating information that is possible to report.

Trial contextualizations by the analyst are the counterpart of trial identifications by the analyst, which are the core of empathy. Just as the analyst must be able to establish a mobile, transient identification with the patient to know what the patient is feeling, so also must the analyst form trial and private contextualizations of what the patient is communicating. I pursue this topic at greater length in chapter 6.

The relation between technique and theory is famously confusing. T. S. Eliot remarked about poetry, "We cannot say at what point 'technique' begins or where it ends."[3] When analysts enter into disputes about technique, they often appeal to theoretic arguments at high levels of abstraction, rather than go back to the original data for evidential challenge. But a number of clinical controversies appear quite different when viewed in the perspective of careful descriptions of how inferences were inductively contextualized from the available data instead of deduced from higher levels of theoretic abstractions or technical rules.[4] Without this contextualizing information, it is far easier to prolong polemics. A specimen of such a dispute is examined here at greater length. I wish to be clear at the outset that my interest in this discussion is not about the pros and cons of technique favored or criticized in the controversy I report here but about the dispute itself as a model specimen about the anatomy of polarized arguments in our literature and discussions.

The article that I discuss to illustrate these problems is "Some Pressures on the Analyst for Physical Contact During the Re-Living of an Early Trauma," by Patrick J. Casement, originally published in 1982.[5] The author subsequently published an expanded version of that article in two books (1991 [as combined from 1985, 1990], 2003) and a response to a number of discussants of this case presentation in its various versions (2000). At the present count, over 25 authors have given major attention to Casement's original report, and the publication of these discussions has become something of a cottage industry to rival other famous cases in our literature. Casement was initially praised for refusing physical contact with his patient (Fox, 1984, 1988; Hoffer, 1991; Katz, 1998; Meissner, 1996, 1998; Roughton, 1993). Later, this case was the topic of an entire issue of *Psychoanalytic Inquiry* (2000, vol. 20, no. 1) wherein Casement was often criticized for this same refusal by a number of other authors (see Breckenridge, 2000; Shane, Shane, & Gales, 2000). Whatever the diversity of views in all these discussions, the one agreement in common was to consider the author's dilemma about technique as predominantly a technical issue. The controversy in this sizable literature is thus about the disagreement concerning the pros and cons of Casement's decision to not hold his patient's hand. The discussants are by no means all in agreement that there should be a rule either way (e.g., Ruderman, 2000), but they are essentially in agreement that this disagreement can be argued on the basis of the clinical needs of the patient without reference to how this patient developed this need during her analysis.

Casement (1982) stated at the outset that he wished to consider an important technical controversy:

> Is physical contact with the patient, even of a token kind, always to be precluded without question under the classical rule of abstinence? Or are there some (extreme) occasions when this might be appropriate, (or) even necessary. I shall present a clinical sequence during which the possibility of physical contact was

approached as an open issue. There seemed to be a case for allowing a patient the possibility of holding my hand. The decision to reconsider this was arrived at from listening to the patient and from following closely the *available* cues from the countertransference. The clinical material clearly illustrates some of the issues involved in this decision. (p. 279; italics added)

Note carefully that the availability of cues is predicated on arbitrarily assumed and unexamined contextualizing criteria. Although I have my own opinions about this dispute, I wish to emphasize that my purpose in this presentation is to neither agree nor disagree with Casement's views or his discussants about whether he should have held his patient's hand. I believe that he is a dedicated, honest analyst who was very helpful to his challenging patient. I further believe that she would have been a difficult patient for me and most other analysts to treat. Instead, I wish to remind you that he said that the decisions that he made in this instance were based on his "*listening* to the patient and from following closely the available cues from the countertransference" (italics added). I attempt to show that his inferential decisions were based on far more complex processes than listening. When we evaluate an interpretation, we simply cannot assume that close listening to the patient or to the countertransference, as advised by Casement and others, is a sufficient guarantee of optimal understanding. I am not referring to what has now become our familiar postmodern insistence on the subjectivity of the analyst. The notion of close listening begs the question of "listening to what?" Even the familiar distinction between listening *to* versus listening *for* is inadequate here. This putative close listening assumes a generic analyst who will hear the same thing as any other analyst if only he or she would pay close enough attention. Of course, the irreducible subjectivists among us will hasten to say, "That is what we have been trying to warn against." But I am not referring here to only the subjectivity of the analyst, which supposedly disqualifies any analyst from being able to observe. I am referring instead to a neglected and widespread problem in the methodology of the manner in which the analyst listens and with which we other analysts evaluate one another's clinical work. It is a problem that deserves to be distinguished from the familiar warnings about the subjectivity of the analyst. I explain what I mean in more detail by using the discussions of Casement's article as an illustration of this widespread problem. In the constraints of this brief discussion, I merely say that my discussion is based on the epistemological assumption that there is an imperfectly knowable real world. It is a position known as *critical realism*. In this view, the term *evidence* connotes the data utilized to support an inferential assumption, and it is not a synonym for perfect and absolute truth. I also therefore assume that an observing analyst is not a contradiction in terms.[6] Because these issues cannot be pursued here, I limit myself instead to an important and neglected problem in the evaluation of interpretations: the consequences of arbitrarily ignoring selected associations of the patient for whatever the reasons—epistemological, countertransferential, irreducible subjectivity, theoretic deficiency, or otherwise. What I emphasize is that the reasons for omitting certain associations from a contextual horizon may be deliberate or inadvertent. The familiar problem I wish to reconsider here is that even two analysts from the same theoretic school will predictably contextualize the same clinical material quite differently and often heatedly. What has been insufficiently appreciated is that we have no explicit agreement about the constituent elements of our contextual horizons, even among adherents of the same theoretic model.

By the term *contextual horizon,* I mean a group of associations that are dynamically linked by the contextualizing criteria utilized by the analyst to capture the major dynamic urgency in a given session.[7] The analyst employing Arlow's contextualizing criteria (1979) of repetition of a theme in the associations of the patient would arrive at a different contextualizing horizon than would the analyst who, at that moment, privileged the information about the relationship with the patient. We learned after 1492 that horizons can be illusory. An advantage to the term *contextual horizon* is its metaphoric insistence that what lies beyond the horizon is not yet visible.

It is often said that our ability to evaluate the usefulness (not a synonym for *validity* or *truth*) of an interpretation depends on the proper understanding of the associations of the patient immediately after the interpretation (Wisdom, 1967). For example, if a patient suddenly recalls a dream or a dynamically relevant memory after an interpretation, it has become part of our oral tradition to assume that the interpretation was correct. But it is not uncommonly the case that bad interpretations can be followed immediately by important new disclosures or new memories or even by the report of a hitherto unreported dream. An additional and less appreciated source of evidence for the evaluation of an interpretation is provided by the associations immediately in advance of the interpretation. These associations provide a contextual and dynamic insight into how the analyst formulated the interpretation and how the patient perceived it. We feel greater assurance about the validity of an interpretation when there is a dynamic congruence between the associations immediately before and after the interpretation.

Casement's Clinical Material

The patient, whom I shall call Mrs. B, is in her 30s. She had been in analysis about 2 1/2 years. *A son had been born during the second year of the analysis (and at this point was about 10 months old).* When she was 11 months old Mrs. B. had been severely scalded, having pulled boiling water on to her while her mother was out of the room. She could have died from the burns. When she was 17 months old she had to be operated on to release growing skin from the dead scar tissue. The operation was done under a local anesthetic. During this the mother had fainted. *It is relevant to the childhood history that the father was largely absent during the first five years.* Soon *after the summer holiday* of the analyst Mrs. B presented the following dream.

She had been trying to feed a despairing child. The child was standing and was about 10 months old. *It wasn't clear whether the child was a boy or a girl.* Mrs. B wondered about the age of the child. Her son was soon to be 10 months old. He was now able to stand. She too would have been standing at 10 months. (That would have been before the accident.) Why was the child in her dream so despairing, she asked. Her son is a lively child and she assumed that she too had been a normal happy child until the accident. This prompted me to recall how Mrs. B. had clung to an idealized view of her pre-accident childhood.[8] I thought she was now daring to question this. I therefore commented that maybe she was beginning to wonder about the time before the accident. Perhaps not everything had been quite so happy as she had always needed to assume. *She immediately held up her hand to signal me to stop.*

During the following silence I wondered why there was this present anxiety. Was it the patient's need still not to look at anything from before the accident unless it was seen as perfect? Was the accident itself being used as a screen memory? I thought this probable.

I briefly interrupt my quotation here to direct the reader's careful attention to what happened next when, in spite of her urgent warning that he stop, the analyst persisted in repeating his interpretation.

After a while I said that she seemed to be *afraid* of finding any element of bad experience during the time *before* the accident (i.e. before age 11 months) as if she still felt that the good that had been there before must be kept entirely separate from the bad that had followed. *She listened in silence, making no perceptible response during the rest of the session.*

The next day Mrs. B came to her session with a look of terror on her face. For this session, and the five sessions following, she could not lie on the couch. She explained that *when I had gone on talking, after she had signaled me to stop,* the couch had "become" the operating table with me as the surgeon, who had gone on operating regardless, after her mother had fainted. She now couldn't lie down "because the experience will go on." Nothing could stop it then, she felt sure.

In one of these sitting-up sessions (i.e., immediately after the crisis session) Mrs. B showed me a photograph of her holiday house, built into the side of a mountain with high retaining walls. *She stressed how essential these walls are to hold the house from falling.* She was afraid of falling for ever. She felt this had happened to her after her mother had fainted. (Here I should mention that Mrs. B.

had previously recalled thinking that her mother had died, when she had fallen out of her sight during the operation, and how she had felt that she was left alone with no one to protect her from the surgeon who seemed to be about to kill her with his knife.) Now, in this session, Mrs. B told me a detail of that experience which she had never mentioned before. At the start of the operation her mother had been holding her hands in hers, and Mrs. B remembered her terror upon finding her mother's hands slipping out of hers as she fainted and disappeared. She now thought she had been trying to re-find her mother's hands ever since, and she began to stress the importance of physical contact for her. She said she couldn't lie down on the couch again unless she knew she could, if necessary, hold my hand in order to get through the re-living of the operation experience. Would I allow this or would I refuse? If I refused she wasn't sure that she could continue with her analysis.

My initial response was to acknowledge to her that she needed me to be "in touch" with the intensity of her anxiety. However, she insisted that she had to know whether or not I would actually allow her to hold my hand. I felt under increased pressure due to this being near the end of a Friday session, and I was beginning to fear that the patient might indeed leave the analysis. My next comment was defensively equivocal. I said that some analysts would not contemplate allowing this, but I realized that she might need to have the possibility of holding my hand if it seemed to be the only way for her to get through this experience. She showed some relief upon my saying this.

On the *Sunday* I received a *hand*-delivered letter in which the patient said she had had another dream of the despairing child, but this time there were signs of hope. The child was crawling towards a motionless figure with the excited expectation of reaching this figure. On the Monday, although she was somewhat reassured by her dream, Mrs. B remained sitting on the couch. She saw the central figure as me representing her missing mother. She also stressed that she hadn't wanted me to have to wait to know about the dream. I interpreted her fear that I might not have been able to wait to be reassured, and she agreed. She had been afraid that I might have collapsed over the week-end, under the weight of the Friday session, if I had been left until Monday without knowing that she was beginning to feel more hopeful.

As this session continued, what emerged was a clear impression that Mrs. B was seeing the possibility of holding my hand as a "short-cut" to feeling safer. She wanted me to be the motionless figure, *controlled* by her and not allowed to move, towards whom she could crawl with the excited expectation that she would eventually be allowed to touch me. Mrs. B then reported an image, which was a continuation in the session of the written dream. She saw the dream-child reaching the central figure, but as she touched this it had crumbled and collapsed. With this cue as my lead I told her that I had thought very carefully about this, and I had come to the conclusion that this tentative offer of my hand might have appeared to provide a way of getting through the experience she was so terrified of, but I now realized that it would instead become a side-stepping of that experience as it had been rather than a living through it. I knew that if I seemed to be inviting an avoidance of this central aspect of the original experience I would be failing her as her analyst. I therefore did not think that I should leave the possibility of holding my hand still open to her. Mrs. B looked stunned. She asked me if I realized what I had just done. I had taken my hand away from her just as her mother had, and she immediately assumed that this must be because I too couldn't bear to remain in touch with what she was going through. Nothing I said could alter her assumption that I was afraid to let her touch me. The following day the patient's response to what I had said was devastating. Still sitting on the couch she told me that her left arm (the one nearest to me) was "steaming." I had burned her. She couldn't accept any interpretation from me. Only a real physical response from me could do anything about it. She wanted to stop her analysis to get away from what was happening to her in her sessions. She could never trust me again.[9]

During the next 2 weeks a harrowing and stormy period of battle continued during which the patient now threatened suicide and the author sought consultation from a respected senior colleague but continued to suffer painful doubts about what course to pursue with his patient about holding her hand. Casement then stated the following:

I reflected upon my dilemma. If I did not *give in to her demands* I might lose the patient, or she might really go psychotic and need to be hospitalized. If I did *give in to her* I would be colluding with her delusional perception of me, and the avoided elements of the trauma could become encapsulated as too terrible ever to confront. I felt placed in an impossible position. However, once I came to recognize the projective identification process operating here I began to surface from this feeling of complete helplessness. This enabled me eventually to interpret from my countertransference feelings. We could now see that if I had agreed to hold her physically it would have been a way of shutting off what she was experiencing, not only for her but also for me, as if I really couldn't bear to remain with her through this. She immediately recognized the implications of what I was saying and replied, "Yes. You would have become a collapsed analyst. I could not realize it at the time but I can now see that you would then have become the same as my mother who fainted. I am so glad you didn't let that happen."[10] (*p. 282*)

I interrupt my direct quotation here to say that it is precisely thanks to Casement's meticulous honesty that we are allowed to know that the ostensible crisis of technique in which she seemed to suddenly demand that he hold her hand as a reenactment of her childhood trauma could be viewed as a consequence of his insisting on repeating his confrontations about her idealizing her infancy even after she implored him to stop doing that.

It is well known that no matter how conscientious the analyst, important information is inadvertently omitted from case reports (Spence, 1982). In this instance, there are two highly important examples of this problem. The first is this: Eleven years after his original 1982 paper, Casement participated in a panel discussion about the work of Winnicott (Blum & Ross, 1993) at which time he added a vitally important piece of information to the history of this patient. I quote Casement from that 1993 panel discussion in his own words:

> Mrs. B. was the youngest in her family. . . . She had suffered severe burns from scalding water at eleven months, shortly after beginning to walk. *Barrier-nursed after this, she could not be held by her mother.*[11] At seventeen months, she had had surgery under local anesthesia to release her scar tissue. It was a dream, with a memory of this trauma that brought Mrs. B. to analysis 30 years later. In the dream her mother had "fainted out of sight" after holding her hands, and she herself was about to be killed by a man with a knife. She "couldn't face it alone" anymore, she said, and was afraid of committing suicide once her own children left home. (Blum & Ross, 1993, p. 225; italics added)

This tragic and total physical separation and isolation of the infant patient from any human contact evidently continued for some lengthy period. It would certainly have been traumatic to a greater degree than the scalding accident and the surgery. It is noteworthy that neither Casement nor most of his numerous post-1993 discussants felt the need for such information in relation to their heated debates about her panicky insistence on physical contact. This information was missing from all earlier reports by Casement before 1993 and was therefore not known to his discussants before that time, but it was certainly available to all of the many discussants after this 1993 publication. After Casement provided this additional information about the barrier nursing, 18 additional articles were published commenting about Casement's patient and his views about technique.[12] Only two of their authors mentioned this information about the barrier nursing.[13]

But my purpose here is to illustrate the consequences of omitting the events preceding his fateful interpretation about her happy infancy when evaluating the subsequent technical discussions of all those authors who took at face value that the primary issue to consider was whether he should have held her hand. We must keep in mind that the author and almost all of his discussants have asked us to join them in the assumption that the issue of technique, of whether or not to hold her hand, could be usefully decided on an abstract level, separate from the interaction between the analyst and his patient, immediately before the crisis.[14] Furthermore, one might ask which issues of technique, if any, should be discussed categorically in terms of rules rather than individually in terms of the dynamic context. Sometimes they can. Certainly, gross boundary violations are always wrong. But this illustrates the tension between the specific and the general, as well as the contrast between inductive and deductive reasoning, which is outside the scope of this discussion. One can at least say that we should be wary of the substitution of rules for understanding when deciding about the incredible complexities of a clinical impasse. An alternative view of these events is to consider this interaction between analyst and patient as an unrecognized enactment of a sadomasochistic transference–countertransference struggle centering on the issue of control of the analysis. The point here is not that I wish to prove that such an alternative view is the truth. Rather, I wish to show that this alternative view derives from a different contextual horizon. Viewed in such a context, the question of whether or not to hold her hand takes on a new significance and leads to alternative strategies. It seems to me that it would have been possible to address these matters in a number of ways and that the salient question was not what the analyst should have physically done but to why and how the dilemma became a dilemma. Experience teaches that it is difficult to reason one's way out of a dilemma that was created unreasonably. Space does not permit reporting further details of the original case report, let alone summarizing the numerous discussions about this case, other than to note the almost unanimous and disturbing agreement with the author that the issue here was one of technique. Many authors applauded Casement's integrity, and a large number criticized his insensitivity. I am suggesting that we view his remarkable insistence on repeating his views over her explicit and dramatic objections as a day residue for the impasse that was enacted. But my suggesting that viewing the events before and after the hand-holding crisis as an enactment accounts better for more of the available facts is, of course, my own bias. What is clear, however, is that my view derives from contextualizing criteria different from those utilized by most of the published discussants.[15] At issue here is not the truth of this alternative contextualization but its plausibility as an alternative. In fact, once the enactment rose to the crisis level that it did, it seems perfectly plausible to me that what Casement did was quite helpful to her. Obviously, there are merits both pro and con to the arguments of most of the many discussants of this case. But to focus on technique isolated from context can sometimes be a sign of a strained moment of insufficient understanding of a transference–countertransference impasse. These polarized discussions of Casement's patient illustrate another fallacy in our literature. Can we assume a generic analyst who could have really altered his perceptions and behavior with this patient by following a simple technical rule? Technique in the background is different from technique as a foreground issue. To put it another way, technique is sometimes what an analyst does when he or she does not understand what is going on and has become embroiled in an enactment with the patient in which the transference fantasies of the patient threaten to degenerate into reality (Tarachow, 1963). The purpose of my discussion is to shift the emphasis away from the question of who is right about technique to highlight the consequences of evidential ambiguity when we evaluate alternative technical interventions in our literature.

We have here a paradigmatic and disquieting example of some two dozen analysts divided into two opposing camps, each of which is in visible disagreement about technique in the abstract but nonetheless share a tacit assumption about the permissibility of omitting important data from evaluating generalized technique strategies. Unlike the Oxford don who had strong opinions lightly held, we analysts seem often to have light opinions strongly held. Heated controversies and polemics are the all-too-frequent character of our disagreements. In this model example, these opposing analysts assume that they are discussing the same case when in fact they are discussing how to use selected aspects of selectively reported material to support their theoretic preferences at far-removed levels of theoretic abstraction. This is one of our most familiar dilemmas about clinical evidence, and it has been widely deplored.

Eight Contextual Criteria

There are additional complexities to consider about the discussion of Casement's article. At least eight major evidential issues deserved to be viewed as contextual criteria that are neglected to varying degrees by most of the discussants of Casement's original work. To the extent that they are even mentioned, these topics are not elevated to the status of potential contextualizing criteria for interpretations different from those of Casement. I propose that we define a contextual criterion as a bridging tool. It is a dynamic theme that links theory, context, and technique. It partially defines the boundaries of a contextual horizon. Because space does not permit detailed discussion of contextual criteria at this point, I shall merely list them.

Criterion 1

The analyst had just returned from his summer vacation. This entire crisis developed immediately after he responded to her dream about a despairing child. The analyst ignores the transferential implications of his recent absence and feels no need to ask for associations to the dream. Instead, he states that the dream prompted him to repeat his prior interpretations about her infancy. Analysts of a different persuasion might regard this intervention as a defensive avoidance of the transference by a retreat into the childhood history. So, an alternative path of interpretation opens up with this different contextualizing criterion. Also, we are told in one version of the case report (Casement, 1982) that at about this time and shortly before the crisis, the analyst had quickly agreed to her proposal to cut down the frequency of the sessions from four to three times weekly. We do not know from the available data whether the analyst believed that his vacation and the patient's wish to cut down the frequency of appointments were related or if this was discussed.[16]

Criterion 2

The analyst and patient have established a prior agreement that they can rationally and logically discuss the accuracy of her memory of her feelings in the first year of her life. Here one might question the transference implications for the patient of such extravagant claims for certainty by her analyst about matters that fly in the face of his claims. In fact, just 6 years ago, Casement's article was cited as evidential authority for the view of the registration of infantile memories:

> Numerous case histories of child and adult treatments *document* the continuing effects of events in the first year. . . . For example, Casement describes an adult treatment case in which the patient was preoccupied by having been severely burned at 11 months. This traumatic event was a major organizing theme in the adult analysis. These sources of *evidence* provide a basis from which to infer that organization, or structure, accrues across the first year. (Beebe, Lachmann, & Jaffe, 1997, *p. 150*)[17]

Experienced analysts are familiar with uncanny examples of stunning reenactments of infantile traumatic experiences. But the issue here is that even the possibility of the fallacy of these protracted discussions about actual infantile memories was not considered by the discussants.

Criterion 3

The patient's father was not largely present in her life until she was 5 years old. The consequences of a one-parent oedipal phase of development were usefully discussed long ago by Neubauer (1960). Would not her father's absence and return have profoundly shaped her attachments to her mother, her sexual development as a child, and her perceptions of men when she became an adult? Would it not have contributed to her sadomasochistic absorption in issues of controlling and being controlled? The patient's father is as absent in all of this literature as he was in her life for her first 5 years. We simply lack any information whatsoever about her relationship with him after the age of 5, and the discussants do not seem to consider this a problem. If this information about her father was omitted for purposes of protecting her privacy, one wonders why it was included at all.

Criterion 4

The patient had become a mother just 10 months before she had the dream that ushered in her crisis. This baby was now just about the same age as the patient at the time she suffered her terrible scalding accident. What is it that revived her identification with a despairing child at just this time in the analysis?[18]

Criterion 5

The patient clearly stated in her report of her dream that the gender of the baby was ambiguous. She reported this dream to the analyst immediately before he began to insist on his interpretation and immediately before the crisis ensued. What she told him was the following: "She had been trying to feed a despairing child. The child was standing and was about 10 months old. *It wasn't clear whether the child was a boy or a girl.*"

We have no consensus among analysts about the extent to which we would wish to have associations to important elements in the manifest dream before venturing an interpretation to the patient, but this question does not arise in the Casement literature. Just as the enactment of his repeating his interpretation over her vigorous objection could be ignored, it was generally accepted by all of the discussants that this manifest element of the dream did not require contextual articulation with the ensuing crisis. Consider that the dream in the note that was hand-delivered to the home of the analyst on a Sunday was a continuation of this dream about the despairing baby whose gender was ambiguous. This omission may reflect the fact that an increasing number of analysts in recent years do not feel the need to have information about most of the important manifest elements in a dream. My experience has been that it is useful to at least be curious about anything that the patient felt it important enough to communicate, which is to say that all of the associations cannot be contextualized but that all of the associations of the patient are laden with potential meaning if we but knew how to discover it. Ideally, we will be just as able to say not only what we left out (as in the unpacking prescribed by Spence, 1982) but also why we left it out. The *why* reflects the consequences of contextualizing decisions by the analyst.

Criterion 6

It was to be 11 years after his original 1982 paper that Casement added the vitally important information that the patient was barrier-nursed after the scalding for some unknown length of time.[19] In a personal communication, Casement informed me in 2004 that he was not free to offer further explanatory details about this barrier nursing and why it was necessary, beyond what he published in 1993, to protect his patient's privacy. But for my purposes, the relevant issue here is that Casement did provide at least this much information about the barrier nursing in his 1993 panel presentation and that it has been so widely neglected. Even had there been no scalding accident at all, we would expect that the rigidly enforced requirement that a human infant be deprived of any holding, hugging, or nurturing physical contact with her mother would be a devastating psychic trauma.

Criterion 7

Earlier, I note that in his most recent discussion of his article some 19 years after its original appearance, he reported another critically important piece of information:

> It had been a feature throughout those first years of this analysis that Mrs. B. would frequently seek to control me, a control that I usually allowed her. Latterly, however, we had been negotiating the beginning of some separation from that near total control of me as analyst. *Occasionally, as when I did not accept her signal for me to stop,* I had stood my ground in the course of some interpretive work. Gradually, through such moments as these, Mrs. B. had begun to allow me a more separate existence and a mind of my own, that was not held totally within her control. I believe that we had to find a way for this gradual differentiation between herself and me as not merged and as not totally controlled by her, in preparation for what was to come later. (Casement, 2000, p. 171; italics added)

So, when he insisted on repeating his interpretation to the patient about her infancy before the accident as not being as happy as she insisted, he was consciously attempting to reduce his prior willingness to allow her to control his behavior with her in the analysis. He seems to acknowledge here for the first time that his insistence on his confronting her with the possible error of her idealized memory of her infancy, even after she held up her hand and told him to stop, was a factor in the ensuing crisis about holding her hand. That is left only implicit. But even more important is the fact that throughout this entire period of crisis, while patient and analyst agonized over whether he should hold her hand, he never once discussed with her that his insistence on the correctness of his interpretation was even a change in his behavior at all, let alone explain to her why he decided at the time to change his prior behavior with her. Of course, it is just such an omission of the role of the observing analyst in evoking the very behavior that is ostensibly being observed in an exclusively one-person model that is often correctly faulted by relational theorists as well as advocates of enactment theory in the conflict model. Only with the benefit of this last piece of information is it possible to interpret this power struggle as an enactment by patient and analyst of an unconscious sadomasochistic fantasy. Four more discussions of Casement's patient have appeared since this last addition of information published in 2000. Once again, this new information seems to be disregarded.[20] In fairness to Casement's scrupulous honesty, he would more than likely have provided this new information about his important change in technique if he had thought that it would be relevant. But that assumption of irrelevance is exactly the problem for all of us. Indeed, the ambiguities concerning such assumed irrelevance is one of the central causes of the famously vexing dissociation between theory and practice in psychoanalysis (Smith, 2003). In this sense, the experience of comparing the divergent discussions of Casement's work is reminiscent of the film *Rashomon*; for example, one of Casement's discussants correctly stated with approval and agreement that Casement "decries the analyst who imposes his ideas upon a patient" (Symington, 1992, p. 168), but that discussant saw no contradiction between that theoretic position of Casement in comparison with his actual behavior with his patient wherein that is exactly what Casement did when he ignored her signal to stop repeating his interpretation to her.

The discussant of Casement's work that has been most sharply critical of him is Albert Mason (1987), a Bionian–Kleinian who had the following to say:

> While I feel a certain sympathy with Casement and what he is saying in his book, and with the hard work and sincerity which are clearly evident there, I find his depiction of many of the problems oversimplified and somewhat naïve. It seems to me that he seeks to contain therapists' anxieties in a reassuring way rather than helping them to become therapists with a full understanding of the psychodynamics underlying the problems involved. . . . This is a book I would recommend to students, residents, and perhaps to *beginning analytic candidates*, but I think most practicing analysts would find it rather elementary.[21] (pp. 714–715)

Our confusion about how to view psychoanalysis as a science is illustrated by the enthusiastic endorsement for Casement's work by one of our most prominent advocates of psychoanalysis as a science. Fonagy (1985) describes Casement's work as being imaginative; he strongly commended Casement for taking "enormous care to illustrate clinically all the ideas he has mentioned just as in a good text of mathematics the author would carefully derive all formulae from first principles" (p. 507). Fonagy too goes on to commend Casement for being nondirective, which is puzzling when we recall Casement's insistence on trying to make his patient admit that he was right by repeating his interpretation. In fact, Fonagy states that Casement "gives students a head start in untangling the confusion of terms surrounding unconscious communication" (p. 507).

Criterion 8

Casement provides no information about the sexual conflicts of his patient.[22] This omission is telling and, by and large, his numerous discussants do not question this omission. This vignette is open to alternative conjectures that would include attention to the patient's unconscious sexual conflicts.

Terminological Summary

I have used and introduced a group of loosely related and overlapping terms that I attempt here to summarize in ascending levels of abstraction. These topics are pursued further in chapter 7.

Contextual Horizon

Contextual horizon refers to a group of associations that are dynamically linked by the contextualizing criteria utilized by the analyst to capture the major dynamic urgency in a given session. I introduce this term to facilitate our comparing our inferential processes with each other more coherently. A contextual horizon is the least abstract of the terms that I have used, and it often refers to material in a single session, although the notion I have in mind may describe inferential processes within a single session or to contextual continuities over varying lengths of time. It is most important that there be alternative horizons available to any one analyst or to any group of analysts who are reviewing the clinical material of another analyst. The idea of trial contextualization that I use refers to the important fact that although there are always multiple plausible contextual horizons in any one session, the analyst very often believes that there is an optimal contextual horizon that best captures the affective urgencies of that session. The problem addressed in this discussion is the ambiguity of our criteria for optimal contextualizations.

I intend the term *contextual criteria* to encompass the vast panoply of theoretic beliefs of the analyst that she or he utilizes to bridge the associations of the actual moment in the treatment process with the entire array of theoretic assumptions of the analyst. Therefore, contextual criteria derive from an array of frames of reference and levels of abstraction. Contextual criteria are the linking assumptions made by the analyst to infer meaning from the raw associations of the patient. An example of a contextual criterion is the decision to privilege several narratives in a session that repeat a common theme. This is distinguished from priorities of intervention wherein the analyst puts associations that express defensive tendencies ahead of impulse tendencies. The analyst uses his or her more abstract theoretic assumptions to select contextual criteria to accomplish the filtering so essential to psychoanalytic inferential processes. To make such an inference is a form of psychoanalytic triage: In the heat of the fray, what do we emphasize and select, and what do we de-emphasize and neglect? These criteria are far more vague and abstract, and it is our willingness to ignore requiring information about the contextual criteria and horizons that perpetuates this vagueness. It is also precisely this confusion about contextual criteria that perpetuates our famous disconnect between theory and technique.

Rules of Evidence

Rules of evidence—to speak of such rules is a utopian yearning at this time in our history. I use the phrase to indicate the hope that our scientific methodology for evaluating clinical evidence will always be evolving. I agree with those who believe that there are many definitions of science (Grossman, 1995), and I use the term *science* to argue against those who believe that clinical evidence is not relevant to psychoanalysis because of the daunting complexity of the analytic process or because the analyst should be epistemologically disqualified as an observer. *Rules of evidence* at this time appears to be a wildly exaggerated phrase, but we psychoanalysts are able to make reliable predictions in certain instances; for example, we can predict that an adult obsessional male patient with distressing obsessive–compulsive symptoms will reveal in the course of psychoanalytic treatment that he struggles with the derivatives of unconscious passive anal sexual conflicts and fantasies (Arlow, 1990, personal communication). This empirical finding has been repeated hundreds of times by successive generations of psychoanalysts. We can repeatedly demonstrate that the sequential patterning of the associations of the patient is meaningful rather than random. We can also often plausibly support and refute individual interpretations (Hanly, 1992; Wisdom, 1967).

These proposed terms to describe our inferential and contextualizing processes do not fit together easily or clearly, but perhaps they will serve as the basis for a wider discussion of this pressing problem and to better, later clarification.

Conclusion

A familiar aspect of the problem of evaluating clinical evidence is that we have never defined the optimal relation between the kinds of data we have available with the kind of hypothesis we wish to test. Consider the difference between three types of problems: Was an interpretation the best available explanation for the available data in a given session? Is self-disclosure useful or not? Was an analysis successful? In general, we are speaking of the differences between processes, abstract principles of technique, and outcome research. We badly need to clarify which kind of evidence is most suitable for the diverse levels of abstraction that characterize psychoanalytic theories. Testing the bricks of a house is quite different than inspecting the completed home. It is often said that a single session tells us little about the vicissitudes of the progression of the treatment, yet one wonders about how to place confidence in outcome studies where there is no report of the data of one or more single sessions that illustrate how the particular analyst inferred meanings from the associations of the patient.

Who is correct in this controversy about Casement and technique is not the point for purposes of this discussion. The important issue is to question why each participant believed he or she knew enough to agree or disagree about Casement's views. Such disagreements cannot lead to a meaningful comparison of views without comparing the different contextual horizons chosen by the opponents. I am not saying that the choice of different contextual horizons was the cause of this disagreement about technique. I am saying that unrecognized assumptions about which contextual horizons were utilized allow and facilitate our confusion. To summarize, it is my suggestion that when we make the contextual organization explicit, it becomes possible to see what we are disagreeing about at a level closer to the original data. That is no small achievement. We can then agree or disagree more coherently.

This confusion about evidence highlights the consequences of our increasing tendency to neglect giving careful attention to the associations of the patient. Furthermore, this erosion of interest in the concealed and latent meanings of these associations coincides with the widespread derogation of clinical evidence. It is probably not a coincidence that this downplaying of the associations of the patient is linked to the waning interest in the sexual and aggressive conflicts of our patients on the part of many authors.

The discussions cited here were geared to the abstract question of technique: Is it good or bad to have physical contact with the patient? What I seriously question is how we can discuss such a question in absolute terms as being proscribed for all patients or included for all patients. Is there no better way in which we could base such a decision on clinical evidence? The examples cited here support the view that our methodology of evaluating evidence would be enhanced if we could refine and clarify what constituted evidence for the reporting analyst. If we were more clear about how clinical evidence was contextualized, it would expose the deeper complexities of our disagreements. Our literature now commonly calls for more details about the personal feelings of the analyst during a clinical interaction. But it is rare to hear a request for the analyst to say why he or she included certain associations of the patient in a given contextualization and why he or she omitted other associations. Tape recordings would not solve this problem either. But these ambiguities about the criteria for contextualizing have been obscured by the debates about the more visible daunting problems of how to present clinical material and how to write case reports. Efforts to address this omission are overdue.

At this time, there are psychoanalytic communities so far from utilizing similar methods for adjudicating such questions that one must wonder about the very possibility of meaningful communication between groups. What I suggest here is that this grim danger is less due to the theoretic differences between all of our groups than to the methodological agreement among so many of us to shrug our shoulders about the problems of evaluating clinical evidence. Pluralism of perspectives and theories is not only healthy but vital to the future of psychoanalysis. But the smug consolation of relativistic smoothing (we all get good results, don't we?) of the differences in our numerous theoretic models is overdue for comparative scrutiny. Ideally, the refinement of the role of contextualization in our evaluation of clinical evidence will enhance the possibility for developing a more rational comparative psychoanalysis. Every contextualization is also a condensation of the associations of the patient. If we wish to fully exploit the benefits of a pluralistic psychoanalysis, we will be well advised to refine our understanding of what information about the patient was used to support the conclusions reported. More important, that will also help us to clarify better which associations of the patient were left out. This may even help us to reverse the steady erosion of interest in our literature about the role of the patient's associations during psychoanalytic treatment.

Notes

1. This chapter was originally published as "Analytic Controversies Contextualized" in the *Journal of the American Psychoanalytic Association* (2005), *53*(3), 835–863, but in a different version. It was also presented to the Toronto Psychoanalytic Society, the Michigan Psychoanalytic Society, and the New York Psychoanalytic Institute and Society.

2. If a contextualizing criterion is a linking criterion, so is a correspondence criterion. Both terms (*correspondence criteria* and *contextualizing criteria*) connote the conceptual linkages used by the analyst. However, the term *contextualizing criteria* arises in the frame of reference of clinical data, and the term *correspondence criteria* arises in the frame of reference of justification and philosophy of science. *Correspondence criteria* is a more modest term than *rules of evidence*, but it suggests or implies a canon of evidence and promises far more validity than the term *contextualizing criteria*. I use the term *correspondence criteria* to connote currently held views by an analytic group

(this is never totally consensual) about the reliability of inferring that certain elements in our theory correspond to actual existing conflicts in the patient (for a similar definition, see Garza-Guerrero, 2000).

3. Quoted by W. Pritchard from Eliot's "The Sacred Wood" in his review of *Collected Poems*, by Robert Lowell, *New York Times*, June 29, 2003, p. 11.

4. The actual interaction of deductive and inductive reasoning is far more complex than indicated by this simple statement, but the relevant issues cannot be pursued here (see Hanly, 1992). For another perspective on the preference for rules for technique, see Levine (2003).

5. This case was originally reported at the 32nd International Psychoanalytical Congress, at Helsinki, in July 1981.

6. The assertion on epistemological grounds that an analyst can never logically be viewed as an observer is a category error. The interested reader can find relevant discussions of this problem in Hanly (1990, 1992) and Ahumada (1994a, 1994b).

7. I use the term *contextual horizon* throughout the book as a synonym for a major organizing theme for the manifest associations of the patient chosen by the analyst to give contextual priority to certain manifest associations of the patient in the session.

8. That would be before the age of 11 months.

9. Holder (2000) viewed the withdrawal of the analyst's offer of physical contact to be the more important issue. Mitchell (1991) believed that the offer as well as the withdrawal of the offer were helpful. Schlessinger and Appelbaum (2000) agreed with Mitchell but cautioned against rigid rules. Pizer (2000) rejected Casement's decisions because they were rooted in an outmoded one-person authoritarian model.

10. Aron (1992) agreed that this was the successful turning point in her analysis.

11. According to Casement (2000),

> Barrier nursing her, that is, not holding her or touching her except with sterilized gloves and then only for the most minimal and essential feeding and cleaning of the child. Whatever she did, the mother must not pick up her baby—however much the baby cried to be picked up—for if the mother did pick up her baby, it might lead to her dying from infection. (p. 178)

12. See Bass (2004); Beebe, Lachmann, and Jaffe (1997); Boyer (1997); Breckenridge (2000); Cooper and Levit (1998); DeMattos (2003); Feiner (1998); Fosshaage (2000); Holder (2000); Katz (1998); Levine (2003); McLaughlin (2000); Meissner (1998); Pizer (2000); Pizer (2004); Ruderman (2000); Schlessinger and Appelbaum (2000); Shane, Shane, and Gales (2000).

13. The exceptions are DeMattos (2003), who does not discuss this point, and Pizer (2004) who discusses these issues in a different frame of reference.

14. It might be argued that, after all, the numerous authors in the special issue on this topic in *Inquiry* were invited to address the issue of technique regarding the pros and cons of physical contact with the analyst. But it is precisely the assumption that this isolation of technique is logical and the willingness to consider this question as an abstraction disconnected from the context of the origin of this clinical crisis that I am questioning here.

15. McLaughlin (2000) and Pizer (2004) note Casement's insistence on his interpretation in the face of the patient's vigorous hand signal to make him stop, but they draw conclusions different from my own.

16. McLaughlin (2000) is the only author to note this important fact. He is also one of the very few who notes the repetitious insistence of the analyst that the patient give up her idealized view of her infancy just before the crisis occurred. I have commented on several of these discussions about Casement's patient in abbreviated form (Boesky, 1998). McLaughlin is also the only author in the special issue of *Inquiry* to note the important differences in the details provided in the various versions of this case that Casement reported. McLaughlin points out that the crisis occurred after Casement's too-quick acceptance of the patient's request to cut her sessions from four to three times weekly. He was also one of the several who noted Casement's insistence on his own theoretic views over the patient's urgent pleas that he stop, but he does not relate these matters to the disagreements about technique between himself and some of the other authors. McLaughlin discusses these issues in terms of criticizing too great a reliance on arbitrary technical rules.

17. For a similar citation of Casement as an authority for the reliance on infantile memory, see Boyer (1997), Cooper and Levit (1998), and Feiner (1998). For a contrasting view of infantile memories, see Tuckett and Tyson, as cited in Blum and Ross (1993).

18. Fosshaage (2000) raises this question but views the crisis quite differently on grounds of relational epistemology.

19. See note 8.

20. See Bass (2004) and Levine (2003). Although DeMattos (2003) notes this as an issue, she does not comment further about its possible implications.

21. In his 1993 review, Bass thought that Casement simplified matters too much, but his 2004 review was generally favorable, and his major criticism was Casement's failure to acknowledge commonalities between his (Casement's) views and those of American relational theorists.

22. This omission continues in each of Casement's cited discussions, including his most recent (2004).

References

Ahumada, J. (1994a). Interpretation and creationism. *International Journal of Psycho-Analysis, 75*, 695–707.

Ahumada, J. (1994b). What is a clinical fact? Clinical psychoanalysis as inductive method. *International Journal of Psycho-Analysis, 75*, 949–962.

Arlow, J. (1979). The genesis of interpretation. *Journal of the American Psychoanalytic Association, 27S*, 193–206.

Aron, L. (1992). Interpretation as expression of the analyst's subjectivity. *Psychoanalytic Dialogue, 2*, 475–507.

Bass, A. (1993). *Learning from the patient*, by P. Casement [Book review]. *Psychoanalytic Dialogue, 3*, 151–167.

Bass, A. (2004). *Learning from mistakes: Beyond dogma in psychoanalysis and psychotherapy,* by Patrick Casement [Book review]. *International Journal of Psychoanalysis, 85,* 247–251.

Beebe, B., Lachmann, F., & Jaffe, J. (1997). Mother–infant interaction structures and presymbolic self- and object representations. *Psychoanalytic Dialogue, 7,* 133–182.

Blum, H., & Ross, J. (1993). The clinical relevance of the contribution of Winnicott. *Journal of the American Psychoanalytic Association, 41,* 219–235.

Boesky, D. (1998). Clinical evidence and multiple models: New responsibilities. *Journal of the American Psychoanalytic Association, 46,* 1013–1020.

Boyer, L. B. (1997). The verbal squiggle game in treating the seriously disturbed patient. *Psychoanalytic Quarterly, 66,* 62–81.

Breckenridge, K. (2000). Physical touch in psychoanalysis: A closet phenomenon. *Psychoanalytic Inquiry 20,* 2–20.

Casement, P. (1982). Some pressures on the analyst for physical contact during the reliving of an early trauma. *International Review of Psychoanalysis, 9,* 279–286.

Casement, P. (1985). *On learning from the patient* [Part I]. London: Tavistock.

Casement, P. (1990). *Further learning from the patient* [Part II]. London: Routledge.

Casement, P. (1991). *Learning from the patient* [Parts I and II]. New York: Guilford.

Casement, P. (2000). The issue of touch: A retrospective overview. *Psychoanalytic Inquiry, 20,* 160–184.

Casement, P. (2003). *Learning from mistakes: Beyond dogma in psychoanalysis and psychotherapy.* New York: Guilford.

Casement, P. (2004). Response to Stuart Pizer. *American Imago, 61,* 557–564.

Cooper, S., & Levit, D. (1998). Old and new objects in Fairbairnian and American relational theory. *Psychoanalytic Dialogue, 8,* 603–624.

DeMattos, S. (2003). *Learning from our mistakes,* by Patrick Casement [Book review]. *Psychologist–Psychoanalyst, 23*(1), 61–64.

Feiner, A. (1998). Notes on touch and the genesis of hope: One touch of nature makes the whole world kin. *Contemporary Psychoanalysis, 34,* 445–457.

Fonagy, P. (1985). *On learning from the patient,* by Patrick Casement [Book review]. *International Journal of Psychoanalysis, 66,* 507–508.

Fosshaage, J. (2000). The meanings of touch in psychoanalysis. A time for reassessment. *Psychoanalytic Inquiry, 20,* 21–43.

Fox, R. (1984). The principle of abstinence reconsidered. *International Review of Psychoanalysis, 11,* 227–236.

Fox, R. (1988). On learning from the patient. *Journal of the American Psychoanalytic Association, 36,* 785–788.

Garza-Guerrero, C. (2000). Idealization and mourning in love relationships. *Psychoanalytic Quarterly, 69,* 121–150.

Grossman, W. (1995). Commentaries. *Journal of the American Psychoanalytic Association, 43,* 1004–1015.

Hanly, C. (1990). The concept of truth in psychoanalysis. *International Journal of Psychoanalysis, 71,* 375–383.

Hanly, C. (1992). Inductive reasoning in clinical psychoanalysis. *International Journal of Psychoanalysis, 73,* 293–301.

Hoffer, A. (1991). The Freud–Ferenczi controversy: A living legacy. *International Review of Psychoanalysis, 18,* 465–472.

Holder, A. (2000). To touch or not to touch: That is the question. *Psychoanalytic Inquiry, 20,* 44–64.

Katz, G. (1998). Where the action is: The enacted dimension of analytic process. *Journal of the American Psychoanalytic Association, 46,* 1129–1167.

Levine, F. (2003). The forbidden quest and the slippery slope: Roots of authoritarianism in psychoanalysis. *Journal of the American Psychoanalytic Association, 51*(Suppl.), 203–245.

Mason, A. (1987). *On learning from the patient,* by Patrick Casement [Book review]. *Psychoanalysis Quarterly, 56,* 711–715.

McLaughlin, J. (2000). The problem and place of physical contact in analytic work. *Psychoanalytic Inquiry, 20,* 65–81.

Meissner, W. (1996). *The therapeutic alliance.* New Haven, CT: Yale University Press.

Meissner, W. (1998). Neutrality, abstinence, alliance. *Journal of the American Psychoanalytic Association, 46,* 1089–1128.

Mitchell, S. (1991). Wishes, needs, and interpersonal negotiations. *Psychoanalytic Inquiry, 11,* 147–170.

Neubauer, P. (1960). The one-parent child and his oedipal development. *Psychoanalytic Study of the Child, 15,* 286–309.

Peirce, C. S. (1955). Concerning the author. In J. Buchler (Ed.), *Philosophical writings of Peirce* (pp. 1–4). New York: Dover. (Original work published 1897)

Pizer, B. (2000). Negotiating analytic holding: Discussion of Patrick Casement's *Learning from the Patient. Psychoanalytic Inquiry, 20,* 82–107.

Pizer, S. (2004). *Learning from our mistakes: Beyond dogma in psychoanalysis and psychotherapy,* by Patrick Casement [Book review]. *American Imago, 61,* 543–556.

Roughton, R. (1993). Useful aspects of acting out: Repetition, enactment, and actualization. *Journal of the American Psychoanalytic Association, 41,* 443–472.

Ruderman, E. (2000). Intimate communications: The values and boundaries of touch in the psychoanalytic setting. *Psychoanalytic Inquiry, 20,* 108–123.

Schlessinger, H., & Appelbaum, A. (2000). When words are not enough. *Psychoanalytic Inquiry, 20,* 124–143.

Shane, M., Shane, E., & Gales, M. (2000). Psychoanalysis unbound: A contextual consideration of boundaries from a developmental systems perspective. *Psychoanalytic Inquiry, 20,* 144–159.

Smith, H. (2003). Theory and practice: Intimate partnership or false connection. *Psychoanalytic Quarterly, 72,* 1–12.

Spence, D. (1982). *Narrative truth and historic truth!* New York: Norton.

Symington, N. (1992). *Further learning from the patient: The analytic space and process,* by Patrick Casement [Book review]. *International Journal of Psychoanalysis, 73,* 168–170.

Tarachow, S. (1963). *An introduction to psychotherapy.* New York: International Universities Press.

Wisdom, J. (1967). Testing an interpretation within a session. *International Journal of Psychoanalysis, 48,* 44–52.

3

Comparative Psychoanalysis: What Should We Compare?

To PARAPHRASE A FRENCH APHORISM ABOUT NATIONS, a theoretic school of psychoanalysis is a group of analysts united by their erroneous ideas about the human mind and the hatred of their neighboring theoretic schools.[1] Surely, we can agree by now that our theoretic pluralism is advantageous. Old walls have crumbled, and our patients benefit from our expanded views. But just as clear is that not every new suggestion is of equal usefulness or validity, and it is time that we refine our methodology for comparing numerous theoretic models without incurring the tendentious distractions of accusations of elitism or politics. Like wine and music, our theories are not equal. But who is to say which is better and why? Teaching comparative psychoanalysis in our institutes has become prevalent. The general tendency in these seminars has been toward searching and open-minded considerations of the problems that each of these diverse models was designed to solve that had not been adequately dealt with in the other preexisting models. But what is compared is usually the content of the various models and the problems that the particular models were designed to clarify. Sorely lacking in the scanty literature on the teaching of comparative psychoanalysis is a more rigorous consideration of what can and should be compared about the clinical evidence generated in two or more different theoretic models.

"We seem to be operating as though we could have a single methodology for evidential support or disconfirmation, even as the various schools proclaim the advantages of pluralism" (Boesky, 1998, p. 1018). But we are dealing not only with a beneficial pluralism of theories. We have not yet sufficiently appreciated that we are also led astray because some of these models are in a different frame of reference than the others and therefore cannot be logically compared. To say that patriotism is purple is to make a category error because it collapses the conceptual boundaries between two different classes or categories.

> [A] category mistake (error) [is] the placing of an entity in the wrong category. . . . To place the activity of exhibiting team spirit in the same class with the activities of pitching, batting, and catching is to make a category mistake; exhibiting team spirit is not a special function like pitching or batting but instead a way those special functions are performed. (Audi, 1999, p. 123)

There is no basis in fact, experience, or logic to assume that we can have a single methodology for the evaluation of evidence if we are also to have theoretic models deriving from different domains and categories. There is a fundamental contradiction in the expectations of those who plead for an eclectic oscillation between the diverse theories and yet, at the same time, assume that we can have a unitary methodology for validating or disconfirming clinical evidence. To be clear, I am in no way criticizing pluralism. Theoretic pluralism has already brought us many advantages. I try to demonstrate instead that with theoretic pluralism comes the task of inventing and refining a pluralism of comparative psychoanalysis. By this, I mean that we will need to recognize which of our numerous theoretic models are in the same frame of reference and which are not. In this chapter, I discuss two theories that are in a different frame of reference, to highlight a neglected problem that is impeding our methods for comparing psychoanalytic theoretic models.

Our comparisons of various theoretic models suffer from the high level of abstraction of some of these comparisons because they are so far removed from the actual clinical data from which the relevant disagreements between theoretic models have risen. This has obscured the fact that some of our numerous models are not commensurate with others. This has been further obscured because many of our oldest terms, such as *transference,* are carried forward into each of the newer models but have different meanings. This problem goes deeper than definitional confusion. An analogous problem illustrates our current situation. In the history of science, the introduction of the metric system in the revolutionary period of France was a celebrated achievement because the system of measurements and weights under the old regime had become chaotic owing to the fact that the same terms of measurement meant different things in various parts of France (Furbank, 2005). And now, in different parts of the psychoanalytic community, the terms *transference, memory,* and *unconscious* have different meanings, as we shall see in the theoretic model proposed by the Boston Change Process Study Group (BCPSG; 1998, 2002, 2005a, 2005b). As I hope to demonstrate, the definitional confusion about these three terms masks the even more misleading assumption that we can alter the domains of memory, the unconscious, and, therefore, transference without serious errors in comparing the data derived from two models that use these three terms in profoundly different senses. But our neglect of the problem of incompatible epistemology in our comparisons of certain theoretic models has been more important than mere definitional confusion.

Of the various proposals for defining a bedrock commonality shared by most of our theoretic models, I consider the inference of latent meaning from manifest content to be a fundamental assumption in each of our numerous theoretic models. No matter whether the analytic relationship or interpretations are claimed to be of equivalent or greater value as mutative factors, sooner or later in all models the analyst thinks it is necessary to explain something to the patient. This explanation is an inference made by the analyst from something that the patient communicated that the patient previously did not understand. I do not here claim exclusive mutative advantage for interpretations over the relationship. But even when the explanations of the analyst are viewed to be mostly just a useful way to have the relationship, the analyst will repeatedly make inferences about the meaning of what the patient is communicating. I introduce the suggestion here that when we compare theoretic models, we should compare in each model the method used to infer such meanings from the associations of the patient, and in this book, I consider the reports of the BCPSG as a specimen example of such a comparison. Finally, I suggest that the discovery that two theoretic models are not commensurate does not prove either model superior to the other but that it does allow us instead to see that disagreements about the advantages of the two models have often involved unrecognized category errors in which the disputants were talking past each other. It is just as though we were comparing the results of treatment with cognitive–behavioral therapy with the results of psychopharmacotherapy. With varying degrees of reliability, we could compare the outcomes of the two treatments in an adequately controlled sample population, but we could certainly not and would not smooth out the profound differences in how the claimed results were obtained in two groups of patients treated with such different modalities. I wish to be clear that I have no interest in the definition of what is the true church or the true psychoanalysis. My views here are predicated on the assumption that in the spirit of the pluralism of the day, we should speak of the family of psychoanalyses and that status and power are irrelevant to this suggestion. At issue is our need to agree that some of our models are better than others for varying purposes; for example, classical ego psychology de-emphasizes the participant relationship of the analyst in the dyad, and some of the more radical current relational theories de-emphasize sexuality. But this is still a reductive view of the problem of how to compare our various models because it has nothing to say about the gathering of data or the formation of inferences by the analysts in each model. We simply cannot disconnect observation, theory, and praxis in any of our models.

A group of analysts (BCPSG) have authored a series of reports concerning their views about the nature of change in psychoanalytic treatment. In 1998, they examined what factors beyond interpretation were mutative in the following way:

> It is by now generally accepted that something more than interpretation is necessary to bring about therapeutic change. Using an approach based on recent studies of mother–infant interaction and non-linear dynamic systems and their relation to theories of mind, the authors propose that the something more resides in interactional intersubjective process that give rise to what they will call "implicit relational knowing." *This relational procedural domain is intrapsychically distinct from the symbolic domain.* In the analytic relationship it comprises intersubjective moments occurring between patient and analyst that can create new organizations in, or reorganize not only the relationship between the interactants, but more importantly the patient's implicit procedural knowledge, his ways of being with others. The distinct qualities and consequences of these moments ("now moments", "moments of meeting") are modeled and discussed in terms of a sequencing process that they call "moving along". Conceptions of the shared implicit relationship, transference and countertransference are discussed within the parameters of this perspective, which is distinguished from other relational theories and self-psychology. In sum, powerful therapeutic action occurs within implicit relational knowledge. They propose that much of what is observed to be lasting therapeutic effect results from such changes in this intersubjective relational domain. (p. 903; italics added)

Several years later (BCPSG, 2002), they discussed their views of change in terms of what could be observed at the local level:

> The usual way of discussing analytic material is in narratives reconstructed by the analyst from memory or with the aid of notes taken during the session. However, videotape observations reveal that these narratives fail to capture many of the micro-events of the complex, multilayered interactive process. This detailed process constitutes what we will term the local level. The split-second world of the local level is a level of small specific *events*, rather than primarily a level of *verbalized meanings*. In this paper we will argue that such an implicit process exists and is organized into complex patterns that it is possible to study. Moreover, our view is that this local-level process constitutes an important domain of therapeutic change, because it is the site of change in relational procedures. (p. 1052)[2]

And their method of observation was to be adapted from the direct observation of infants:

> How exactly do we study interaction? . . . Here, models and insights from developmental research and dynamic systems theory seemed particularly pertinent. The observational methods of developmental research, which rely on repeated viewing of videotaped interactions between infants and their mothers, have illuminated a wealth of detail in the split-second microprocess. The minutiae of interaction, body language, gestural and facial expressive elements, vocal rhythms, tonal elements and timing can be observed and coded. For adult analytic patients, this meta-communicative or meta-content level is conveyed partially through the verbal medium, via nuances of word choice, timing and prosody of speech. . . . It seemed to us that it would be potentially useful to put clinical process under the micro-analytic lens in an analogous fashion. Perhaps this split-second world is critical to understanding change in therapy with adults as well. In infant observational studies, this split-second world is where relational life happens. Although the therapeutic medium is linguistic, the interactions we observe here and the patterns that emerge are largely implicit, in that *much of what transpires does not enter reflective consciousness.* (p. 1053; italics in original)[3]

These last words (in italics) are the only visible sign of one of the category mistakes here because of the statement that "much of what transpires does not enter . . . consciousness"; that is, it does not specify what the authors consider to be the explanation. If the authors really mean what their suggestion strongly suggests, then their explanation for the muchness that does not enter consciousness is something other than defense.

If the patient and analyst communicate in terms of a nondefense model, a gradual and vast accumulation of experiences develops expectations in the patient about how she or he will be understood that profoundly differ if the analyst were using a conflict-defense model or an object relations–defense model. It might be that the model of implicit relational knowing will prove superior to our traditional explanation of unconscious conflict and defense. The point here is that the data from the patient were processed by the analyst in a frame of reference that is in an incommensurate category. This is analogous to the difference between temperature measurements in centigrade versus Fahrenheit. I intend *incommensurate* to be understood in its connotation of a lack of parity between classes or categories.

The authors have stated their intention to offer a reconciliation of these two frames of reference at some point in the future. One is the dynamic unconscious, and the other is what they call the "dynamical" unconscious. One is the repressed unconscious, and the other is the unrepressed unconscious. Further evaluation of their intended reconciliation must await its publication. In their searching discussion, House and Portuges (2005) correctly point out that the implicit relational knowing that is at the heart of their theorizing is really only based on an analogy to what can be observed in infants, which the authors have simply carried forward to the mental life of adults.[4]

The mutative factors in the particular relational model espoused by the BCPSG are co-created changes that produce nonlinear shifts that are new and were unpredictable. In the BCPSG view (2005),

> [the] psychoanalytic therapeutic interaction is an inherently sloppy process. This sloppiness arises from the intrinsic *indeterminacy* of the co-creative process between two minds. Sloppiness here refers to the indeterminate, untidy or approximate qualities of the exchange of meaning between patient and analyst. (pp. 693–694)

Litowitz (2005) made the following astute observation about the relation between sloppiness and interpretation: "'Sloppiness' is not 'something more than interpretation'; rather, when more clearly defined, it is at the very heart of interpretive processes in general, and the co-creation of meaning specifically" (p. 757).

I added italics to the word *indeterminacy* to direct attention to another category contradiction. If the elements of the local-level exchanges of meaning between analyst and patient are indeterminate, they are beyond evidential challenge or pursuit, at least insofar as the comparison would be made with a model that does use a determinacy epistemology. Here we can see that the consequence of trying to compare these two theories is like comparing apples to oranges because in one theory, evidence for the justification of inferences is based on indeterminacy and, in the other model, evidence derives from psychic determinism. We therefore would have to devise a separate methodology of evidence for the two models. We analysts would do well to recall that psychic determinism has been every bit as much a bedrock epistemic constituent of psychoanalysis as have childhood sexuality or the unconscious been its theoretic foundation. If the inferred meanings are indeterminate, then the inferences of meaning cannot be derived from the associations of the patient that preceded this interaction. If this epistemic difference in the methodology of inference is unrecognized when we attempt to compare the meanings inferred by analysts from two theoretic models that use radically different epistemologies of determinacy, then the two analysts would be talking past each other. The conclusions would be incommensurate.

Perhaps, the basis for the differing epistemological views of the BCPSG (2005) can be traced to the following statement:

> We believe it is a fundamental error—one carried forward in psychoanalytic thinking—to base meaning (and mediation) in semantic meaning. Language and

abstract forms of thought build on earlier modes of making and representing meaning, but these earlier modes are not symbolic, nor are they superseded by the symbolic. A variety of work proves that both complex rule-learning and the learning of affective valence *can* occur in the absence of the capacity for explicit, declarative forms of memory. (p. 764).

In this statement, we see the claimed authority for discarding the epistemic importance of the associations of the patient. Because the verbalized associations of the adult patient were developmentally not semantic, they do not warrant epistemic value. This curious attention only to the baby's presemantic learning throws out the adult of later developmental semantic evolution and learning with the bath of ignoring the developmental nonsemantic roots of learning. This is a classic example of the genetic fallacy in which developmental alterations are ignored. It is erroneous to assume that direct extrapolation from infant to adult mental life is possible. At the same time, traditional psychoanalytic theory neglected the important role of nonverbal communication in the psychoanalytic process. This latter error was a serious omission, but the former error endangers much of what we have learned in the course of a century of psychoanalytic progress.

The authors also say the following: "We feel that observing the moment-to-moment exchange of meaning and relatedness in the two-person therapeutic exchange is . . . a rich and generative level of inquiry" (BCPSG, 2005, p. 769). With regard to the difference between the dynamic and dynamical unconscious, the authors state that they intend a later reconciliation. But this last statement is the announcement of a more radical proposal because it omits reference to the intrapsychic domain altogether. And the question of a future reconciliation is not mentioned here. The abandonment of the intrapsychic domain would be consonant with the abandonment of our epistemological reliance on the determinacy of the associations of the patient.

The next category difference that I discuss has to do with the BCPSG view regarding the indeterminacy of the patient's associations. The term *indeterminacy* has several connotations. Its most relevant connotation in this context is "not predetermined by some external force: not constrained: acting freely: spontaneous" (*Webster's*, 1986).[5] Thus, the authors advocate a definition of indeterminism that would be exactly opposite to the principle of psychic determinism.

For over a century, psychoanalysis has utilized a deterministic epistemology. Given this, we have postulated contextual determinants in the associations of our patients. We usually cannot predict associations or events forward in time from those determinate associations, but in the treatment situation, in our literature, and in supervision, we look back in time to the prior associations as being more generative of meaning in light of our later information.

But as the BCPSG uses the term *indeterminate* in the context of nonlinear, dynamical systems and complexity theory, this is also a reciprocal indeterminacy from a temporal point of view. Not only could an event not have been predicted forward in time, it cannot ever be traced backward to verbalized "determinants" within the framework of the manner that these authors speak of complexity and emergence theory. We psychoanalysts have long been accustomed to our ability to only explain backward. Perhaps, the most clarifying discussion of this problem was offered by Kris (1956) in his classic discussion of the fallibility of memory. This is famously true of our psychoanalytic theories of pathogenesis. We analysts can only explain backward about the evolution of our patients' symptoms. But that is hardly a basis for discarding everything that we have learned in a century about psychopathology. Similarly, it is one thing to maintain that we could not have predicted the reactions of our patients to our interventions (although we often can; ask any supervisor); it is that we are instructed by the BCPSG that we are logically forbidden to think of the associations of the patient as being organized in a determining, shaping, or causal manner in the patterning of these associations. An epistemology of indeterminacy and one of determinacy are as categorically different as the domain of quantum mechanics and the physics of stars and planets.

More than a century of psychoanalytic work has been predicated on the assumption of the principle of psychic determinism. That principle assumes that mental events are determined or caused in the same manner as physical events. This basic premise of psychoanalysis has been the basis for data gathering and the derivation of inferences of meaning by analysts all around the world. Our assumption has been that the sequential patterning of the associations of the patient are meaningful. The technical consequences of this assumption are visible in the ubiquitous curiosity of the analyst about the question "Why does the patient want me to know this now, at this particular time?" It is the technical analogue of our diagnostic curiosity in the beginning of treatment to investigate why the defense organization of the patient failed at a particular time. The removal of the principle of psychic determinism might some day be deemed to provide better explanations for the emotional suffering of our patients, but that will mean that all prior inferences derived from the principle of psychic determinism will require revision. And that might some day be the case, although I doubt it. But more important, the notion of indeterminacy is not a slight proposal. It is a conceptual earthquake that is not introduced as a profound alteration here. In fact, the authors promise a reconciliation at a later date. If they are able to reconcile these utterly incompatible frames of reference, then we will be left with the task of deciding when the experiences of the patient can be viewed to be determined and when they cannot.[6]

If these assumptions of the BCPSG are true, then we will have to give up the idea that the context of the patient's associations has any relevance to useful inferences that can be derived from the actual associations. The authors might argue that in their planned reconciliation of dynamic and dynamical frames of reference, this would not be so; but at the very least, they clearly intend that the clinical material offered in their work is to be understood best in terms of their own theory. A century of psychoanalytic clinical experience has been based on a profoundly important assumption that is neglected in the views of the BCPSG: the term *association* means "connected" or "grouped with." It is a paradox of "free" associations that we expect that the illusion of freedom provided by the safety of the analytic situation will create enhanced conditions for the appearance of connected ideas that are not free of contextual influences.

If the epistemology of a theoretic model excludes psychic determinism, many events during treatment will appear to be "new" or surprising. Actually, something emerging as "new" is an old idea in psychoanalytic developmental theory. It has been traditionally described as developmental discontinuity. But instead of being informed of an integration with or even an explicit challenge to existing developmental literature in child psychoanalysis, we are told that complexity theory has the advantage of compatibility with brain science. The authors of the BCPSG (2005b) give short shrift to the child psychoanalytic literature:

> Previous psychoanalytic theory has tended to equate non-verbal forms of representation with the preverbal functioning of infancy, current neuroscience makes clear that implicit forms of representation are fundamental to complex adult functioning as well as to infant functioning. (p. 697)

It seems paradoxical that these discussions of the emergence of unexpected and surprising new behaviors during the course of psychoanalytic treatment with adult patients by authors who favor the methodology of developmental infant and child research omit any reference to the extensive literature by child psychoanalysts who for some time have been studying developmental discontinuities in children and adolescents. Anna Freud (1965) said,

> In fact, what we regard as surprising are not the relapses but occasional sudden achievements and advances. Such moves forward may occur with regard to feeding where they take that form of a sudden refusal of the breast . . . or at later ages a sudden relinquishing of food fads. They are known to happen with regard to habits as a sudden giving up of thumb sucking or of a transitional object, of fixed sleeping arrangements. . . . In toilet training, instances are known of almost instantaneous change-over from wetting and soiling to bladder and bowel control; with regard to aggression, its almost overnight disappearance with change-over

to shy, restrained, diffident behavior. But convenient as such transformations may be for the child's environment, the diagnostician views them with suspicion and ascribes them not to the ordinary flow of progressive development but to traumatic influences and anxieties that unduly hasten its normal course. According to experience, the slow method of trial and error, progression and temporary reversal is more appropriate to healthy psychic growth. (p. 99)

I return to this point in my later discussion of the clinical example presented by the BCPSG wherein the patient suddenly announces her desire to terminate the analysis. Peltz (1986) summarized,

The genetic/developmental point of view in psychoanalysis contains the often overlooked premise that development proceeds both continuously and discontinuously. An example of developmental continuity is the theory of a continuous anxiety stream that alerts the ego to inaugurate defense. An example of developmental discontinuity is the theory that what evokes the signal anxiety changes across development: loss of the object, loss of the object's love, castration anxiety and guilt. Our theory holds that each successive anxiety signal emerges as the consequence of new psychological structure not inherent in the prior organization. (p. 245)

Against the BCPSG (1998) about unpredictable, new developments that seem to pop up out of nowhere, Abrams (1983) said,

In its more restricted conventional usage, a development is a specific happening; *the outcome of a sequence of related events whose causal links may be tracked. Functioning as historians, analysts trace such developments retrospectively by establishing the logical connections in a set of antecedent events. This type of development (i.e., outcome) may evoke surprise, be viewed with satisfaction or dismay, be seen as desirable or disagreeable.* In an analysis a completely new symptom may appear, a lost phobia from childhood may surface, or a patient may make transference demands. Such developments are aspects of the treatment and always require study. (pp. 113–114; italics added)

And consider the following from Abrams and Solnit (1998):

Growth is both continuous and *discontinuous*. The step-by-step changes from infancy to adulthood are informed by an inherent maturational blueprint or timetable of potential steps in organization that becomes realized in the form of a progressive sequence of developmental hierarchies. Each new organizational configuration builds on antecedents (continuities) *while bringing in novel structures and functions unavailable in earlier forms (discontinuities)*. In effect, psychological development unfolds in a series of systems or "minds," each containing new, drive-related experiences as well as innovative defenses, affects. (p. 89; italics added)

Blum (1987) pointed out that genetic continuity, such as transference neurosis, could paradoxically coexist with developmental discontinuities. For these reasons, I am very much in agreement with Fonagy's view (1996): "A hypothetical model cannot be presented as an alternative to actual empirical observations; far less can it be used to undermine its frame of reference" (p. 415). Neubauer (2001) further commented,

> That new organization can emerge without antecedents needs further clarification. We have accepted the notion that unresolved conflicts in one stage of development will be carried into the next stage in a state of transformation without resolution or co-existence with previous conflicts in a new organization. . . . In which area can we expect the shifts from one stage to the next—beyond developmental fixation or regression—and in which will new organizations, new psychic hierarchies emerge? *What can and what cannot be predicted?* . . . This raises the question of whether what is adaptive for one developmental phase may become maladaptive later. What are the differences between compromise formation and adaptation? (p. 21; italics added)

Galatzer-Levy (2002) clearly linked the concept of emergence to chaos theory, complexity theory, and nonlinear dynamic systems. If I understood him correctly, he was in agreement with the BCPSG's use of the term *surprise* (discontinuity without traceable antecedent determinants). This recent interest in complexity theory is allied with unacknowledged challenges to existing psychoanalytic theories of infant and child development.[7] Challenges are essential, but without their acknowledgment, we are unable to assess how the authors perceive the prior views they are contradicting. In our traditional views of the relation between child development and adult functioning, we have abundantly confirmed the value of Hartmann's concept (1955) of the genetic fallacy: "The actual function is equated with its history, or rather reduced to its genetic precursors, as if genetic continuity were inconsistent with change of function" (p. 14).

There is another unrecognized problem with the dynamical, nonlinear type of surprise mapped by complexity theory. As clinicians, we are now confronted with two kinds of surprise in two different frames of reference. The fact is that we have had plenty to worry about with clinical surprises since the dawn of psychoanalysis. Not all of these clinical surprises have been good ones. If "surprises" were taken at face value, then we would lose the possibility of viewing unpleasant surprises as being defensively motivated. Furthermore, every supervisor is acquainted with the surprises that derive from the blind spots as well as the dumb spots of the analyst. In fact, one of our most challenging problems has been the bad surprises—for example, the patients who suddenly announce that they will terminate treatment. But some of those surprises could have been predicted, and as such, many candidates learn a great deal in supervision from impasses discussed with a supervisor who could foretell in the material that a crisis would occur because of issues that had been ignored.

To be sure, the BCPSG authors offer us the reassurance that they do not reject the concepts of unconscious defense and dynamic unconscious and that they intend to reconcile the concept of a dynamic unconscious with the concept of unconscious implicit relational knowing at a later time. But they give us a disquieting hint about what the nature of this future reconciliation of these frames of reference will consist of:

> We do not reject the concept of the dynamic unconscious. Rather, we think in terms of a range of unconscious phenomena. Traditionally, the dynamic unconscious, construed as verbal or symbolic, and as unconscious only by reason of repression, is in psychoanalysis the only unconscious phenomenon considered "psychodynamic," the locus of all affectively important representations. However, there is also implicit knowledge that is non-conscious, has no verbal or symbolic label and does not require repression [*sic*] to remain unconscious. (BCPSG, 2005b, p. 696)

This constitutes a smoothing of a category error. Two different frames of reference are not at all integrated by nonrejection of the validity or usefulness of either by the other. The BCPSG authors are misleading when they speak of a range of unconscious phenomena because the word *range* implies a nonexistent continuum or an easy translatability of the one category into another— for example, the neural substrate (brain) is also unconscious, but the continuing failure to resolve the mind–body problem illustrates that the dynamic unconscious cannot be located in the same range as the unconscious of the neural substrate. In fact, the problem of an unrepressed unconscious occupied Freud's attention extensively in his writings (Freud 1900/1953a, 1915/1953b, 1923/1953c, 1933/1953d, 1940/1953e). The authors would need in their planned reconciliation to integrate their views of a nondynamic unconscious with prior views of the unrepressed unconscious described originally by Freud as primal repression, as well as the additional nondynamic unconscious described by Matte-Blanco and Lacan (1988, as cited in Lindell, 2003).[8]

The BCPSG discussion (2005b) of spontaneity and surprise conflates several distinctly separate issues.

> As the therapeutic relationship moves along, shared implicit knowing and shared intentions emerge bit by bit from the co-creative relational overtures each provides the other. The dynamical dyadic system has emergent capacities for creating new and unpredictable forms of shared implicit knowing in the interac-

tants as new ways of being together are co-created in the treatment. . . . Most of the affectively meaningful life experiences that are relevant in psychotherapy are represented in the domain of nonconscious implicit knowledge. This also includes many manifestations of transference. Therefore, much of what happens at the local level is psychodynamically meaningful, though not necessarily repressed. The fact that the dynamically repressed unconscious can also be an active influence at the local level is not our focus. We are *simply* calling attention to a different level of process. (pp. 697–698)

It would be more correct to say the authors are calling attention to a different frame of reference for understanding what they call the *local level*. It is not necessarily true that two different processes are occurring simultaneously but that one process can be understood in two different ways:

We have noted that co-creativity is the upshot of an unpredictable, improvisational process and that fuzzy intentionalizing depends on variability and redundancy. We do not mean to imply that everything that happens in a session is unpredictable. Rather we emphasize that the interplay of two subjectivities inevitably throws up unpredictable and surprising phenomena at the local level. (p. 709)

Is there no more reliable method for this determination of unpredictability than the fact that the analyst feels surprised? Most analysts could think of experiences when they were surprised and, in retrospect, realize that they should not have been. And, certainly, inexperienced analysts have this experience more often than they will later in their careers.

It is one thing for an analyst to be surprised by the patient; it is another to argue that on logical grounds, the analyst cannot be allowed to go back over the material preceding the surprise to reconsider whether he or she had misunderstood something.[9] The assurance that certain events could never have been predicted is not the question. Certainly that is so, but the problem then is to decide how best to explain that the event had not been predicted. To say merely that it would have been logically impossible seems to give the analyst a justification to stop analyzing that particular interaction. That strategy seems paradoxical for a relational theorist.

Note the BCPSG's methodology for inferring meaning from these indeterminate communications in the relational knowing of the interactions they describe:

The sloppiness of a therapeutic dyadic system emerges in part from a core feature of therapeutic interaction that we will refer to as fuzzy intentionalizing. When any two creative and independent agencies interact, a central problem they encounter is that while actions are observable their intentions or meaning must be inferred. We would claim . . . that this process of inferring intentions, through parsing of actions is central to how the brain works ["brain" not "mind"] and to how we understand others. (2005b, p. 699)

On what evidential ground would the supervisor wish to advise the student that the student's views were not as useful as that of the instructor? It also seems paradoxical to claim that evidence is dubious because of indeterminacy but that the authors' views are more correct than others. Either evidence is relevant in both ways, or it is not relevant in either way. If evidence is relevant, do the authors foresee any problems with an attempt to reconcile their dynamical model view of evidence with the traditional dynamic model view of evidence?

Will there be deeper implications for the fate of our prior notions about clinical evidence? Would we simply have to take the word of the analyst as a co-creator because the molten, inchoate flux of implicit relational knowing is beyond evidential pursuit? The authors (BCPSG, 2005b) state,

We use the term co-creativity rather than co-construction for several reasons. The latter has connotations inconsistent with a *dynamical* systems model. The word construction implies a directed process in which preformed elements are brought together according to an a priori plan. In contrast, with co-creativity *there is no blueprint for assembly.* Instead the elements assembled are themselves formed during the process of the interchange. (p. 701; italics added)

With this last argument, are we absolved of the requirement to support truth claims with clinical evidence? Do the authors mean that they themselves in the aftermath of the co-creation by patient and analyst are not able to describe their "blueprint" for the assembly of meaning? Second, do the authors believe that the inferred meanings derived by any and all analysts who use a deterministic epistemology are preformed from a blueprint for assembly in the same sense that Freud viewed the meanings of symbols or typical dreams or those of the symptoms of actual neurosis? Is it their view that all of us who are not strong constructivists simply decode the communications of our patients? That would contradict much of the clinical literature of recent decades.

The authors state with approval the coordination of their views with modern neuroscience. It is unclear why they feel it more necessary to reconcile their views with neuroscience and the brain than with the broad body of existing psychoanalytic literature about the relation of memory to the mind. They state that, traditionally, the dynamic unconscious, construed as being verbal or symbolic, was unconscious only by means of repression. That appears to be a reductive reading of Freud's views about the relation of primal and secondary repression. This, they say, is in contrast to implicit knowledge that is nonconscious and has no verbal or symbolic label and does not require repression to remain unconscious. Here they also ignore the incommensurate disconnect with the large body of psychoanalytic theory about defense in which defense has not been synonymous with repression for over 80 years.

Don't the authors really mean to say that we will have to radically alter the manner in which we adjudicate the claim that any one theory is or is not more supported by clinical evidence? The reason is that the very notion of evidence must also be radically redefined based on an ontological assumption: It is incapable of existing in the inchoate matrix of intersubjective co-creativity. At least the available methodology for evaluating moment-to-moment transactions of the type they have discussed until now has required the assumption of psychic determinism. We have evaluated interpretations based on assuming a deterministic shaping influence of the associations before and immediately following an interpretation. Can we just slip that method out of a stack of cards as though it didn't have other far-reaching consequences? Once again, we have an incommensurate disagreement because we are observing what appear to be similar phenomena (the moment-to-moment interactions with our patients), but we are using two radically different frames of reference. Before, we were told that we were barred from speaking of reliable and valid comparisons of different explanations to see which one best explains certain phenomena because of our irreducible subjectivity (Renik, 1993). Now evidence is barred from playing a role in our disagreements because of the irreducible indeterminism of the events occurring in the interaction of patient and analyst. Note the following, for example:

> Neither analyst nor patient can know in any specific detail what the two of them will need to do together to reach their goals. Indeed, both analyst and patient can only grapple with the immediate dilemma of what to do to take the next step in the interactive process. This grappling is, of course, the point at which all of the analyst's dynamic [*sic*] training and humanity come into play. It is here that the analyst's grasp of some healing direction, some selection of what to "recognize" in the patient's words and actions, will be operationalized. But this indeterminacy of the "how to" of therapy is inescapable, regardless of technical stance, and emerges necessarily from the irreducible fact that both patient and analyst are [the] source of independent agency and subjectivity and at the same time are constantly influencing each other. (BCPSG, 2005, p. 699)

There are puzzling contradictions in the following clinical example, provided to illustrate the views of the authors. They provide three portions of the transcript of an audiotaped session of an analysis conducted by one of them (the full transcript is usefully available as an appendix to their article). The authors state that the beneficial changes illustrated in their clinical example were the result of sloppiness, fuzzy intentionality, and co-creativity. They insist that "the interplay of two subjectivities inevitably throws up unpredictable and surprising phenomena at the local level" (p. 709). They also say,

> *Sloppiness is to a two-person psychology what free association is to a one-person psychology.* They each add the unexpected specific details. They create the surprise discoveries that push the dyad to its uniqueness. However, there is also an important difference. *Free associations are assumed to lead to and from pre-existing networks of meanings. . . .* Sloppiness, by contrast, is not part of any established organization, even though it, too, is influenced by the past. Sloppiness, like free association or other unanticipated pop-up events, can be used creatively only when framed within a well-established therapeutic system or within a well-functioning dyad. Without the direction and constraints of those dyadic systems, the improvisational elements can veer toward chaos. (pp. 721–722; italics added)

There are profound epistemic consequences to this exchange of sloppiness for free association. That is also true of their description of an upside-down reversal of the determining role of the past and the here and now in their epistemology:

> Even though we view each individual as having a past and as bringing a set of potential ways of relating into the new encounter, we see the dyadic situation as dominating the past events. In our view, the way the past of the two participants influences their interactions is the way transference and countertransference expressions present themselves in this model. It is the present interaction of the participants that *recontextualizes* the transferential manifestations of the past. (p. 717)

We are left to wonder what these constraints of dyadic systems consist of. The authors seem to imply the technical restraints that characterize well-intentioned, ethical, and benevolent therapeutic behavior—also, the theoretic constraints of consistency between their theory and their technique. But they are silent about the problem of evidential constraints, which are, according to their own views, disconnected from free associations.

To make the ensuing discussion of comparing the relational theory used by the members of the BCPSG with the type of conflict theory with which I compare it more clear, I wish to remind you of the notion of a scientific domain. The familiar reductive distinction between one- and two-person theoretic models does not address an important distinction between our various models. Each of the interactional theoretic models is formulated in the two-person perspective. A scientific domain defines what data are observed in any scientific enterprise. As such, any scientific theory addresses possible answers to explain phenomena generated in a finite and circumscribed domain of data. We can discuss stars only when we use telescopes and cells only when we use microscopes. The tension between general relativity theory and quantum mechanics illustrates two different domains of data: very large objects and very small objects. Contrary to a still prevalent and erroneous view, conflict theory or structural theory can no longer be viewed as only a one-person model as a consequence of the influence of the various two-person models upon traditional structural theory. Enactment theory is one example of this influence (see Chused, 1991; Chused & Raphling, 1992; Jacobs, 1986; McLaughlin, 1991; Poland, 1992). A number of analysts do still adhere to the view of a conflict model as a one-person model. But a number of other analysts who use the conflict model, including myself (Boesky, 1990), view the participation of the analyst as being powerfully influential in shaping the interaction with the patient. This group of analysts oscillates in its observations of the intrapsychic and interpersonal domains. In chapter 4, I give a detailed example of this and discuss how it differs from the Sullivanian participant observer. The language of the BCPSG is derived in the interpersonal domain, and my discussion is written from the standpoint of the intrapsychic domain. If this difference in these two categories is omitted, serious misunderstandings about reconciliation arise.

The particular contrast to which I direct your attention is this: In the two-person perspective–structural theory using the intrapsychic domain, rather than the interpersonal domain, the mutative factors are thought to be alterations in the defense organization and self and object representations as a result of interpretations as well as relational factors. The interpretations in this theory are based on inferences from detailed contextualizations of the moment-to-moment associations of the patient. These inferences depend on the assumption that the associations of the patient are shaped by psychic determinism and unconscious defenses. Let us turn now to the BCPSG's clinical report to consider that last point. As you will see, the inferences derived from the following clinical example reported by the BCPSG are themselves derived from a very different category of epistemological assumptions.

Clinical Example of the BCGSP

A condensed introductory summary of the views of the authors about how they explain therapeutic change in their patient will pave the way for my discussion of their clinical report that follows. Before their clinical example in their *Journal of the American Psychoanalytic Association* article (BCPSG, 2005b) the authors explain,

> Any therapeutic interaction . . . [lends] itself to a discussion of psychodynamics, [but] it also has an organization at the local level (i.e. moment to moment level),

regardless of the particular analytic technique adopted. The negotiation of intention and direction will look quite different with different techniques, but such negotiation will always be present. And the reality of the features we are describing is *not apparent unless one looks very closely at this moment-to moment level.* ... We will therefore demonstrate what we mean by sloppiness in the co-creative process as it occurs at the local level, relational move by relational move. We will illustrate the process of fuzzy intentionalizing. ... We will also comment on how these features of sloppiness are intrinsic to the creation of shared meaning. (p. 702; italics added)

In my discussion, I demonstrate that these proposals have profound consequences for our methodology of justifying truth claims based on psychoanalytic treatment data.

The patient had come for analysis 4 years before, for suicidal thoughts related to being sexually abused in her family:[10]

The Monday session to be described followed an *extra session* the preceding Friday that the analyst had proposed, having sensed increased distress in the patient during their last scheduled meeting [Thursday]. In the extra [Friday] session, the analyst suggested that the patient might have felt coerced to come, but the patient had disagreed. (p. 702; italics added throughout, except where indicated)

We are not informed about the basis for the urgency felt by the analyst that prompted him to advise her to come in for an extra session the next day, when they evidently did not ordinarily meet. We are told only that the analyst sensed increased discomfort in the patient during their last scheduled meeting but not what that discomfort was about. We are next told that in this Monday session (which was reported in detail) that followed the extra session Friday, the patient reported two dreams and used the dreams "to enter new territory." In the first dream, which occurred on Friday night (the night immediately after the extra session proposed by the analyst), the patient was in a group therapy meeting that reminded her of a sexual abuse group that she had attended. She said that that meeting (in her dream) disturbed her because, by emphasizing her victimization, it made her feel worse, not better.

At this point, I offer two conjectures about the session up to this point. These are based on a theoretic model using psychic determinism and the concepts of unconscious defense. The analyst might then infer from these associations that her Friday-night dream had to do with frightening fantasies about the emergency session suggested by the analyst and that the anxiety that she felt had to do with feeling worse, for two reasons. First, if her analyst believed that she needed that session so badly and could not ask for one herself, then it was necessary for him to carry out these functions for her, which implied that she was worse off than what she had thought. Second, it is possible that the dream of a group therapy session for sexual abuse patients meant that she feared that there were links between the analyst's wanting her to have the extra session and the memories of her having been sexually abused in her family.

The second dream occurred the night before (Sunday) and contained humorous material in which imperfections of the analyst made him seem more human and normally fallible, not someone totally in control of his life and therefore more as if she was more like him. The next day (Tuesday), the patient began the session sitting up, which was quite unusual for her.

> It began very differently, with the patient wanting to sit rather than lie on the couch. For the first time, she began talking while sitting up on the couch and looking at the analyst. (p. 719)

Later in the session, she said that she felt more connected and in control of what they were talking about, in a way that was unusual, and that it was as though she had an agenda today. The analyst said wryly,

> "It's hard to have an agenda other days?" She replied "Yeah." The two then burst into laughter, enacting a sense of shared fittedness of initiatives. This shared recognition of fittedness is the period, or sometimes the exclamation point, that marks the creation of a new joint intention that *contextualizes* the interaction. In fact, it did later in the session when for the first time the two began to realistically discuss termination. (p. 720)

The statement about her unusual refusal to use the couch clearly indicates that the analyst was surprised, as well he might be, given that this was apparently the first time in 4 years that she had done this. Later in that same session, they began for the first time to talk about termination in a way that felt realistic and reasonable to them both. The authors next ask the question "How did they arrive at this *new territory* from having begun at a point of distress?"

It is not common for authors in our literature to state their contextualizing criteria explicitly, and we should be grateful to the BCPSG for doing so here. This makes it possible to compare contextualizing criteria across models. They said that this shared recognition of fittedness and shared fittedness of initiatives (which includes the shared agreement that termination would be realistic) is what contextualized this interaction for them. However, for a conflict model analyst, the developments at the end of the session that, in their contextualization, meant shared fittedness would have meant unrecognized unconscious anxiety. A conflict analyst would have contextualized this session in the larger context of the prior emergency session and the first dream. Then, her surprising refusal of the couch would have seemed paradoxically contradictory to the view that termination in this session was simply to be taken at face value. Even those differences are secondary to the importance of seeing clearly here the consequences of two different systems of contextualization. At issue is not primarily which is the truer understanding of what was going on (although there are visible differences of interpretation) but the clear chance to see that the contextualizing criteria of the BCPSG are incommensurate with those of the conflict model. To paraphrase another French aphorism, to understand everything is to forgive everything. If we understand when we are in a disagreement with colleagues that they and we have contextualized the associations of the patient differently, then we can compare conclusions with more light and less heat.

It is important to note that the context of their discussion of this new territory clearly indicates that for them it included the agreement to terminate the analysis and that this agreement was a desirable sign of therapeutic change free of defensive implications. The problem that they set for themselves then is how to account for this good change from the distress that the patient manifested in her refusal to use the couch to her comfort about termination.

They answer that question by presenting a line-by-line report of this session, illustrating what they call the local level of the interaction, which they assume gave rise to the more visible macrochanges experienced by this analytic dyad. Let us remember that one of these changes was the mutual agreement that termination would be reasonable. If we compare our two methods of making inferences, the authors regard her wish to sit up as a surprise evoked by indeterminate events, and the conflict model analyst would view it as a sign of intense anxiety evoked by her emergency session and her dream of taking part in a sexual abuse group. The second difference, if we compare models here, is that the authors regard the mutual agreement to discuss termination immediately after the emergency appointment as a sign of desirable change, and the conflict model analyst would view it as a paradoxical avoidance of pursuing the question of why the topic of termination was coming up at just this particular time. It might indeed have been reasonable to terminate this analysis, but it is paradoxical that this agreement comes so quickly after the analyst thought it necessary to advise the patient to have an emergency appointment. The reason is that it would then seem that she herself was deemed by the analyst as being not capable of making either that judgment or the request:

> Below, she describes the second dream [concerning the analyst's imperfections and her feeling more like him] as a contrast to that first dream. As can be seen, the analyst does not stay with her talk about the Sunday night dream but directs her back to the idea of calling him after the dream concerning the group therapy. (p. 704)

Now we backtrack a bit. On the Saturday morning after the Friday extra session, the patient thought of phoning the analyst. The reason she gave was that

"I had seen you on Friday and felt there was like a thread of consciousness that had flowed into that dream" (p. 706). However, she decided that she could wait until Monday to tell him.

Remember that we were told that the patient originally came for treatment because of her recurrent suicidal thoughts as her only way to assert herself in the family in the aftermath of her family's having sexually abused her. We are given no information about these traumatic sexual experiences nor about how her sexual conflicts were understood in the analysis nor about the status of her sex life at the time that termination was mutually accepted. Instead, this active analyst steers her away from the dream of the night of the emergency session with its obvious allusions to her sexual conflicts and instead directs her to talk about her idea of phoning him.

I now report a brief excerpt of that process material and the selected excerpts from the authors' running commentary about it:

> Patient: So there are two completely different . . . the dream that I had last night [i.e., the second dream from Sunday night] left me feeling really connected to you, and you know it made me feel—I don't know, I guess closer to you, that you would tell me that you were not perfect. (p. 704)

The authors explained, before quoting this excerpt, that this second dream

> contained somewhat humorous material in which imperfections of the analyst made him seem more human and normally fallible, not someone totally in control of his life. Here the patient felt that the analyst, contrary to her previous notions, was much more like she was. (p. 703)

We are told later in the article that she had said in this same Monday session,

> I haven't quite figured out how to make that scar [by *scar*, she meant "feeling like a sick person"] fit in to my image of myself. . . . And because of that, every time I come here I feel like I have to come with that wound, that gaping wound being the most visible thing. (p. 713)

Actually, this last statement appears in the third excerpt of three extracted from the Monday session and clearly not construed by the authors as associations to her dreams. This scrambling and inversion of the temporal sequence of the patient's associations in their report is possibly related to the de-emphasis by the authors of the role of context of the association in the inferential processes established by the analyst. The authors then interject a comment:

> She has presented two dreams with some discussion and analysis but at this point she proceeds with the second one. Why? While there may have been many

reasons for her choice—defensiveness, closeness in time, etc.—this is an example of the indeterminacy in communication regarding the direction the person intends to take, what we refer to as fuzzy intentionalizing. Was there more to learn from the first dream? We don't know, because what she talks about, the feeling of closeness in the second dream, is where she has taken us. And even within the choice she has made, she introduces some minor uncertainties, saying things like "I don't know, I guess . . ." These declarifications could be resistances, show a reluctance to engage the topic, or suggest a real question about what she was saying. In any case they add to the fuzzy intentionality, or indeterminacy, in inferring where the patient wants to go. (p. 704)

Note that, once again, the authors do not say that they invoke their ideas about indeterminacy to explain the patient's feelings. Instead, they locate what is merely their inference about the indeterminacy of her associations, as though they had directly observed indeterminacy in her instead of in their theories about her. This confusion of observation and inference is an ancient source of trouble in the history of psychoanalysis. I now resume by quoting from their clinical report at the point where I interrupted it.

> Analyst: Uh-huh.
> Patient: Um.
> Analyst: You actually thought about calling me on Saturday about this other dream.
> (Here we have the first surprise, an example of the unpredictability in the sloppiness. The analyst exercises his own initiative and shifts the discussion to the other dream. In fact, not even to the dream but to what she thought of doing *after* [original italics] the dream. Why? He seems to have radically altered the direction of things. Did he know why at the moment of doing it? The word actually stands out. It is either a request for clarification that she really did think about calling him or a statement of his own surprise that she did. Or it could be related to his concern that he had coerced her into accepting an extra hour. In any case, his intentions are probably multiple, and not yet well formed. It turned out fine [*sic*], but that does not mean he knew what he was doing at the time. The analyst's shift, his abandonment of the second dream appears, the one from Sunday night, is also surprising because the second dream appears to contain hotter transference material.)
> Patient: Yeah!

At this point, the authors interrupt their report of this process material to comment as follows: "She works through some of the fuzziness by focusing on only one piece of unclarity" (p. 705).

I return later to some important assumptions in those statements, assumptions that, in my opinion, are misleading. For now, I direct your attention to the confusing overlap in the terms *sloppiness, fuzziness, unclarity,* and *indeterminacy.*

Analyst: Which would have been, uh, and the reason you were thinking of that, that kind of very real connection, was what? . . .
Patient: What are you referring to, the calling?
Analyst: Yeah, the calling.
Patient: Well, because I had seen you on Friday and felt there was like a thread of consciousness that had flowed into that dream. . . .
Analyst: Yeah. (pp. 705–706)

Later the authors provide a summary explanation as follows:

How does the co-creative, sloppy nature of the local-level process operate in this segment to contribute to change? It is in the implicit jockeying back and forth, patient and analyst checking out at each step how much each can contribute and respond to the emergence of a new shared direction, that a new shared meaning is co-created (this, rather than change in symbolic meaning leading the way through shared understanding of the patient's dreams and associations). As patient and analyst search for a fit with each other, while at the same time referencing their own agendas, they are co-creating a shared intention. This new intention reorganizes and recontextualizes each of the old agendas in the process of its emergence. (p. 708)

At this point, the authors have interrupted their verbatim reporting of the process material that is available at the end of the article, where these two sessions are reproduced in their entirety. In the material, they do not include in the main body that the patient says something to the analyst that can be read to imply a most meaningful irony about the manner in which the analyst is working with her. She told him,

And [Ferenczi] said it's not the free [association] itself that is the cure. It is that if you can free associate, you're cured. (chuckles). He says: "Uh-huh." She says, "And I thought, you know, that really struck me as relevant to what you and I have been talking about." He says: "Yeah, uh-huh, how specifically about you and me?" She says, "Well, that you know my problem seems to be that I'm still way too much in control of what I'm aware of thinking." (p. 725)

At precisely this point, the authors state that several lines of the transcript were deleted. The authors resume later in the session, about the issues of the first dream, which returns the discussion to what follows:

She says: "[Talking with the group therapist] makes me feel too vulnerable, and it makes me feel something I don't feel I can afford to feel. Y'know, I would rather . . . I would rather focus on—I don't know, the part of me that feels strong—than to be in touch with the part of me that felt like *I was going to be stabbed to death* [a reference to some of the sex play that occurred in her familial sexual abuse].

It just makes me think I could never, I couldn't have tolerated doing therapy with her [the group therapist is first identified here as a woman] or something [*sic*] like her because that really would make me fall apart, and it feels like I would be disintegrating in such a way I could never reconstruct myself. I would be too, like I'd have no confidence in myself at all, as opposed to the way my relationship with you has always been. You and I both know that there is a part of me that is strong. . . . I don't know where any of this is going, but . . ."

Analyst: Well, where, I, I mean I guess I was thinking, do you feel that in the second dream this, are you, how strong are you vis a vis me? I . . . you told me how strong I am raising these children and yet . . . I tell you that, you know. (p. 725)

Note that the analyst once again interrupts her associations to the sexual aspects of the first dream and directs her attention to the second dream. After he did that, she almost immediately fell silent for over 2 minutes, and he then expressed no curiosity about the timing of this unusual silence. There is an unrecognized irony then in the authors' commentary about this shared intention of the patient and the analyst. They wonder,

> How in this brief exchange did they come to "agree to" what their shared intention was? It was not explicitly articulated. The key to this joint accomplishment lies in the recurrences in the patient's and analyst's statements. These recurrences are not redundant in the sense of being unnecessary or boring. The cycling of the pair's recurrent turn taking is crucial to how they co-created a shared relational intention. It is an exploratory process of slow, incremental steps toward co-creation of shared meaning and shared direction. (p. 714)

An alternative reading of this interaction is that the analyst and patient have indeed created a shared unconscious resistance in the transference based on a collusive wish to avoid the erotic–sadistic transference fantasies of this patient, rather than a nondefensive sharing of benevolently mutative intentions. In short, this interaction could be alternately viewed as an iatrogenic enactment (Boesky, 1990) in which both patient and analyst have unconsciously participated in a collusive avoidance of her terrifying transference fantasies ("I was going to be stabbed to death") expressed in both dreams in two different defensively altered representations.

The authors quietly say that they do not reject the use of free associations, but they propose substituting *sloppiness* for free associations as the basis for forming inferences about the patient in this vignette. But they fail to state how they wish to preserve the use of the concept of associations. In fact, at certain points, the authors seem to advocate shifting away from the use of the associations of the patient. For example, when discussing alternative pathways that the analyst in their example could have employed, they say, "The analyst might have chosen to give priority to free association and so not have interrupted the free-associative process with his comment early on about the patient's thoughts of telephoning him" (p. 721).

This view of free associations conflates the use of free associations as a technique in pursuit of the fundamental rule with the connotation of associations as an essential part of the epistemic fabric of psychic determinism. I pursue this point in chapters 5 and 6. Many analysts would agree that the manner in which the patient and analyst communicate with each other shapes the experience of everything that the patient feels from the inception of the treatment until the last hour. If all of the events in every session are tacitly understood to be at least potentially meaningful because they have been determined by prior events, it is hard to see how the patient and analyst could repeatedly suspend that assumption and shift to fuzzy intentionality, sloppiness, and indeterminacy. If the authors do not wish to repudiate the use of the associations of the patient while, at the same time, sloppiness were to be substituted for associations, what would be the criteria for switching back and forth between the epistemology of sloppiness to the epistemology of associations?

It is not possible to separate the epistemology of different models from the manner in which data are generated and inferences are assumed. The epistemologies of sloppiness and psychic determinism are categorically different. But the authors see no contradiction in claiming that they wish to preserve the use of the concept of free associations as well as sloppiness. Sloppiness in their definition does not mean imprecise. Their *sloppiness* is a form of epistemology in which the data generated in the interaction between patient and analyst are indeterminate.

The authors here are unclear about their use of indeterminacy when they speak of sloppiness and indeterminacy. According to Cavell (1993), "when we say a thing is determined sometimes we mean it is caused, sometimes forced, sometimes that it has a determinate nature" (p. 172). The determinism in the phrase *psychic determinism* means only the latter. To say that associations are determined does not mean they are caused by their prior associations, it means only that there is a contextually meaningful determinate relation between the associations in a given contextual horizon.[11] This also relates to the disagreement between Wittgenstein and Freud about Freud's views that certain reasons could be viewed as causes and Wittgenstein's views that reasons cannot be causes unless experimentally verified (Cavell, 1993). It is logically incoherent to say that something is both indeterminate and determined. It cannot be both unless we are using different definitions of *determinacy*. I believe that that is the case here. Sloppiness as an epistemology is in a different conceptual category than psychic determinism is and will thus generate incommensurate data when compared with data from a determinate or psychic determinism epistemology.

I add here that I am in agreement with the authors that the analyst must look closely at the moment-to-moment interaction with the patient, but I am not in agreement that we have a consensus about what to look for when we look closely at this interaction. In the view of these authors, "sloppiness is *intrinsic* to moment to moment relating" (p. 701) rather than sloppiness is intrinsic to their assumptions about moment-to-moment relating. The data are not sloppy. They believe rightly or wrongly that sloppiness is the best way to describe these data. This is a critical distinction. As they see it, sloppiness contributes to the generation of change in the patient, and this is where they deploy their views about co-creativity:

> We think of co-creation as a self-organizing process of two minds acting together that takes advantage of the sloppiness inherent in the interaction to create something psychologically new. *What comes into being did not exist before and could not be fully predicted by either partner.* . . . Nonlinear dynamical systems as seen in dyadic interaction by their nature reassemble interpersonal and mental events in ways that are not predictable and that emerge spontaneously as a function of the interaction. Therefore, interactive processes make nonlinear leaps or qualitative shifts. For this reason, new intentions, feelings and meanings are some of the creative products of interest in a nonlinear dyadic system. Although meanings, feelings, intentions are not usually thought of as created products that pop up unexpectedly from a dyadic process, they are arguably the most important and complex products that emerge from human interaction. . . . We use the term co-creativity rather than co-construction for several reasons. The latter has connotations inconsistent with a dynamical systems model. The word construction implies a directed process in which preformed elements are brought together according to an a priori plan. In contrast, with co-creativity there is no blueprint for assembly. Instead the elements assembled are themselves formed during the process of the interchange. (p. 701)

I return to this point later in the discussion because it conflates unpredictability with a disconnect between all that precedes a moment in analysis with what follows and it is directly in opposition to many decades of psychoanalytic empirical experience.

Viewed from the conflict theory frame of reference, we confront another contradiction. If the analyst was sufficiently concerned about the welfare of the patient to suggest an extra appointment at the end of the Thursday session, it is puzzling that in the Tuesday session, after her unusual refusal of the couch, that they both agreed that termination was realistic and reasonable to them both. This may have to do with customary prior interventions by this analyst that were not made explicit, but it is a sufficiently jarring contradiction to hear about an emergency session on Friday and mutual agreements preliminary to actual termination in just a few days afterward that one would expect the authors to clarify for their readers what appears to be such a contradiction. But we are only left to guess.

The authors discuss three excerpts from the audiotapes of the entire Monday session. At issue here is not the so-called "correct" way to understand this material but a more interesting question: Can there be a coherent disagreement between the views of these authors and those of analysts from other theoretic models if the communications of the patient are contextualized in theoretical systems from radically different frames of reference? But just such a difference clearly emerges when the authors state the following:

> One can see that there is no consistent narrative structure at the local level, and no way to tell what would follow any of the relational moves. Even the most insightful analyst cannot know what the patient will say in the very next sentence. Even if the general topic is clear, the exact form it will take is unpredictable. Yet the exact form of what the analyst says will create the context and thus influence what happens next. *This important feature of what actually happens in the therapeutic process is not revealed by a focus on dynamic unconscious meanings.* (p. 711; italics added)

Thus, context does not arise in the dialectic of interaction in the dyad as viewed by the analyst in the intrapsychic domain. Instead of the collaborative contextualization that could be constructed by the analyst, the analyst co-creates change by generating unpredictability, sloppiness, and creativity.

It would be reductive to parachute into this dauntingly complex clinical interaction with alternative readings about "what it all means" based on my own preferred model because the material available to us was gathered in a frame of reference utterly different from that in which I would view the material. It is more interesting and important to determine whether we can even compare our impressions about each other's work than to presume to "correct" each other.

I return now to the question of the surprised analyst. We might speak of bad surprises and good surprises. It is an oversimplification, but it puts the problem here more clearly. If there is to be a new category of mutative surprise that is only benign and has no defensive function, in contrast to the bad surprises that need to be analyzed, how do we distinguish the one from the other? Are we to simply refrain from investigating the good surprises and take them at face value? Was the surprise of the analyst in the clinical example reported when the patient refused to use the couch unrelated to the surprise of this reader about the agreement established between patient and analyst to stop the analysis at the same time that emergency appointments were felt necessary by the analyst? Freud once warned about the uncritical face value acceptance of a patient's demand to avoid secret topics, with his analogy of guaranteed safety for thieves in the cathedral. Pretty soon the population of thieves in the cathedral would increase. The BCPSG write,

> In our view the way the past of the two participants influences their interactions is the way transference and countertransference expressions present themselves in this model. It is the present interaction of the participants that recontextualizes the transferential manifestations of the past. . . . *We believe that the center of gravity lies in the interaction between two parties, not in the individual past of either person.* In agreement with current views of memory, we believe the present moment contextualizes what will be remembered but also transforms that memory as it is recontextualized in light of the present interaction. (p. 717; italics added)[12]

To support their views, the authors then cite noted authorities in brain science.[13] This view of the dialectic between past and present is not novel, but it is incomplete. What is novel is the reversal of roles from the pathogenic force of the past in creating symptoms in traditional psychoanalytic views in contrast to the authors' formulation of the primary memory-creating power of the present interaction. It follows from the authors' views that if the present moment is the key determinant of memory formation, then the sexual past is irrelevant to the present transference at least insofar as it would deserve contextualizing priority at any time. This might indeed account for the striking absence of consideration of the sexual elements in the reported clinical illustration about this sexually abused patient—for example, her dream about a group discussion of sex abuse and her sudden and unexpected refusal to use the couch, as she and the analyst burst into laughter about how she enjoyed feeling in control with him.

When two theoretic models prove to be incommensurate, what recourse do we have for comparing their advantages and disadvantages? We certainly do not need to resort to the futile solution of saying that one method is real psychoanalysis and the other is not. Many different forms of psychoanalysis now exist. If some of them are categorically not comparable to others, then we still have recourse to empirical outcome studies to determine which has the better results; but it is going to be complicated and difficult for us to arrive at a consensus about the definitions of therapeutic change. Defining the criteria of stable change is difficult enough within the parameters of just one model. Doing so across models is immeasurably more complex. An example of which is the discussion about successful termination in this clinical instance.

I conclude by quoting the closing statement of the reply of the BCPSG (2005a) to the discussants of their article:[14]

> One of the central challenges for science will always be to find the level of description of a phenomenon that leads to generative insights regarding funda-

mental processes. We feel that observing the moment-to-moment exchange of meaning and relatedness in the two-person therapeutic exchange is such a rich and generative level of inquiry. (p. 769)

I am in complete agreement with this statement, but I take little consolation from that fact, because this agreement is valid at only a high level of abstraction. What is disquieting is the likelihood that other apparent agreements at such an abstract level in our comparisons of all of our models might conceal important ambiguities, problems, and disagreements.

The term *comparative psychoanalysis* promises too much at this point in our confusion about the methodology for justifying the inferences of latent meaning in the psychoanalytic treatment situation. Can we assume that we really know how to compare theories that use categorically different epistemologies? The problem with this question is that it evokes memories of the days when dissidents were accused of not being real analysts. But the purpose of a meaningful comparative psychoanalysis is not to establish elitist definitions. Nor will egalitarian proclamations solve the problem of our crude methodology for comparing evidential claims. We need a better way to know if we can compare data generated in incommensurate theoretic models. Can we clarify that question without resorting to the orthodoxies of "what is really psychoanalysis" and "what is not"? Congenial inclusiveness will not help enough.

Notes

1. Earlier versions of this chapter were delivered at meetings of the Association for Psychoanalytic Medicine and the Columbia Psychoanalytic Institute, as well as the Michigan Psychoanalytic Society,

2. "We will attempt to describe the process of psychoanalysis at what we have called the local level. The local level is the second-by-second interchange between patient and therapist consisting of relational moves composed of nonverbal and verbal happenings. . . . Each relational move at the local level is seen as revealing an intention to create, alter, or fine-tune the immediate nature of the therapeutic relationship. Any exchange will have a local level" (Boston Change Process Study Group [BCPSG], 2002, p. 694).

3. These assumptions about carrying over from the direct observation of infants to the intrapsychic events in the adult psychoanalytic patient were extensively debated by Daniel Stern and Andre Green (see Sandler, Sandler, & Davies, 2000).

4. I cannot pursue here the other excellent questions about BCPSG's views concerning the various forms of implicit memory and symbolic systems (see House & Portugese, 2005).

5. The definitions of indeterminate include "uncertain, vague, indistinct; not fixed or settled, not known in advance." But for purposes of the present discussion, the most

relevant definition is this: "not predetermined by some external force: not constrained: acting freely: spontaneous" (*Webster's*, 1986, p. 1148).

6. The conundrum that determinism means that there is neither free will nor responsibility is rooted in a similar logical error. The fact that there are causes for events does not mean that contingency has been erased. See also, House and Portuges (2005) for similar comments about the contrast between the modest and quiet tone of the language of established science used by the BCPSG and the truly radical discrediting of the foundational significance of the use of the free associations (and transference) of the patient to infer meaning.

7. Peter Woolf (1996) said,

> The current consensus among psychoanalysts holds that direct infant observations are one means for testing the developmental propositions of psychoanalytic theory; that the observations have already falsified some of the theory's basic propositions; and that they hold the key to a qualitatively different developmental theory of psychoanalysis. The consensus, although not universal, has motivated a wide range of research programs on early infancy, whose findings are commonly interpreted as disclosing psychoanalytic metapsychology and clinical theory in an entirely new light. . . . On the basis of these explorations it is concluded that psychoanalytically informed infant observations may be the source for new theories of social-emotional development, but that they are essentially irrelevant for psychoanalysis as a psychology of meanings, unconscious ideas, and hidden motives. (p. 369)

8. For a selected survey of some of this literature see Cohen (1994); Corbett (2000); Dyess and Dean (2000); Etchegoyen, Jorge, and Ahumada (1990); Frank (1969); Keene (1998); Kinston and Cohen (1986); Malin (2002); Matte-Blanco (1988); Rayner and Tuckett (1988); Taylor (1988).

9. See, for example, the unexpected clinical crisis in Casement's case report in chapter 2. I shall return to the topic of the surprised analyst later in the discussion.

10. In quoted clinical excerpts parentheses indicate BCPSG quotations and brackets indicate author's insertions. Text in quotes is excerpted verbatim and otherwise is paraphrased. Italics added.

11. See also chapter 5 where I use "contextual horizon" to connote the inference of a major organizing theme of the manifest associations of the patient.

12. See note 5. Here the authors cite Imber's review (2002) of Beebe and Lachman's book *Infant Research and Adult Treatment* because Beebe and Lachmann do focus on the moment-to-moment interaction. But compare the difference here between the views of the BCPSG and what Beebe and Lachmann infer from this interaction in the following quote from the Imber review:

> While few analysts should have trouble accepting the importance and benefits of the "non-specific" aspects of the analytic setting that allow a sense of safety and trust to exist between patient and analyst, the authors are suggesting something more intriguing. In a reversal of the conventional wisdom, they are proposing that these factors, heretofore conceived as background, which they show have their roots in the earliest months of interpersonal life, should in fact be placed in the foreground. While they say they are not proposing a new

technique, they are changing the traditional psychoanalytic emphasis from an exclusive focus on dynamic issues to an awareness of "mutually regulated nonverbal exchanges" that are constantly ongoing in treatment. What many analysts may have trouble accepting is the idea that what has traditionally been considered background or preparation for the "real" work of analysis—namely, interpretation of transference and resistance—may only be what the participants are overtly engaged in while the actual transformative processes are occurring nonverbally. (p. 669)

13. Greenberg (1992) said the following about this appeal for validating support to disciplines outside of psychoanalysis:

We often hear that it is urgent for us to coordinate psychoanalytic observations and hypotheses with those of so-called "adjacent" disciplines. Many analysts seem to think that we can bootleg a measure of legitimacy if our findings agree with those of the neurologists, or the anthropologists, or, most recently, the developmental psychologists. In contrast, I feel a certain amount of skepticism; I suspect that we can stand on our own as a discipline, without deferring and without conceding that our findings are contingent upon those that come from other fields or that grow out of other observational methods. (p. 278)

14. See House and Portuges (2005), Mayes (2005), and Litowitz (2005).

References

Abrams, S. (1983). Development. *Psychoanalytic Study of the Child, 38,* 113–139.

Abrams, S., & Solnit, A. (1998). Coordinating developmental and psychoanalytic processes: Conceptualizing technique. *Journal of the American Psychoanalytic Association, 46,* 85–103.

Audi, R. (1999). *Cambridge dictionary of philosophy* (2nd ed.). Cambridge, England: Cambridge University Press.

Blum, H. (1987). Analysis terminable and interminable: A half century retrospective. *International Journal of Psycho-Analysis, 68,* 37–47.

Boesky, D. (1990). The psychoanalytic process and its components. *Psychoanalytic Quarterly, 59,* 550–584.

Boesky, D. (1998). Clinical evidence and multiple models: New responsibilities. *Journal of the American Psychoanalytic Association, 46,* 1013–1020.

Boesky, D. (2005). Analytic controversies contextualized. *Journal of the American Psychoanalytic Association, 53,* 835–863.

Boston Change Process Study Group. (1998). Non-interpretive mechanisms in psychoanalytic therapy: The "something more" than interpretation. *International Journal of Psychoanalysis, 79,* 903–921.

Boston Change Process Study Group. (2002). Explicating the implicit: The local level and the microprocess of change in the analytic situation. *International Journal of Psychoanalysis, 83*(5), 1051–1062.

Boston Change Process Study Group. (2005a). Response to commentaries. *Journal of the American Psychoanalytic Association, 53,* 761–769.

Boston Change Process Study Group. (2005b). The "something more" than interpretation revisited. *Journal of the American Psychoanalytic Association, 53,* 693–730.

Cavell, M. (1993). *The psychoanalytic mind from Freud to philosophy.* Cambridge, MA: Harvard University Press.

Chused, J. (1991). The evocative power of enactments. *Journal of the American Psychoanalytic Association, 39,* 615–639.

Chused, J., & Raphling, D. (1992). The analyst's mistakes. *Journal of the American Psychoanalytic Association, 40,* 89–116.

Cohen, J. (1994). A view of the moral landscape of psychoanalysis. *Journal of the American Academy of Psychoanalysis, 22,* 699–725.

Corbett, K. (2000). Toward the coexistence of effort and lack: Commentary on paper by Cynthia Dyess and Tim Dean. *Psychoanalytic Dialogues, 10,* 775–786.

Dyess, C., & Dean, T. (2000). Gender: The impossibility of meaning. *Psychoanalytic Dialogues, 10,* 735–756.

Etchegoyen, R. H., Jorge, L., & Ahumada, J. (1990). Bateson and Matte-Blanco: Bio-logic and bi-logic. *International Review of Psycho-Analysis, 17,* 493–502.

Fonagy, P. (1996). Commentaries. *Journal of the American Psychoanalytic Association, 44,* 404–422.

Frank, A. (1969). The unrememberable and the unforgettable: Passive primal repression. *Psychoanalytic Study of the Child, 24,* 48–77.

Freud, A. (1965). Regression as a principle in normal development. In *The writings of Anna Freud: Vol. 6. Normality and pathology in childhood: Assessments of development* (pp. 93–107). New York: International Universities Press.

Freud, S. (1953a). *The standard edition of the complete psychological works of Sigmund Freud: Vols. 4–5. The interpretation of dreams* (J. Strachey, Trans.). London: Hogarth Press. (Original work published 1900)

Freud, S. (1953b). *The standard edition of the complete psychological works of Sigmund Freud: Vol. 14. The unconscious* (J. Strachey, Trans.). London: Hogarth Press. (Original work published 1915)

Freud, S. (1953c). *The standard edition of the complete psychological works of Sigmund Freud: Vol. 19. The ego and the id* (J. Strachey, Trans.). London: Hogarth Press. (Original work published 1923)

Freud, S. (1953d). *The standard edition of the complete psychological works of Sigmund Freud: Vol. 22. New introductory lectures on psycho-analysis* (J. Strachey, Trans.). London: Hogarth Press. (Original work published 1933)

Freud, S. (1953e). *The standard edition of the complete psychological works of Sigmund Freud: Vol. 23. An outline of psycho-analysis* (J. Strachey, Trans.). London: Hogarth Press. (Original work published 1940)

Furbank, P. (2005, May 26). *Science and polity in France: The revolutionary and Napoleonic years,* by C. C. Gillispie [Book review]. *New York Review of Books,* pp. 39–40.

Galatzer-Levy, R. (2002). Emergence. *Psychoanalytic Inquiry, 22*(5), 708–727.

Greenberg, J. (1992). Discussion. *Contemporary Psychoanalysis, 28,* 277–285.

Hartmann, H. (1955). Notes on the theory of sublimation. *Psychoanalytic Study of the Child, 10,* 9–29.

House, J., & Portuges, S. (2005). Relational knowing, memory, symbolization, and language: Commentary on the BCPSG. *Journal of the American Psychoanalytic Association, 53,* 731–744.

Imber, R. (2002). *Infant research and adult treatment: Co-constructing interactions:* Beatrice Beebe and Frank M. Lachmann [Book review]. *Journal of the American Psychoanalytic Association, 50,* 666–670.

Jacobs, T. (1986). On countertransference enactments. *Journal of the American Psychoanalytic Association, 34,* 289–307.

Keene, J. (1998). Review of *Unconscious logic: An introduction to Matte Blanco's bi-logic and its uses. International Journal of Psycho-Analysis, 79,* 1033–1040.

Kinston, W., & Cohen, J. (1986). Primal repression: Clinical and theoretical aspects. *International Journal of Psycho-Analysis, 67,* 337–353.

Kris, E. (1956). The recovery of childhood memories in psychoanalysis. *Psychoanalytic Study of the Child, 11,* 54–88.

Lacan, J. (1988). Logical time and the assertion of anticipated certainty: A new sophism. *Newsletter of the Freudian Field, 2,* 4–22.

Lindell, J. (2003). Discussion of Bent Rosenbaum's paper: "The unconscious. How does it speak to us today? Or the story about the unspoken and the not heard." *Scandinavian Psychoanalytic Review, 26*(1), 58–62.

Litowitz, B. (2005). When "something more" is less: Commentary on the BCPSG. *Journal of the American Psychoanalytic Association, 53,* 751–759.

Malin, B. (2002). Review of *Who is the dreamer who dreams the dream? A study of psychic presences,* by James S. Grotstein. *International Journal of Psycho-Analysis, 83,* 982–986.

Matte-Blanco, I. (1988). *New library of psychoanalysis: Vol. 5. Thinking, feeling, and being.* London: Routledge.

Mayes, L. (2005). Something is different but what or why is unclear: Comments on the BCPSG. *Journal of the American Psychoanalytic Association, 53,* 745–750.

McLaughlin, J. (1991). Clinical and theoretical aspects of enactment. *Journal of the American Psychoanalytic Association, 39,* 595–614.

Neubauer, P. (2001). Emerging issues. *Psychoanalytic Study of the Child, 56,* 16–26.

Peltz, M. (1986). *Continuities and discontinuities in development:* Edited by Robert N. Emde and Robert J. Harmon [Book review]. *International Review of Psycho-Analysis, 13,* 245–248.

Poland, W. (1992). Transference: An original creation. *Psychoanalytic Quarterly, 61,* 185–205.

Rayner, E., & Tuckett, D. (1988). An introduction to Matte-Blanco's reformulation of the Freudian unconscious and his conceptualization of the internal world. In I. Matte-Blanco, *New library of psychoanalysis: Vol. 5. Thinking, feeling, and being* (pp. 2–42). London: Routledge.

Renik, O. (1993). Analytic interaction: Conceptualizing technique in light of the analyst's irreducible subjectivity. *Psychoanalytic Quarterly, 62,* 553–571.

Sandler, J., Sandler, A., & Davies, R. (Eds.). (2000). *Clinical and observational psychoanalytic research: Roots of a controversy.* Madison, CT: International Universities Press.

Taylor, S. (1988). Matte Blanco and Skelton: Systems of logic and logic of systems. *International Journal of Psycho-Analysis, 69,* 427–429.

Webster's third new international dictionary, unabridged. (1986). Springfield, MA: Merriam-Webster.

Woolf, P. (1996). The irrelevance of infant observations for psychoanalysis. *Journal of the American Psychoanalytic Association, 44,* 369–392.

4

Memory Recovery as Viewed Through the One-Person (Versus the Two-Person) Theoretic Model

A NUMBER OF ANALYSTS DISAGREE that the analyst can be an observer of the patient's associations, because they assume that observation requires a one-person model.[1] This argument holds that such a one-person model omits vitally important components of the interaction of the analyst with the patient. This welding of the observing function of the analyst to a one-person model conflates the function of observing with the field of observation. The analyst certainly influences the associations of the patient but can still be capable of stepping back and observing the ensuing associations of the patient to make conjectures from the associations of the patient about the effects of the participation of the analyst. That is exactly what happens in enactments such as the one I discuss next. Some interpersonal authors maintain that this view is merely a belated concession of the truth of Harry Stack Sullivan's description (1953) of the analyst as a participant observer. But that view also conflates two different frames of reference. The Sullivanian participation involves interpersonal behavior viewed in the interpersonal, or two-person, domain. The participation of the analyst who inadvertently and unwittingly participates in an enactment is better mapped as interpersonal behavior evaluated by the contextualization of the ensuing associations of the patient in the intrapsychic domain.

In the past 25 years, the view of enactments has provided an opportunity to facilitate the integration of the intrapsychic and interpersonal domains of observation within one theoretic model. A number of authors from more than one school (model) clearly advocate a two-person/interpersonal domain combined with the traditional intrapsychic methods of contextualizing (see

Boesky, 1990; Chused, 1991; Chused & Raphling, 1992; Hirsch, 2003; Jacobs, 1986; McLaughlin, 1991; Poland 1992). Chodorow (2007) has designated this trend to use both observation and interaction perspectives by such conflict theorists as *intersubjective ego psychology*. The terms *model* and *domain* are confusing because they are used in different ways by different authors. I use the word *domain* (in this instance) to designate the data to be observed and the term *theoretic model* to mean the body of theory claiming to map this data.

U.S. analysts were slow to recognize the advantages of the British contributions to the literature on countertransference (e.g., Heimann, 1950; Racker, 1953, 1957, 1958). An early change in my views occurred toward the end of the 1980s. I had until then not really appreciated these contributions to the problem of countertransference and had thus given little thought to the role of the participation of the analyst in the psychoanalytic process and to the question of the effect of this participation on what the analyst was observing. In the one-person perspective that I used at that time, countertransference was like a cold—one certainly had to be resigned to catching one sooner or later, but ideally, it would be mild and then disappear.

My portal of entry into a reconsideration of the precepts of my own earlier training was the vexing confusion then extant about the notion of counter-transference. It became apparent to me that our British colleagues had caught on to the fact that there was far more to this concept than the pejorative connotation of the personal conflicts of the analyst. I concluded that the use of a one-person model prevented us from providing a theoretic home for the ubiquitous emotional participation of the analyst (Boesky, 1990). I further suggested at that point that the iatrogenic contributions of the analyst to the resistances of the patient were not only unavoidable but provided an essential tool for the analyst to better understand the patient.

Clinical Example

I now give a clinical example illustrating the following points. I relied on observing my countertransference reaction to contextualize an affectively charged transference–countertransference enactment. This led the patient to the recovery of an important previously repressed traumatic memory. The recovery of that memory was an important therapeutic change that became visible during the second of two sessions, which I describe in detail.

I wish to demonstrate that depending on the way that one contextualizes my interaction with the patient in these sessions, the explanation of this change will appear to be quite different. These two sessions occurred in the analysis of a middle-aged man whose presenting complaints were premature ejaculation, depression, anxiety, and lack of self-confidence. My subsequent understanding of the events in these two sessions evolved slowly over the span of several months. I originally selected the first session for attention, with no expectation that I would wish to report the session that followed it. I originally chose the first session to illustrate the frequent occurrence of sessions in which I was unsure of the optimal contextual choice. At the end of the first session, I felt dissatisfaction about my confusion in deciding whether to choose one contextual path or an alternative. My inner tension had to do with my concern about inducing higher and dangerous levels of anxiety in the patient in the face of the ominous recurrence of his serious psychophysiological illness. I worried that my wish to extend further our work of the prior week about his passivity with his daughter and his sexual passivity with his wife would be too painful for him. In the past week, he had dealt more openly with his conflicts about tacitly encouraging his wife and daughter to taunt and demean him. His wife would become especially abusive in their daughter's presence if she felt that he had withdrawn from her sexually. She taunted him for being a wimp and a failure as a man and in the past had accused him of being gay. Their daughter was a pawn in their battles and alternated between complaining to the patient about not protecting her from her mother and joining her in laughing at the patient. With both his wife and daughter, the patient alternated between masochistic submission and violent temper outbursts.

The session I report here occurred on a Monday, and I had previously canceled the Friday appointment for that week. It is important to know also that these sessions took place during a period of discontinuity in the analysis because of an impending planned vacation interruption and, a few months before that, an unplanned interruption when I had been ill.

The First Session

The patients starts saying that he cannot accept my offer of an alternative appointment for tomorrow morning (Tuesday) to make up for my canceling on Friday. His wife had asked him to go to some party tomorrow night. He notices that when he returns from a business trip, he starts to become tense again. He is often so relaxed when he is away for a few days or even longer, but on the plane last night he started to bite his nails. He got a headache, but that is starting to clear up now. That reminded me that we had both been worried in the prior week about the possibly ominous recurrence of his chronic psychophysiological symptoms.

I then said, "Speaking of bodily symptoms, how's your other pain?" He said it was 85% better, and with a minimizing tone he assured me that when these things happen, he gets over it in a few days. He had spoken to his wife about my saying on an earlier occasion that he should see a specialist about this problem and that she had agreed with me, but he does not see the point. He will have his routine tests next year either way. So what is the guy going to tell him? *He had a dream last night.* He is driving his daughter in an old neighborhood near a college campus. This reminds him of his dream last week. Did I recall that one? He was driving during that dream in this undeveloped neighborhood in the suburbs. In that one, a rooster attacked him. But that was north of here, and it was a beautiful house. As he was telling me about the interweaving of this dream and the earlier dream of the prior week, I became gradually and unpleasantly aware of feeling confused about which dream was which, and I was also becoming drowsy and struggling to stay alert. For what I hoped was a brief moment, I was drifting in and out of sleep, and I interrupted him because as I shook myself awake, what he was saying sounded confusingly real rather than like a dream. But I felt deceitful as I debated whether to tell him that I had drowsed off or to just ask him to clarify what he had been saying. It felt deceptive for me to ask in a disingenuous matter, as though I was pretending only to have not heard him while fully alert. It would be later that I realized that this inner debate with myself was part of the very enactment that made me sleepy in the first place, and I discuss that a bit later. He next said that there would not be such a luxurious house in that particular neighborhood now.

I then did ask him if this was actually true or only in the dream, and he said that it was in the dream, not in reality. But it then turned out that the confusion that I just described in me was similar to what he had felt in the new dream. He had felt confused in the dream itself. It did not make sense that this beautiful luxurious house . . . like an architect-designed house . . . should be in this poor Black neighborhood. And it was on a main thoroughfare, but there was a beautiful median on the street, just like an affluent street near that spot in the old days. He asked if I had seen the newspaper story about Ferry Street. That was spelled F-e-r-r-y. It had a time line showing how the original homes on the street were the mansions of wealthy gentiles. That has always been the pattern in this city. The gentiles flee the Jews, who then move out to where the gentiles fled, and the Blacks move into the Jewish neighborhood. Ferry Street was the old college neighborhood. He and his wife had dinner with her friend Lois. She is the daughter of Sadie and Warren X. Do I know who they are? I tell him that I knew them by name but that I had never met them. He really liked Warren. When he was younger, they had met at a health club, and he told Warren that he was a model for the patient. He said teasingly, "I want to be just like you when I grow up," and Warren had laughed. Warren retired altogether many years ago and just played golf every day. He and his wife go on cruises all the time all over the world.

But that Sadie is really a tough woman. If she likes you, okay, but if she does not, you had better get out of her way. He asked if I recalled the awful time when he discovered that an employee of his was an incompetent thief. At the meeting, he got so mad, and Warren had heard about it. People froze when they saw how mad the patient got at the meeting. When he decided to fire that guy, Warren sensed how nervous he was and said, "Have him come to your office, and I will be there with you." He told Warren that he didn't have to do that but Warren insisted. He said we'd do it together. And they did.

When he had his major surgery many years ago, his own parents didn't bother to come to see him, but when he woke up the next morning out of the anesthetic, there was Warren at his bedside. Warren told him not to get upset. He wouldn't stay long. He just wanted to be sure that the patient was okay. At that point, I said, "It must have meant so much to you. Your own parents didn't even show up." He laughed ruefully. "You better believe it." I then said, "You two guys really loved each other, didn't you?" Here I was deliberately testing to check the safety of this topic of loving a man. He said that was true. But he immediately went on to speak about how both Warren and Sadie didn't ever take much of an interest in their own kids or in their grandchildren. They were really no better than his own parents. Warren had an affair with a flight attendant, and Sadie told him he better cut it out or she would divorce him and take him for all his money. But, actually, everyone knew that she had had an earlier affair with Warren's friend. Sadie could be loyal to her women friends. He recalls her grief when one of them died. Not long ago, Sadie and Warren had built this very fancy house (the dream house?). But she didn't like the side drive, so they never moved in. Then they bought this even bigger place at a resort, and now he just heard they are buying still another place out there because it's even fancier. He laughed and said to their daughter Lois, "Your dad must have the patience of a saint. Doesn't he ever say no to anything she does?" Lois married a house husband. He doesn't work at all. He does whatever Lois wants. The patient told him that he is stressed out by work, and this guy told him, "Not me. I'm relaxed all the time." He's nothing but a houseboy for her. He publicly tells their friends that Lois doesn't respect him but that he can make a perfect martini.

The First Session: Discussion

Based on my experience with him, his initial declining of my offer of an alternative time for the Friday session that I had canceled was predictable. He never cared if I canceled. Others had to depend on him so that he would never need anyone. One of the unconscious determinants of his choice of his wife was her profound dependence on him. She was the vicarious projected receiver of the nurturing and guiding mothering that he could not tolerate needing himself. I noted also that his conscious anxiety started to mount not with separation but with his return home. When he gets back home from his numerous business trips, his wife and daughter invariably give him the cold shoulder, as though they were both his little kids who had to helplessly submit to his leaving them and who would get their revenge through passive hostility when he returned. When he referred to his headache early in the session I took that as an occasion to inquire about his other physical symptoms. As I did so, I wondered if that had really been necessary or whether I was unduly concerned about a recurrence of his psychophysiologic disease. He then told me indirectly that my prior intervention at the end of last week about his neglecting his health had been unwanted by him and unnecessary. We had spent quite a bit of time up to this point about his complex efforts to embroil me in an externalization and enactment of his conflicts about resenting and needing more from his formal and distant mother. He would speak of some example where his internist had failed again to return his calls or order a necessary test, and if I inquired about this, he would defend the internist as though I were the one who was mad at the doctor and thereby pushing unwanted maternal nagging on him. To need parental or maternal concern from me was, in his view, unmanly. When he was ill as a child, it would be his father who would get up at night with him and never his mother. These conflicts resonated with a pivotal memory of his first trip to Europe. He had sex with a Jewish prostitute, but when he became ill, a local doctor came to his hotel room at night and refused to accept any money from him.

I am here retracing my own steps in going back over this session and attempting to recall my own state of mind as I was listening to the patient in the session. But it is difficult to distinguish what I was actually thinking then from the thoughts occurring to me as I went back over this material. I arbitrarily included the memories about the trip to Europe to provide contextual background for my intervention with the patient wherein I inquired prematurely about his physical symptoms. This was a continuation of my prior concern about his getting adequate medical attention. On reflection, I thought that my nudging him to take better care of himself was an enactment of a countertransference fantasy. It was the first of a group of behaviors by me that I now view as parts of the larger enactment that occurred in these two sessions. The patient next predictably declined what I think he felt to be my parental nudging by telling me that his wife agreed with me that he should consult a specialist but that he disagreed with both of us. I say *parental* because it was the father and not the mother who cared for him in a more nurturing way when he was sick. It was at precisely that point when I resumed this enactment with him in which I worry about his health that he told me his dream from the night before the session. My sleepiness and confusion about his dream then ensued, and I began to think simultaneously of the recent nightmare about the rooster that had attacked his hand with its sharp beak. An old adage about dream interpretation states that the last association before the dream is the first association to the dream. That is also an example of a contextualizing criterion. I think this supports the conjecture that my enactment with him was stirring up an intensification of the passive homosexual father transference.

His elaborate need to spell the name of Ferry Street seemed to be an effort to flag my attention via a denial. It was definitely not a street for fairies or gay people; it was spelled differently. The issue of his feminine identification and negative oedipal conflicts and his passive longing for a father who would nurture him were on very different levels, developmentally and dynamically. This was hard for me to sort out in this session. I would now view the attacking cock in terms of his anger with his sleepy analyst as being displaced to the dishonest, incompetent employee who deserved to be fired. The theme of the conflicted longing for the love and protection from Warren and his contempt for Warren's passivity with Sadie, his biting and attacking wife, were well trodden ground from our prior work with identical views of his passive father and tough mother. It is as though his flattering idealization of Warren evoked so much narcissistic gratification for Warren that he in turn stood by the patient more than the patient's own parents. But Warren, his son-in-law, and the patient's father were all castrated figures. Indeed, the patient himself felt keenly the depressed sense of being on a leash with his own wife.

So those were the reasons that I believed that I was testing the waters when I said to the patient, "You guys really loved each other, didn't you?" I was worried here about the recurrence of his physical symptoms if I were to interpret his sexual feelings about me. At that point, I was not yet aware of his anger with me in this interaction. He verbally agreed that he loved Warren, but he immediately started to disavow this by stressing how Warren and his wife neglected their own kids and grandchildren just like his own parents do. I later thought that this was his first disguised reference to my sleeping. He expressed contempt for Warren as a cuckold and for his pathetic affair with the airline flight attendant but most of all for how scared and passive Warren was with his wife about her extravagance. I thought first that this immediate shift from an idealized and libidinized picture of Warren to a devalued image signaled too much anxiety about my observation that he and Warren loved each other. In other words, I took it as a contextualizing criterion that this outpouring of negative feelings about Warren instantly followed when I asked him, "You guys really loved each other, didn't you?" I did not want to stir up more anxiety in him, and I thought that direct attention to his transference conflicts

about needing me to love him instead of excluding him by canceling still another session would either scare him or fall on deaf ears or, more likely, both.
I did not yet consider that his negative reaction about Warren immediately
after my intervention was more than his disagreement with my intervention.
At that point in the session, I had forgotten my earlier sleepiness altogether. I
merely believed that my question about his loving Warren was arousing his
castration anxiety. It would only be in the next session that I began to realize
that his reaction to my intervention about loving Warren had to do with my
sleeping.

The lag in my understanding at the end of the first session added to my
sense of an excess of contextual choices and alternatives for intervention. The
theme of loss and separation in the story of Sadie and the death of her friend
were visible. But so was the theme of his depressing and frightening wish for
the love and nurturing of a father who would protect him from his dangerous
mother and console him for the lack of her love. It seemed plausible to me that
the canceled appointment on the Friday of this week and his refusal of a
makeup hour were related to my prior cancellations. But, as noted, past experience taught me that it was extremely difficult for him to be in touch with
needing me for anything or caring about my being unavailable to him. Any inquiry that I had made in the past about his disguised reference to my cancellations usually met with his amusement and denials. Anything I thought of selecting seemed premature or too frightening or not useful to him at this
moment. Instead, I asked him near the end of the session about how things
are turned upside down and reversed in the dream because these wealthy people are moving back instead of leaving. It was my hope that my saying that
would put us at least in one of several useful areas without worrying him that
these topics were too toxic or that I would collusively join him in not speaking of them at all. But at the end of the first session, I was puzzled and dissat-
isfied with simply leaving this marker in my comment about reversal in his
dream. It felt thin and intellectualized. The crucial point here is that during
this session, I was unaware that my enactment of secret sleepiness, rather than
a candid acknowledgment that I had drowsed off, would have been an important contextualizing criterion. As the session ended, I recalled my sleepiness
and debated whether I had been right to decide to wait a bit before telling him
that I had drowsed off during his dream. I rationalized that I had had some
experiences like that with other patients wherein I found it useful to bring this
up in the following session because patients would then have a chance to see
that they had a defensively altered need to deny my countertransference behavior in their own unique way. So, for better or worse, I decided to wait for
the developments in the next session. Little did I know what was in store for
both of us.

The Second Session

The second session was on Wednesday. The day before today was the Tuesday that he had refused as a makeup hour because of a charity event. He started this Wednesday hour by saying that he found out that he could come in tomorrow (Thursday) although he had thought that he would have to cancel for a trip. I reminded him that he had already told me that. That surprised him, and he assured me that he had not. So he was listening to Howard Stern talking on the radio with this other guy, and Stern said that after he divorced his wife after 20 years of marriage, he had this really hot girl, but he got so excited he came in 2 seconds; so, he got it up again in an hour and again she was so hot that he came right away. A lot of guys come too fast (one of the patient's major concerns). This guy he was talking to himself the other day said that he also came too fast, especially with a new girl. It's the novelty. It's more exciting, but it's common to come too fast with a new girl. Then a woman called in to Stern and said her husband had that trouble, so he used four rubbers to keep himself from feeling anything so that he wouldn't get so excited. Then he started using three and then two, until finally, he got the hang of it and could do it. The patient reflected on his surprise that these people could speak about such embarrassing stuff so publicly. It would only be later that I could see this as an allusion to my keeping my sleeping a secret.

So, Saturday—or, he wondered, was it Friday night—he had vaginal intercourse with his wife for the first time in a long time. He had not said anything at all about that important fact in the Monday hour. This was a highly important piece of withholding because the couple almost exclusively used a complex masturbatory ritual instead of intercourse. But just as he had feared, when he attempted vaginal intercourse, he could only last a couple of minutes. He thinks that she had a couple of orgasms; he thinks that she had an orgasm during the intercourse. I sensed his embarrassment and asked him if he was doubtful about that, and he countered with the question, what is the normal length of time for a man to come? Is it 5 minutes or is it 10 minutes? Some of these porno movies, the guy lasts 15 or 20 minutes. I told him that one way to talk about this was in terms of how many minutes. But another way was to think in terms of the couple and whether they both had intense excitement together much of the time and how that went with how they felt about each other. Could they truly love and trust each other and really care about each other? I also asked him if his worry about being normal had to do with feelings of shame about not being as good as other men.

Howard Stern complained about one brand of rubber. The patient said that he couldn't use latex rubbers because they make his skin burn, so he prefers the natural lambskin rubber. I asked him if it was hard to compromise between too little excitement versus too much excitement, and he quickly and enthusiastically agreed. Then he again wondered, how long does a normal man last? In retrospect, I thought that during this interaction, he and I were in a tense disagreement about what we should be talking about. He wants to know if he is abnormal, and when I relate that to his fear of shame, he speaks again about using rubbers. I had not yet realized that my sleeping represented for him my loss of control analogous to his premature ejaculation. This guy on the radio said that he came before he even got his penis out of his pants. Awful. Then there's this stain on his underpants. The guy on the radio said that he couldn't go back into the bar with that stain—reminds him of when he was a teenager, when he came in his underpants and then had to go home with that wet stain on his pants. I said, I wonder if he didn't marvel that these two guys were talking on the radio to millions of people about something that he felt was so shameful. Well, maybe it's a physical problem. After all, why should he be able to control when he comes? But it's true that he marveled at them talking so openly. That guy Stern is smart and has made millions of dollars because he's willing to talk about stuff that most people are ashamed to discuss. But then he denied feeling shame. For him it's not the shame that matters; it's the stain. I sensed his distress at this point, so we had an interaction about his even feeling ashamed to be ashamed and feeling depressed about himself. I said that he seemed to fear that if he couldn't satisfy his wife, he would feel like a failure compared to other men and that his avoidance of intercourse for so long had spared him this humiliation from coming too fast. I also reminded him of his nightmare about the rooster that bit his hand and said if that is what the woman's vagina was like, wouldn't it make sense that he would either not want to stick it in or get out in a hurry? When he agreed, I asked him what enabled him to take this risk on Friday night. It sounded as though he had felt safer. I also asked him if he had any thoughts about why he hadn't told me about this sexual experience during his Monday session, given that I would have thought this had been good news for him because he had made it clear in the past that he wished that he could attempt intercourse more often. I also thought privately that he was at about the maximum of tolerable affective distress here and that it would help him to have some acknowledgment of the genuine progress he was making. He said that his wife had asked him to insert his penis, so he thought, what the hell? What if he does fail? Let's get on with it.

This sexual attempt may have been a day residue for the confusing Monday session dream, and I now felt vindicated about my decision to say so little about that dream in the prior session. Moreover, this new information now placed the narratives about Sadie and Warren in a sexual context that had been unavailable then. Somewhere at this point, he recalled that he left stains on his mattress for his mother and the maid to discover. He was always in a hurry to masturbate, to get it over with. Here the repetition of the phrase "get it over with fast" from his prior descriptions of his premature ejaculations links and therefore contextualizes the current sexual symptom to his prior masturbation conflicts. A normal guy would take a *Playboy* magazine and stroke his penis and enjoy it, but he couldn't do that. His friend's brother even collected his semen from masturbating in a jar. He didn't even know at that time what masturbating was. Maybe his shame came from sitting down with his mother to have that sex talk. This was an allusion to an often-revisited memory of his sister being present during this talk and laughing at the patient because he had so much trouble understanding what his mother was saying to him. His mother was indiscreet to have his sister there. I said, you must have felt so terribly ashamed and humiliated when she laughed at you. He said that it was terrible and that in school, when he didn't catch on to something, he always felt that same kind of shame. "How come you don't get it? What's the matter with you?"

At this point I told him that I know that we had previously discussed toilet accidents and that he had not recalled any but that his thoughts today about stained underwear, losing control of his semen, and feeling terribly ashamed made me wonder again if he had forgotten some toilet accidents. When I had asked about that in the past, he had denied any memory of that happening. Once again, he said that he didn't recall any. But then to my surprise, he hesitantly added except maybe a few times. I felt a sudden sharpening of interest and some excitement, as I asked if these were bowel or bladder accidents that he might recall, and he said that he might have wet his pants during the day. This was the first emergence of these painful memories after several years of analytic work. He next recalled wetting the bed when he slept over at a friend's house, so he had to go home in the middle of the night. I said, you must have felt so embarrassed and, if you were sleeping over, you were probably more than 5 or 6 years old. Then he quietly said that he recalled that in kindergarten, he had to take extra pants to school so if he wet himself, he'd be okay. These were all new memories. I then said that I could imagine how awful that would have been for you. What if you had to ask permission to go change your pants, and what if the other kids saw the wet stain? I also reminded him that his younger brother had just been born before he started kindergarten and that it was common for a kid with a new baby in the house to want to be home instead of at school and to be like the baby in diapers. I was quite unclear at that point about what enabled him to recover this memory, and I resolved to take notes later in the day about this session, just as I had done for the previous hour. At that point, it had not yet occurred to me that my falling asleep could be used as a contextualizing criterion for his memory recovery.

He next recalled a really awful bitch of a teacher in the third grade. She made him bring his mother to school because he was swearing. I thought here that swearing could be linked to his enuresis as the sign of poor control of his stream of speech. But his kindergarten teacher was so sweet and warm. I wondered about the sharp contrast between the two women, like two images of his wife and mother. I then reminded him at that point of his image of the nasty Sadie at the end of the last session and added that I had been puzzled about his description of her. He was surprised that I brought that up. He thought that he had been boring. He himself couldn't understand why I didn't fall asleep (my loss of control). He thought he had wasted the hour. Why was he talking about her, and I said, "I thought you were associating to your dream." The minute that he said that he could not understand what had kept me from falling asleep, I experienced a sinking feeling of embarrassment. But I knew instantly that he was telling me that just as I had expected and feared, he knew that I had fallen asleep and that he was both denying this and sarcastically needling me with his sardonic surprise. It was the last moment of the session, and I decided to wait until the next session to tell him about my falling asleep during his dream. At this point, I merely reminded him of his other denial at the start of the session when he had started by saying that he didn't recall telling me that he would be here tomorrow. He jokingly said that maybe now he would remember to come.

The Second Session: Discussion

It was only while reviewing my notes of the hour (taken after the hour) 2 months after this session that I could see these events in a different context. It was only after this delay that I realized that my falling asleep had been a plausible determinant for the emergence of his memory of wetting himself. During that interval of time, I had been puzzled by the two sessions and had especially wondered what allowed the patient to recover this important and traumatic childhood memory of wetting his pants at just that point. This question "why now?" has, of course, always been a crucial concern for psychoanalysts. But it is not sufficiently appreciated that the crucial importance of this question is that it is essential to ask it to establish context. I had reviewed in vein the events of the first session to understand this dramatic recovery of memory during the second session. This long delay was, of course, a continuation of the original enactment itself. My purpose in this detailed description of the enactment is to support the claim that it is useful to include this enactment as a contextualizing criterion to illustrate my use of both a one-person and a two-person model.

There is no consensually accepted standard definition for the term *enactment*. What I mean by the term is the joint and interactive behavior of the analyst and the patient that actualizes a repudiated unconscious fantasy of the patient and the analyst. This touches on another tendentiously polarized controversy about one-person versus two-person models. This example illustrates the deployment of a two-person perspective within an intrapsychic frame of reference. It is a misleading fallacy to equate the one-person perspective with the intrapsychic frame of reference and the two-person perspective with the interpersonal or intersubjective theoretic models. This view of enactment entails the necessity that the analyst be able to make mobile shifts from the subjective, interacting, and participating perspective to the objective, observing perspective.

I think it is valid to describe this temporary memory recovery as a sign of a destabilization of his defense organization. What I refer to in this example as a reconstruction is my conjecture that he suffered as a child from enuresis. This reconstruction was initially related to the unusual concern that the patient expressed about many different kinds of shame issues united by the element of his fear of losing control throughout his life. I was also struck by the manner in which the patient described his symptom of premature ejaculation as a humiliating experience. Furthermore, this was contextually linked to his adolescent memories of repeatedly leaving his semen on the sheets of his bed and consciously fearing but secretly wishing detection by his mother. The semen left yellow stains. Another evidential source for the reconstruction came from the literature and the often-noted link between enuresis and premature ejaculation, beginning in 1917 with the classic paper by Karl Abraham (1917/1960).[2]

In the clinical example I am reporting here, I had hoped that the recovery of memories of the patient's enuresis in childhood would help him to establish a heightened conviction of the childhood links to his adult conflicts about shame, premature ejaculation, and fantasies about losing control of his emotions. My purpose was to help him to see the dynamic continuities of his conflicts about shame that arose in his childhood and persisted in his adult symptoms and in the transference. But my intent was to view his symptoms as compromise formations rather than to utilize an exclusively topographic view of the revival of repressed memories, which would now have a directly mutative effect by virtue of their mere accessibility. Such a view would fly in the face of the modern views in structural or conflict theory concerning the central mutative importance of a reintegration of the entire defense organization of which repression is but a part.

The subsequent fate of the patient's recovered memory of his enuresis is remarkable. Some 2 years later, his analysis was terminating with substantial improvement in his sexual symptoms and conflicts, as well as his depressive symptoms. Intervening events at this point led me to remind him of this childhood memory of enuresis that he had recalled on the occasion of my

falling asleep. He responded with surprise and denied any such memory whatsoever. It was just as though all of the events that I have reported here about
his memory recovery had never happened. What the subsequent fate of the
memory will be, I do not know, but it is well known that such dynamic shifts
of repression of memories are not uncommon even in one session.

The irony is that his recovery of this memory was not only or even necessarily a therapeutic change. It was itself a compromise formation in which he
identified with my own poorly controlled behavior. Instead of reveling in the
forbidden and frightening *schadenfreud* that he felt about my sleeping, he revived a memory of his own shame when he lost bladder control. It was not
primarily the recovery of the memory itself that was helpful to the patient. It
was instead the memory recovery at this point in the analysis that made it con-
vincingly possible for him to fully realize in an emotionally meaningful way in
that session that he was scared by the pleasure that he felt about my shameful
behavior when I fell asleep. He could then better see that there were important
continuities between his wishes to shame me and his previously forgotten
childhood shame about his enuresis. Furthermore, it was helpful to the patient to see the striking linkage between his childhood shame, the shame that
he wished that I would feel in the transference, and his adult shame about his
sexual problem. In short, it was not the lifting of a repression that was mutative in this session (*useful* would be a more modest term). It was the rebal-
ancing of his defense organization. In this instance, the recovery of the memory was better viewed as a momentary loss of amnesia in response to my
falling asleep. In this restricted sense, it could be viewed as a conflicted and
temporary flight into health evoked by the affective pain of the patient in response to his gratification and fear about my countertransference behavior.
Thus, his memory recovery (or his miniature cure) was structured exactly as
a symptom would be. Whether it was helpful or mutative is important, but
that is in a different frame of reference than the question of better understanding how and why the memory recovery happened. Viewing this memory
recovery as a compromise formation (Brenner, 1982) is an advantageous way
to do so. Accumulated clinical experience for many decades supports the view
of a highly complex dialectic relationship between the patient's conscious
knowledge of the past and upward reconstructions (Loewenstein, 1951).[3]

We usually discuss therapeutic change on the basis of two assumptions. The
first is that good changes in the patient are only due to good interventions or
good relating by the analyst. The second assumption is that it is sufficient, instead of useful, to speak about therapeutic changes in the patient on the basis
of the visible macrochanges that appear near the end of a successful analysis
(outcome studies) without clarifying the necessary antecedent transient microchanges that must occur much earlier. I am suggesting the possibility that

the change in my patient, heralded by the recovery of his memory, may have been facilitated by a serious countertransference intrusion (i.e., my falling asleep). I cannot prove that my enactment facilitated his recovery of his memory of losing control of his bladder. My point is rather to illustrate the role of choosing between contextualizing criteria in expanding and shaping the inferences that one can make about such events.

It was not until I began to write about these two sessions a few months later that I realized that there was a striking unrecognized enactment running throughout this entire interaction with him in which he and I were both fearful of shame and humiliation. Notice that my understanding of the complexity of my enactment increased only slowly. It is important also to remind you that if I had not told him that I was puzzled about Sadie at the end of the first hour, he would not have expressed surprise that I had been awake. That interaction between us was pivotal in what ensued in the next session, when he recovered his memories of enuresis. Note also that his memory recovery was not spontaneous but followed after my directly asking about such a memory, contrary to Fonagy's warnings (1999) against such a pursuit of childhood memory. In retrospect, I could see that this question about Sadie was my first step in the slow process of realizing how complex my enacted behavior with him had been. I gradually came to understand that the importance of my enactment was not only that I fell asleep but that I created a shameful secret of my own for him to know about. I knew better than to trust my hope that he hadn't found me out. My delay in finding opportunities to decide to discuss my falling asleep, which is what I have ordinarily done, was parallel to his embarrassment about the times in his life when he had stained himself with urine or semen, by masturbating or premature ejaculation. It then became possible for me to realize that my identification with him was related to some distressing earlier events in my own life. It is important to note that it is only when I make available the numerous details of what happened in these 2 hours, including my interaction with the patient, that it becomes less difficult for the reader to decide the degree to which my contextual organization of these events is credible or not.

In this clinical example, I find evidential support for Loewenstein's notion (1951) of reconstruction upward. I used that idea to contextualize my understanding of the role of public shame in the past as it resonated with his present transference fantasies in our mutual enactment. Viewed in this manner, it seems quite misleading to exclude the past experiences of our patients as being not only difficult to discern but irrelevant to our aims. It is one thing to delude ourselves into thinking that we can reconstruct the events on the staircase with the governess, as in the famous caution by Ernst Kris (1956). It is another thing to proclaim the death of reconstruction. The inherent dialectic between the past and present is ancient knowledge. Santayana (1922/1967) observed that repetition is the only form of permanence that nature can achieve. Loewenstein said,

> Interpretations aim at connecting the (past and the present), and that this connection works both ways. Interpretations, consequently, deal also with *what* connects the past with the present. One knows that this is one reason that interpretations of transference are so effective. Transference, indeed, reactualizes the past. (pp. 5–6)

The contextualizing I did here included the events of my enactment from the prior session as relevant to the opening of the next session, instead of my separating these events by using different contextualizing criteria. When I initially forgot my sleeping, I inadvertently deprived myself of the conscious choice of deciding between one- and two-person contextual perspectives at the moment in the session when he remembered wetting his pants, and it would indeed be only much later in reflecting on these events that this option occurred to me. This shift in contextualizing priorities has profound consequences for inferential opportunities. What if I had reported this clinical example describing this patient recovering his memory and I had left out my falling asleep? Wasn't it important for the reader to know that my listening was under the sway of my ongoing enactment that was as yet unrecognized?

Not surprisingly, when I told him in the third session that I had fallen asleep during his dream, his response was to deny that he had had any awareness of that. He merely thought now that this confirmed his suspicion that I was bored with him, but I told him that such inexcusable behavior by me was actually due to some personal reaction I had to what he had been telling me in his dream. It would only be later in reviewing these notes that it occurred to me for the first time that my enactment might have been a determinant for the recovery of his shameful memory. Poetry has been defined as passion recollected in tranquillity, and later, in more tranquil moments, I was able to learn from this countertransference poem. What matters for our purposes now is to compare the contextual alternatives I chose at the time of the session with those that open up with this additional information about enactment. If we review the events of the second session in the light of my enactment in the first session the contextual opportunities change radically. Context, like God or the devil, is in the details.

As I see these events, the inclusion of this knowledge of my enactment facilitates an understanding of his ability to recover his traumatic experience of enuresis at precisely this time in the analysis. The actualization of his defensive, unconscious wishes by my enactment gave him a real reason to perceive me as the one who was concealing a guilty secret. My enactment validated the reality of his wishes. This information adds immeasurably, in my opinion, to our understanding of the timing of the reemergence of his enuretic memory. It is as though he was saying that when he recovered his memory, he and I shared a shameful secret and we both wanted to cover up a stain. What looked like a simple recovery of a memory was actually, in this view, a scary and defensively altered actualization of an unconscious fantasy and revival of a humiliating memory that expressed and concealed his wish to laugh at me just as his sister had laughed at him. Now it was I who was out of control and publicly shamed. His new memory was, of course, a sign of progress, but that functional evaluation is from a different frame of reference. That would be an evaluation and comparison of his previous functioning as a patient, rather than an explanation of how and why the change occurred at exactly this moment.

My sharing a shameful experience with my patient illustrates the falseness of the polarized opposition of the views of the analyst as an observer/discoverer versus the analyst as a participant/co-creator or that of the one- versus two-person model. In the polemics about this polarized view, the one-person camp argues that the analyst who is willing to consider his or her contributions to the patient's views of the analyst is guilty of ignoring deeper transference realities by advocating a co-created transference. Such an analyst is viewed as committing the Ferenczian fallacy of active analysis. The patient must be considered the sole creator of the transference. The opposing argument arose with the ascendance of the relational view. In that argument, the analyst is incapable of observing—first, because she or he is irreducibly subjective and, second, because on epistemological grounds, there is no reality to observe given that the analyst is at every moment a participant and co-creator of the very phenomena that she or he claims merely to have observed. I disagree with both of those arguments.

I propose that in this example, my affective experience in developing a shame experience with the patient became a valuable contextual criterion that facilitated my inferences about what the patient may have felt now in the transference and much earlier when he was a child. At issue is not the truth of this assertion but its ostensible illustration of the simultaneous deployment of a contextual criterion from a two-person model, as well as inferences deduced from a one-person model. I further suggest that the notion of contextual criteria and contextual horizons facilitates the integration of one-person with two-person models and renders specious the tendentious opposition of these two frames of reference. One would of necessity hold suspect a methodology of inference that failed to account for the interaction of the emotional life of the analyst with that of the patient.

Another question that remains unclear is whether in any instance the contextualizing decisions of the analyst "originate" in the observed data or whether these decisions are prejudiced by theoretic preconceptions of the analyst. Was this an example of deductive or inductive reasoning on my part (Ahumada, 1994; Hanly, 1992, 2005)? Such a dichotomy of choice would be a naive way to think about this question. There is, of course, no such thing as an observation that is innocent of bias, and the anatomy of the dialectic interaction of deductive and inductive reasoning in the mind of the working analyst is an unresolved problem. This question also borders on the topic of a large literature about psychoanalysis as science that is outside of my competence and is also beyond the scope of this discussion.

Memory as a Curative Element

The very idea that memory recovery could have a curative role will seem quaint to many contemporary analysts because there have been profound changes in the trends of discussion about the curative role of memory in our modern literature. That has certainly been true in the proliferation of numerous theoretic models. It is not sufficiently appreciated that there are important differences between the mutative role of memory recovery in the era of the topographic model before approximately 1920 and the helpful role of memory recovery in structural theory that was later called ego psychology and, more recently, conflict theory. In his searching discussion of the fate of memory as a curative element in clinical theory, Bohleber (2007) traced the manner in which remembrance and reconstruction acquired therapeutic evidential status by proposing direct causal connections with the continuing psychic effects of the event:

> This view of the therapeutic efficacy of remembrance and reconstruction has been dealt a massive blow by the emergence of the more recent forms of object-relations psychology and the move towards narrativism and constructivism. According to the narratological view, we never make contact with the actual memory, but only ever with its description by the patient. Truth does not therefore exist as something hidden that can be directly found, but is constantly integrated into a narrative that only acquires truth status when it gains plausibility for the patient (in accordance with Spence, op. cit.). . . . In this conception of memory, the discovery of real events disappears from view. . . . Historical truth is replaced by narrative truth . . . and the connection with the real world goes unmentioned. . . . The fundamental problem with these narratological and constructivist conceptions of psychoanalysis consists in their exclusion or obscuration of any connection with the reality behind the narration. (p. 333)

Bohleber continues,

> Whereas Freud worked from the premise of a unified memory system, today object-relational patterns . . . and autobiographical memories are localized in two fundamentally different types of memory process. The connection between a behavioral repetition of old relational schemas in the here-and-now and remembering life-historical events largely seems to break down (Fonagy, 1999).

In that cited article, Fonagy clearly expressed his criticisms of the view that remembering actual events was therapeutically useful:

> The aims of psychoanalysis have been greatly elaborated over the hundred years since Freud's original model of undoing repression and recovering memory into consciousness . . . But these advances have not brought with them an updating of the role of memory in the therapeutic process, nor a clear and consistent theory of therapeutic effect. Some still appear to believe that the recovery of memory is part of the therapeutic action of the treatment. There is *no evidence* for this and in my view to cling to this idea is *damaging* to the field. (p. 215; italics added)

The Fonagy–Blum Disagreement About Memory

At the invitation of the editors of the *International Journal of Psychoanalysis*, Blum (2003a, 2003b) and Fonagy (2003) debated the latter's views of transference and memory. Among the diverse issues about which they differed, their central disagreement had to do with the role of memory recovery and transference as sources of data and as mutative factors in psychoanalytic treatment. Fonagy faulted Blum for overlooking the contributions of cognitive science and neuroscience to the nature of memory and for ignoring the concept of *nachtraglichkeit*, and Blum faulted Fonagy for omitting the large literature about genetic development and the defensive nature of transference as opposed to a face value view of the manifest content of the transference.[4] Fonagy (1999) stated, "The removal of repression is no longer to be considered a key to therapeutic action. Psychic change is a function of a shift of emphasis between different mental models of object relationships" (p. 218).[5] Fonagy (2003) later stated, "As is so often the case in such debates in psychoanalysis, there are some problems of definition, some issues of differential emphasis, some of probable misconstrual, and finally, genuine disagreements" (p. 304).

Fonagy omits from this list of problems contributing to this disagreement differences in the epistemology used by those in this disagreement. We can observe this in his citation of the methodology of Stern et al. (1998; also known as the BCPSG). In arguing for his views against the therapeutic efficacy of remembrance, Fonagy cites with approval the clinical claims of Stern et al. as his authority about this problem.

> Using an approach based on recent studies of mother-infant interaction and non-linear dynamic systems and their relation to theories of mind, the authors propose that the something more (than interpretation) resides in interactional intersubjective processes that give rise to what they will call "implicit relational knowing." This relational procedural domain is intrapsychically distinct from the symbolic domain. In the analytic relationship it comprises intersubjective moments occurring between patient and analyst that can create new organisations in, or reorganise not only the relationship between the interactants, but more importantly the patient's implicit procedural knowledge, his ways of being with others. (p. 903)

But the work of the BCPSG is based on epistemic assumptions of indeterminacy. And as noted in chapter 3, Stern's dynamical unconscious is in a different frame of reference (category) than the dynamic unconscious of traditional psychoanalysis. Stern stated that in the future he would reconcile these two frames of reference, but he has not done so to date. This promise of a reconciliation is based on the tensions between the two memory systems, but it omits any reference to the necessity of integrating two incompatible epistemic systems—psychic determinism and sloppiness (indeterminacy). At this point, then, if one assumes that Fonagy approves of the epistemology of the BCPSG, as he implies, then the Blum–Fonagy disagreement about memory recovery (Blum, 2003a, 2003b; Fonagy, 1999, 2003) cannot be settled on the basis of comparing clinical evidence, because the two frames of reference here are incommensurate.

At issue in these comments is not the correctness or incorrectness of Fonagy versus Blum. The question I raise is how this debate could ever be settled on the basis of clinical evidence if that evidence includes the raw data of single sessions. Instead, this disagreement serves as a model similar to the controversy about Casement's paper (see chapter 2). It is a specimen model of many psychoanalytic disputes that cannot be settled by the comparison of the same clinical data, because the epistemology of determinism and indeterminism cannot be compared coherently (this problem is discussed at some length in chapter 3). Neither can we compare the same clinical data with dynamical and dynamic views of defense and memory. The same data will convince those who adhere to the differing epistemologies of quite different conclusions that cannot be settled with detailed data from individual sessions. That problem will therefore invade comparisons all the way up the ladder of abstraction.

I agree with Bohleber (2007):

Even if Freud's theory of the memory-trace has become obsolete and the metaphorical comparison of the analyst's work with that of the archaeologist is no longer considered apposite, the metaphor of the trace nevertheless conveys something that derives from clinical knowledge. The "trace" accords the past an element of autonomy that is left out of account by modern theories of memory base on transcription and construction. . . . Traumatic memories can exercise a distressing power and intrude violently into the present life context without being transmitted with it. Trauma is a brute fact that cannot be integrated into a context of meaning at the time it is experienced because it tears the fabric of the psyche. This creates special conditions for its remembrance and retroactive integration in present experience. (p. 335)

Scientific Domains and Category Errors

There is great value to the cross germination of interdisciplinary research between brain science, cognitive science, and psychoanalysis. We must be sure that our psychoanalytic theories do not contradict established observations derived from other frames of reference. But too often, in such seemingly straightforward transfers of the concepts of one domain to another, there has been a failure to deal with the problem of category errors in which data derived from one frame of reference are viewed as being easily translatable into a different scientific domain. It is noteworthy that the repeated calls in our recent literature for integration with neuroscience and cognitive science is at the same time accepting of the disappearance of the past from psychoanalysis as well as the disappearance of detailed sexual information in our case reports. Another tranquillity in our recent literature is the assumption that we do not need to reconcile the unconscious with what is nonconscious. This conflation of what is unconscious and what is nonconscious is a serious error.

An example of such a category error was a recent debate on the Internet among analysts about the lowest possible level of neuronal organization in the animal kingdom that would make conflict possible. The error here is the totally different meaning of the word *conflict* to animal psychologists, neurobiologists, and adherents of the structural theory of drive and defense. This confusion between indecisive earthworms, confused dogs, and anxious human beings simply repeats the famous errors of Masserman's experiments with so-called animal neurosis (Tarachow, 1963). It is noteworthy that in this debate there is no mention of the valuable contributions made by psychoanalysis to the field of cognitive psychology (Bucci, 2000).

The concept of scientific domains is helpful in considering the translatability of one scientific domain into another.

No scientific discipline has as its objective the explanation of "everything." A discipline takes as its intended domain a realm of more or less clearly defined phenomena, about which there are specific kinds of questions. The discipline, if it is able to explain anything or answer any questions at all, will be able to explain these phenomena or answer these questions. (Edelson, 1986, p. 576)

Mutative Factors and Change

We know that necessary and important changes in treatment represent new compromises rather than the destruction of old conflicts (Brenner, 1982). Major changes are possible because of the emergence of adaptive compromises that allow greater pleasure and less self-punishment. This view of change differs from the pragmatic definition of change cited by Renik (1998).[6] In that view, change is whatever works for the patient. Accepting that definition risks losing the hard-won knowledge that many things that seem to work consciously are linked to conflicts that are still pathogenic. If we accept as our criterion of validation whatever seems to work manifestly and consciously, we lose sight of vitally important conflicts that endanger the stability and duration of therapeutic change. Thus, pragmatism becomes a license to dismiss the need for evidence. Explanations of change are too often global, vague, and abstract. That is especially the case with statistically organized outcome research studies that omit meaningful information about the actual treatment process.

The bigger the hypothesis, the easier it is to escape evidential challenge (Edelson, 1984). In this sense, it is easier to do outcome studies than single-case research. In this special sense, it is easier to understand the outcome of an entire analysis than a single analytic session. A related issue about the diversity of levels of abstraction of context is that we have no consensually agreed conventions that establish the fit between an author's conjectures and the nature of the differences in evidence required for those conjectures up and down the ladder of our theoretic abstractions. The closer the assertions are to what the patient actually said and to what the analyst felt and thought, the more data are available to support the assertion. The more sweeping and general the assertions are, the more distant the available data become to support those assertions. To put it another way, it is easier to support trivial assertions and much harder to support important groundbreaking clinical generalizations.

Reductive polarized alternatives flourish in the heady stratosphere of abstractions. They cannot be supported or refuted—for example, was it his relationship with me or my verbal interventions that enabled him to recover his memory? When one has detailed data available, it is far easier to see that such a polarizing dichotomy of choice is misleading. It is easier with the detailed information to show that it is both the relationship and the interpretive activities of the analyst that are operative. It is both–and rather than either–or, plus the possibility for the admission of other factors yet to be described.[7] Even to say only that it is both relational and interpretive factors that are mutative is reductive. Exactly what was going on in the relationship that enabled him to recover his memory and why at just that point?

It would be incorrect and unfair to say that many analysts believed that there was only one major factor that was mutative; but, to remind the reader of some of the major mutative slogans, we need think only of empathic attunement, the new object, containment, and insight. The names of Ferenzci, Kohut, Loewald, and Winnicott are often linked to such views of change that favor a few factors that have been passed down as shorthand allusions to the complexities of the actual work of these authors. It would be unfair to any of these authors to imply that this would have been their sole explanation for therapeutic change. Another issue in this discussion is the question of our misleading assumptions that we can reliably define what we mean by change. If the presenting symptoms have not been improved, then something failed in the treatment; but *pace* the pragmatists among us, major symptomatic changes, as we have known for many decades, can take place without contact with the major pathological conflicts of the patient. These issues are widely recognized. What is less often appreciated is that the concretization of the notion of change is deterring us from a deeper understanding of what changing is about. Once again, the noun *change* reifies the process of changing. We are sorely in need of a better understanding of the myriad of subtle microchanges that precede more enduring and visible change. In the work of certain relational theorists, we see a revival of the claim that the corrective emotional experience is mutative. Which emotional experience was corrective and why? If all that matters is that the patient is satisfied, then that question can be deemed to be irrelevant on pragmatic grounds. The enactment that my patient and I co-created was certainly part of the relationship. Yet, it was not simply benevolent, nor was it only progressive. In this case, some undesirable behavior by the analyst can be viewed as facilitating a modest forward change in the patient. If so, why?

Conclusion

Two disagreements in the psychoanalytic literature were discussed in this chapter. The first was the debate between Blum and Fonagy about memory. Specifically, Fonagy claimed that the pursuit of memories during psychoanalytic treatment were damaging to our patients and our field. My clinical illustration does not prove that the recovery of his childhood patient was directly mutative, but there was good reason to believe that it was one of a group of elements that were helpful to him in quite a complicated way. But, certainly, there was no evidence that my pursuit of his memory was damaging to him. Much about his later amnesia for these events in the analysis that I have reported here is beyond my understanding but does not support either view in the Blum–Fonagy debate.

The second disagreement in our literature concerns the tendentious and polarized opposition of one- and two-person models. This is ripe for inclusion in our history of misleading either–or controversies. Whether explicitly or implicitly, the literature of enactments over the past 25 years richly illustrates the use by an increasing number of analysts of both an intrapsychic and interpersonal domain of observation. The clinical illustration in this chapter is such an example. It also illustrates the value of using detailed clinical material to evaluate such abstract disagreements between one- and two-person models.

In that regard, adding explicit information about how and why the associations of the patient have been contextualized in a certain way should be added to the authorial intentions (Michels, 2000) that we wish to know about when we read about clinical material. This is too often left implicit. This is the other incompleteness to which Freud alluded in the Dora case (see Freud, 1905/1953a). Our literature still too often reflects this same incompleteness. Making such information explicit would facilitate more logical comparisons of various clinical models and perspectives. What I am suggesting then is the importance of using explicit contextualizing criteria for improving our methodology of comparative psychoanalysis.

The use of substantially different contextualizing criteria by different analysts will lead to the generation of inferences that are not easily intertranslatable. It would be difficult to reconcile Freud's dictum (1912/1953b) "For when all is said and done, it is impossible to destroy anyone in absentia or in effigie"[8] (p. 108) with the BCPSG concept of implicit relational knowing. Reconciliation, on a highly abstract level by those who disagree, is no substitute for a careful comparison of the contextualizing criteria deployed with detailed clinical data from each perspective. Without having detailed information about the contextualizing criteria of the authors who disagree, then we as readers will continue to argue about opinions instead of acquiring new knowledge.

Notes

1. The clinical material in this chapter was presented in different forms at a panel discussion regarding nonverbal interventions at the midwinter meetings of the Amer-

ican Psychoanalytic Association, January 19, 2007; at meetings of the Philadelphia Psychoanalytic Center, October 3, 2002; and at the Michigan Psychoanalytic Society, October 17, 2002.

2. Abraham (1917/1960) reported the following observations about enuresis and premature ejaculation: "They were bed-wetters up to a late period of childhood, and that they easily react to excitement of any kind with an irresistible desire to urinate" (p. 282). See also, Blum (1971), Kafka (1971), and Yorke (1990), to name but a few.

3. Loewenstein (1951), in a now neglected classic article, stated,

> Genetic interpretations aim at the establishment of a reciprocal relationship between the present and the past. If the term reconstruction is used for the establishment of a forgotten childhood event from its more recent derivatives, one might use the term *reconstruction upward* to denote the type of interpretation we employ in reconstructing the more recent consequences of a former event. (p. 142).

4. For an incisive discussion of this issue, see Arlow (2002).

5. This is a puzzling statement in view of Freud's proclamation in 1926 "where id was shall ego be," which was, of course, the formal announcement of a radical shift in the technical goals of psychoanalytic treatment and the final formal shift by Freud from the topographic to the structural model. One of the cardinal reasons for Freud's introduction of the structural model in the several years before 1926 was precisely his realization that the memory recovery called for in the topographic model was ineffective. He therefore advised analysts to no longer attempt to simply make conscious what had been unconscious. Fonagy prefers (and, of course, it is his right to do so) to view this as a shift to the object relations model rather than to the structural model. And many analysts in the United Kingdom as well as in the United States would agree on that point. The complex history of the very different views of many British and U.S. analysts about the comparative advantages of the topographic and structural models and the extent to which the latter supercede the former cannot be pursued here.

6. For a closely related view, see Goldberg (2002).

7. See also, Wallerstein (1990) and Rangell (2002).

8. See Freud (1912/1953b) for a similar idea.

References

Abraham, K. (1960). Ejaculatio praecox. In *Selected papers of Karl Abraham* (5th ed., pp. 280–299). New York: Basic Books. (Original work published 1917)

Ahumada, J. (1994). What is a clinical fact? Clinical psychoanalysis as inductive method. *International Journal of Psychoanalysis, 75*, 949–962.

Arlow, J. (2002). Transference as defense. *Journal of the American Psychoanalytic Association, 50*(4), 1139–1150.

Blum, H. (1971). On the conception and development of the transference neurosis. *Journal of the American Psychoanalytic Association, 19*, 41–53.

Blum, H. (2003a) Repression, transference, and reconstruction. *International Journal of Psychoanalysis, 84,* 497–502.

Blum, H. (2003b). Response to Peter Fonagy. *International Journal of Psychoanalysis, 84,* 509–513.

Boesky, D. (1990). The psychoanalytic process and its components. *Psychoanalytic Quarterly, 59,* 550–584.

Bohleber, W. (2007). Remembrance, trauma, and collective memory. *International Journal of Psychoanalysis, 88*(Pt. 2), 329–352.

Brenner, C. (1982). *The mind in conflict.* New York: International Universities Press.

Bucci, W. (2000). The need for a "psychoanalytic psychology" in the cognitive science field. *Psychoanalytic Psychology, 17,* 203–224.

Chodorow, N. (2007). McLaughlin's *The healer's bent: Solitude and dialogue in the clinical encounter* [Book review]. *Psychoanalytic Quarterly, 76,* 617–630.

Chused, J. (1991). The evocative power of enactments. *Journal of the American Psychoanalytic Association, 39,* 615–639.

Chused, J., & Raphling, D. (1992). The analyst's mistakes. *Journal of the American Psychoanalytic Association, 40,* 89–116.

Edelson, M. (1984). *Hypothesis and evidence in psychoanalysis.* Chicago: University of Chicago Press.

Edelson, M. (1986). Heinz Hartmann's influence on psychoanalysis as a science. *Psychoanalytic Inquiry, 6,* 575–600.

Fonagy, P. (1999). Memory and therapeutic action. *International Journal of Psychoanalysis, 80,* 215–223.

Fonagy, P. (2003). Rejoinder to Harold Blum. *International Journal of Psychoanalysis, 84,* 503–508.

Freud, S. (1953a). *The standard edition of the complete psychological works of Sigmund Freud: Vol. 7. Fragment of an analysis of a case of hysteria* (J. Strachey, Trans.). London: Hogarth Press. (Original work published 1905)

Freud, S. (1953b). *The standard edition of the complete psychological works of Sigmund Freud: Vol. 12. The dynamics of transference* (J. Strachey, Trans.). London: Hogarth Press. (Original work published 1912)

Goldberg, A. (2002). American pragmatism and American psychoanalysis. *Psychoanalytic Quarterly, 71*(2), 235–250.

Hanly, C. (1992). Inductive reasoning in clinical psychoanalysis. *International Journal of Psychoanalysis, 73,* 293–301.

Hanly, C. (2005). *Deductive reasoning in psychoanalytic theorizing.* Freud lecture given at the Psychoanalytic Institute, New York City.

Heimann, P. (1950). On counter-transference. *International Journal of Psychoanalysis, 31,* 81–84.

Hirsch, I. (2003). Analysts' observing-participation with theory. *Psychoanalytic Quarterly, 72*(1), 217–240.

Jacobs, T. (1986). On countertransference enactments. *Journal of the American Psychoanalytic Association, 34,* 289–307.

Kafka, E. (1971). On the development of the experience of mental self, the bodily self, and self conciousness. *Psychoanalytic Study of the Child, 26,* 217–240.

Kris, E. (1956). The recovery of childhood memories in psychoanalysis. *Psychoanalytic Study of the Child, 11,* 54–88.

Loewenstein, R. (1951). The problem of interpretation. *Psychoanalytic Quarterly, 20,* 1–14.

McLaughlin, J. (1991). Clinical and theoretical aspects of enactment. *Journal of the American Psychoanalytic Association, 39,* 595–614.

Michels, R. (2000). The case history. *Journal of the American Psychoanalytic Association, 48,* 355–375.

Poland, W. (1992). Transference: An original creation. *Psychoanalytic Quarterly, 61,* 185–205.

Racker, H. (1953). A contribution to the problem of counter-transference. *International Journal of Psycho-Analysis, 34,* 313–324.

Racker, H. (1957). The meanings and uses of countertransference. *Psychoanalytic Quarterly, 26,* 303–357.

Racker, H. (1958). Counterresistance and interpretation. *Journal of the American Psychoanalytic Association, 6,* 215–222.

Rangell, L. (2002). The theory of psychoanalysis: Vicissitudes of its evolution. *Journal of the American Psychoanalytic Association, 50*(4), 1109–1137.

Renik, O. (1998). The analyst's objectivity and the analyst's subjectivity. *International Journal of Psychoanalysis, 79,* 487–498.

Santayana, G. (1967). *Soliloquies in England.* Ann Arbor, MI: University of Michigan Press. (Original work published 1922)

Stern, D. N., Sander, L. W., Nahum, J. P., Harrison, A. M., Lyons-Ruth, K., Morgan, A. C., et al. (1998). Non-interpretive mechanisms in psychoanalytic therapy: The "something more" than interpretation. *International Journal of Psychoanalysis, 79,* 903–921.

Sullivan, H. S. (1953). *The interpersonal theory of psychiatry.* New York: Norton.

Tarachow, S. (1963). *An introduction to psychotherapy.* New York: International Universities Press.

Wallerstein, R. (1990). Psychoanalysis: The common ground. *International Journal of Psycho-Analysis, 71,* 3–20.

Yorke, C. (1990). The development and functioning of the sense of shame. *Psychoanalytic Study of the Child, 45,* 377–409.

5

Free Associations:
Which Ones Count?

A NEGLECTED REASON WHY WE ARE NOT YET PREPARED to deal with a genuine comparative psychoanalysis is that we have not yet devised methods to deal with the important disagreements between adherents even within one given model.[1] In the controversies between models—for example, the relational versus the modern conflict theorists—we are warned not to lump all the members of the opposing camp into the same group. Rightly so. But there is precious little attention to the fact that our comrades in arms within our own favored group have many important differences of opinion. I suggest here that we would be well advised to set our own house in better order and pay extensive attention to our intramodel disagreements. What follows is a report of just that kind of disagreement, arising from a clinical report by an Israeli analyst, Dr. Ilany Kogan, that was discussed by Drs. Charles Brenner, A. Ferro, and J. Herzog.[2]

The Kogan–Brenner Disagreement:
The Role of Context in a Clinical Disagreement

There has been a recent proliferation in our journals of a new clinical format. An author presents a detailed case report as a target paper, and various discussants, usually from different theoretic models, discuss the case. Of course, this has been done at our scientific meetings both nationally and internationally for a long time, but in the published format, there is space and time for a more detailed consideration of the inevitable disagreements. This is an emerging format for comparative psychoanalysis. It seems to be assumed in our various editorial boards and program committees that it will provide a more balanced view of the main paper to be discussed so that readers or those at a meeting will have the opportunity to hear diverse views about the same clinical material. One problem with this solution is that the participants in an ensuing disagreement are not listening to the same material at all because, as we know, listening is far more than a merely passive, auditory experience. Listening as an analyst includes silent, rapid contextualizing choices, parallel to the listening that simultaneously filters and sorts what is heard. Different contextual choices by the analyst have a profound effect on what is heard. That has been insufficiently appreciated. Second, I wish to call attention to a neglected distinction between free associations as an aspect of the fundamental rule versus the epistemological significance of the associations of the patient. I discuss my own disagreement with Brenner's criticism of Kogan to illustrate the role of contextualization criteria in creating a clinical disagreement between Dr. Brenner and myself, who are affiliates of the same theoretic model.

Kogan's patient Nurit was the child of two Holocaust survivors, each of whom had suffered the tragic loss of a child before their own marriage and before Nurit's birth. Nurit was an accomplished scientist, married, and the mother of three children, and she was fluent in several languages. Both of her parents had been married before they married each other and had Nurit, and both of them had a child murdered in the Holocaust during their prior marriages. There was persuasive evidence that emerged in the analysis that each of Nurit's parents nurtured the fantasy that Nurit could replace their lost child. The complex pathological, developmental consequences of her feeling herself to be a replacement child rather than being loved in her own right had occupied extensive analytic attention before the sessions to be discussed. Indeed, the title of Dr. Kogan's moving paper was "On Being a Dead, Beloved Child." Dr. Kogan had learned from her prior work as an analyst in Israel that the child of survivors whose prior children had been murdered senses that she or he is destined to be a replacement for the dead child. In addition, she or he will concretize the parent's unconscious fantasies and expectations about the replacement child. Not the least of these is the feeling that the price for being loved is to fulfill the destiny of the lost child. It is a matter of some importance to note that Dr. Kogan had also learned in her prior work with such patients that children who have been assigned such roles, which cannot be fulfilled, would often develop difficulties in thinking and reality testing. As we shall see, that theoretic assumption was the basis for the intervention with which Dr. Brenner later disagreed.

Now I report further selected aspects of the published case presentation. Nurit was a married scientist and the mother of three who sought help for her compulsive behavior. She described distressing obsessional symptoms earlier in her life. Now she had to check and recheck that she had turned off the gas stove, closed the refrigerator door, set the alarm clock, and so on. The immediate occasion for her seeking help was a series of arguments with her eldest teenage daughter. She was an attractive, tall, slim, and elegantly groomed woman with a regal quality. She was intelligent and talented. Her sophistication reflected her travels and her cultivated life. Although, as mentioned, she was fluent in several languages, her voice was devoid of emotion and had a metallic quality.

As stated, Nurit was the only child of two Holocaust survivors. Her mother's entire family perished in the Holocaust. At 19, the mother married a considerably older man, who fled to Russia while her mother remained in the Warsaw ghetto with their only child, a girl of 7. This child was murdered while the mother was at work one day, and Nurit's mother was later sent to Bergen-Belsen. When the war ended, she went to Israel, where she met Nurit's future father. He, too, had left a wife and child in Poland and fled to Russia, and he, too, suffered the murder of his child as well as his wife and father. The father's daughter may have been the same age when she was killed as the daughter of Nurit's mother. Suffice it here to say that when Nurit was born in Israel, both of her parents were about 40 years old. Her father was highly successful, and Nurit described an affluent and happy childhood. The family lived in a number of different countries, but she returned to Israel at 18 to live with her father's mother. There she married happily, had her children, and succeeded in her own career in biology. In stark contrast to her memories of a happy childhood, she described terrible experiences with her mother from the age of 11 to 18. Her mother was by then paranoid and thus subjected Nurit to a series of humiliating and frightening experiences. She refused to speak to Nurit for days at a time; she had unexpected outbursts of anger; and she made many accusations about her. Nurit described all of this in a detached and unemotional manner. The following are brief excerpts from one session in the third year of the analysis (Kogan, 2003, pp. 736–739). Dr. Kogan was impressed by the emotional flatness of Nurit's tone throughout this session:

> Nurit walked into my office, arranged the pillows the way she always did before lying down, and suddenly said, "There's a hair on the pillow. *Whose hair is it? Who are your other patients?*" After a moment of silence, she continued by relating a memory. "I remember a time in my childhood when I first noticed a picture of a little girl on my father's desk and asked who she was. I was told that it was a picture of my sister, who had died a long time ago. I thought this meant that she was Father's daughter. When I was older, I found out that she was actually Mother's daughter. This made me feel very insecure. I used to wonder, 'Who does the child belong to—Father or Mother?'"

The analyst listened silently. Nurit continued: "You know, sometimes, when I was walking down the street and saw a cat or a dog that was run over, I tried to look away." To this, the analyst responded, "Do you think your reaction might be the same as your reaction to your sisters, who were run over by the Nazi machine?"

Nurit replied, "Well, yes. When I was younger, I would try to block out the stories of the dead. I wanted to grow up without letting them affect me."

ANALYST: It couldn't have been easy growing up in the shadow of the dead.

NURIT: The truth is I enjoyed being an only child. I had so many privileges.

ANALYST: Today, when you noticed a hair on the pillow, you asked me who my other patients were.

NURIT: Right. I never actually thought about the others. For me they just don't exist, even though of course I know that they come here.

ANALYST: You wish you were an only child, and like with your sisters, you try to ignore my other patients so that their existence won't affect you.

NURIT: [*After a silence*] When I first came to you, I was so worried about my oldest daughter. She is such a talented girl, but she was an underachiever in school. She also had this awful boyfriend from a low-class family; maybe he was even on drugs. She was always rebelling against us—her successful, achievement-oriented parents. I always felt that what she was doing was directed against me; she was so angry with me.

ANALYST: Perhaps you were angry with your mother and your sisters in the same way your daughter was angry with you.

NURIT: [*After a moment of silence, she spoke nonchalantly*] That's an interesting piece of information.

The analyst was struck by the remote, intellectual nature of Nurit's reaction. She felt her interpretation had fallen on deaf ears. She decided to drop the topic of comparing her daughter's way of relating to her and her own way of relating to the analyst.

NURIT: I never did that to my mother [i.e., got angry with her]. I was a good girl, a good student in school. My parents never had to worry about me. But, as soon as I became a teenager, my mother was no longer pleased with me. She accused me of being egoistic and selfish. I was terrified by the threats. She told me that I would never have any friends because I was so cold and inconsiderate. I remember my mother saying, "You'll see—your child will do exactly the same thing to you that you're doing to me!"

The analyst was struck by this reaction and reminded of aspects of her relationship with her own mother. She then said: ""You probably felt she was cursing you."

NURIT: Definitely. Today I know that I have good relationships with people; a lot of people like me. But then I didn't know that and I believed her. It completely shook my self-confidence. You know, when I was around eleven years old, Mother became so demanding—everything had to be done perfectly! I remember the first time it happened, it left such a strong impression on me. Mother accused me of not turning off the light in my grandmother's room. I was so sure I had turned it off that I argued bitterly with her about it. But in the end, I felt confused and wasn't really sure any more. This began happening so often that I no longer knew when I was right and when I was wrong. Maybe this caused the symptoms that I'm suffering from now.

The analyst confides to us: "Nurit's distress left a deep impression on me. Evidently, years of being told that she was completely untrustworthy had left her feeling that she could not trust her senses. At that instant Nurit suddenly blurted out a question: 'This plant in your office, wasn't it much smaller two days ago, or am I imagining it?'"

Dr. Kogan is quite candid with the reader in disclosing her quandary as to how to best reply to her patient's question about her plant. She reflected as follows: "There were various ways to react to this question. I could have inquired further about what she thought of this. I could have tried to link her anxiety over the replaced plant to her anxiety and guilt over being a replacement child for her parents[3]—but this was an idea that we would be able to deal with only later in the analysis. I chose instead to reassure the confused child revealed in the analytic situation. At the time, I felt that this was the only way to help her regain faith in her perception of reality."

ANALYST: Your question about the plant brings into the room the confused child who could not trust her senses. Yes, you are right. The plant was much smaller. I brought in a new, larger one yesterday.

The analyst then tells us that we can observe her trying to avoid touching on unconscious "dangerous" subjects, such as Nurit's wish that her siblings had never existed and her hatred of her mother. Instead, she thought it better to totally accept her conscious feeling of being the victim of a mother who had undermined her child's perception of reality: "Nurit was afraid that I would not believe her version of the reality of life in the parents' home." But the analyst also feared that something was missing in this analysis and that was the work of making the unconscious conscious, due to the fear of the analyst about arousing Nurit's anger and becoming her victim. The following statement showed that Nurit, too, felt that something was absent: "In the beginning of analysis, I expected you to ask me all sorts of questions so that you would know more about me, but you never did."

In view of the main topic of contextualizing associations, what the analyst said next is remarkable:

> Since from the start, I had explained the role of free associations to Nurit, I speculated over the deeper meaning of her remark. Was she referring to questions regarding her feelings toward me in the transference that I did not dare to bring up? Or perhaps to elements hidden in her story that I did not know about? I chose to pursue the latter, feeling that that would be more acceptable to her (and possibly safer for me as well at this stage of the analysis).

She then said to the patient, "Perhaps you see me as yourself, the little girl who wanted to know so much about the secret past of her parents, but never dared to ask . . . ?" They were both silent and then the session ended.

At issue in what follows is not to advocate for a perfect way to deal with the two questions. The advantage of this clinical example is the clarity of the consequences of the differing contextualizing choices of three analysts, especially because two of the analysts, Dr. Brenner and I, are adherents of the same theoretic model. Both she and Dr. Brenner did not privilege the contextual links between the first and the second question. They probably had different reasons for that choice, but they agreed in that choice and disagreed about their choice for their own preferred interventions. What I find important here is that in the moment of reflection about the choices she made in the session about how to intervene, Dr. Kogan had not once but twice indicated her choice to disregard the congruence between the two questions in her contextualizing priorities: Whose hair is on the pillow, and is that a new plant? This contextual disconnection deprives the analyst of certain choices of intervention. This is analogous to a physician who would find it much harder or perhaps impossible to make a diagnosis that had not occurred to him or her as a possibility. Concerning the first question, about whose hair was on the pillow, the avoidance of the transference seems to have been unintended, but we simply don't know if that is so or not so. Her disconnection of the two questions of the patient throughout this discussion was not questioned by any of her three published discussants. This was actually a major contextualizing decision by all four of the analysts participating in this discussion. In every instance, the opening question to the analyst about whose hair is that on the pillow was never contextually linked to her second question: Is that a new plant? It is just that omission from the contextualizing horizon that led directly to the contextualizing strategies deployed by each of the discussants, as well as by Dr. Kogan.

I now define two terms. By *contextualizing criteria*, I mean the widely diverse links between associations and theory that constitute the choice by the analyst for forming a contextual horizon. By the term *contextual horizon*, I mean a group of associations that are dynamically linked by the contextualizing criteria utilized by the analyst to capture the major dynamic urgency in a given session. It is the impossible-to-fulfill task of the patient to speak as freely as possible, and it is the corresponding impossible-to-fulfill task of the analyst to listen to everything that the patient says as freely as possible. But it is an epistemological rather than a technical requirement that requires this from the patient and the analyst. This is not a technical compliance with the fundamental rule. The tension between these two impossible tasks is the very stuff of the psychoanalytic process. The listening of the analyst requires that she or he eventually begin to contextualize what the patient is saying. We prioritize the associations in terms of dynamic relevance. We privilege certain associations for that reason and de-emphasize others.

The opening question of this patient is echoed in her later question but in a different manifest guise: "Whose hair is this?" could mean "Who preceded me, and am I replacing someone?" or "Will someone replace me?" But the two questions will sound very different if they are de-linked. There is a contextual synergy to these two questions. Each enhances our possible understandings of the other. That is, of course, the evidence of the hermeneutic circle in which the part and the whole are synergistically linked as generating meaning by their very relatedness.[4] This is embedded in the later question about the plant: Can I believe my own eyes, or is that not a replacement plant? To recognize the contextual link of these two questions allows us to wonder privately, why exactly now, and in such a selective manner, can she not trust her senses? This would allow the analyst to think about what kind of major affective danger is evoked by the theme of replacement. In this large array of possibilities, we should employ one other important contextualizing criterion. The first communication of the session (and often the last) has superordinate contextualizing significance. The opening question about the hair and the later question about the plant were related like theme and variation in a musical score. So, knowing that the opening question must have given affective priority to the transference would have led me to my own contextualizing choice to give priority to the transference in this session. Something has happened to scare the patient about replacing another patient or being replaced by another patient. This undoubtedly reflects the traumatic events in her childhood, but the opening question would have signaled me to approach these issues in the transference. Suffice it to say here that the contextualization of the associations of the patient is a form of triage in which we assign dynamic priorities, usually with lightning speed and usually unconsciously or preconsciously.

Among the various ways that analysts listen to their patients, we differ a great deal in the way that we organize the associations of the patient as we are listening. Often the word *listen* in discussions on this topic is a loose synonym for *contextualize.* Putting to one side the confusing effects of different theoretic models in determining how we contextualize and therefore prioritize the associations of the patient, it is time that we stopped overlooking the profound effects of the inconsistencies in the way that analysts within the same theoretic model listen to the associations of the patient. When Dr. A and Dr. B, who adhere to the same model, listen to an entire session, it is wrong to assume that they will necessarily have attached the same importance to selected portions of the session. The reasons why are complex, but the neglect of this problem adds an unnecessary burden to the daunting problem of evaluating clinical evidence.

Brenner faulted Kogan for the omission of contextual information about the onset in her life of her obsessional symptoms. Knowing when they had developed might have shed important light on the pathogenesis of some of her other problems. He also objected to the omission of details of her sexual history. He thought it possible that this was an omission in reporting rather than in her understanding, in view of the final excellent clinical results. I agree with those observations, and so did Kogan in her reply to Brenner's comments. However, perhaps his sharpest criticism was about her answering the second of the patient's two questions in the session—and that is the point about which I disagree with him.

When the patient asked about the plant, Brenner (2003) said,

> I suggest that it would have been preferable to say something like "You were just talking about your mother making you uncertain about your memory. Now you feel uncertain about your memory here. What do you think about that?" I suggest, in other words, that it would have been not only possible, but actually preferable, to be *analytic* rather than trying to be reassuring by answering Nurit's question directly. (p. 774; italics added)

I disagree with Dr. Brenner about what is "analytic" at such a moment. Dr. Kogan had a different understanding of what being analytic means. So did I. In fact, we have a bewildering number of definitions today about what it means to be an analyst, partly because of our confusion about the incompleteness of our understanding of the relation of our interpretive inferences to our theories about what is mutative. I would have preferred to link the question that the patient asked at the beginning of the hour about whose hair is this to the question at the end of the hour about whether this is a new plant. With that in mind as the better way to contextualize the events of the hour, I too would have answered her question instead of refusing. But I would have said, after telling her that it was indeed a new plant, that I wondered if her question about whose hair that was on the pillow was related to this question about this being a replacement plant. These contrasting technical strategies can then be viewed as the consequence of three different analysts' choosing three different contextual horizons—despite the fact that two of the analysts are from the same theoretic school—to organize their inferences about the meaning of the patient's associations. There is an irony here: Dr. Kogan and Dr. Brenner agreed, by de-emphasizing the link between the two questions, and disagreed about answering one of them. Dr. Kogan and I agreed about answering the question, but I disagreed with both of them about privileging the contextual link between the two questions. In my own view, the issue is not what the proper analytic behavior was; it was, which way of listening or contextualizing afforded richer opportunities for understanding the patient better? In that sense, all three of us were trying to be analytic. But isn't every analyst, regardless of theoretic persuasion, trying to be analytic? And none of us would do what we do with patients if we did not believe that we were being analytic. But there are those who use that view to justify nihilistic relativism and simply shrug their shoulders about such questions as this. That is why we need a discipline that could be called comparative psychoanalysis.

Therefore, I want to be clear that the question of who is more correct is not the issue. I think, instead, that more can be learned from the questions that arise about this vignette and its ensuing disagreements than from answers about the disagreement. The complexity of what transpires in the mind of the analyst at work is certainly daunting.

When analysts feel discomfort about technique, when there is uncertainty about what to do, instead of an understanding of what is happening, we are often in the midst of an enactment wherein the patient and the analyst are actualizing the same unconscious fantasy. The conscious reliance on rules is not rarely a sign of just such uneasiness—but not always and it's a risky business attributing motives to a colleague who is either for or against certain interventions. These are ad hominem arguments. They can always be turned both ways. There are also some rules that should always be observed. One should under no circumstances ever misuse the trust of the patient or harm a patient. That is a rule that has no exceptions. But we have a number of other guiding precepts that have to be administered with discretion and judgment. One of the problems with rules—such as the rule of never answering a question that the patient directs to the analyst—involves the problem of the generic analyst.[5] We have seen this problem in the view of some of our Kleinian colleagues who speak of the patient's putting feelings into the analyst. Would all analysts become the same receptacle for feelings? The enormous variation in emotional responses by various analysts argues against blaming the patient for what the analyst feels. I suggest here that contextualizing an interaction with the patient often resolves such questions in a better way than that of relying on technical rules. There is a greater likelihood of remaining in emotional contact with the patient if we understand that we often reach for a rule when we don't understand that the patient is trying to solve a problem. But I don't think that there should be a rule against rules for all analysts or even for most of us. I think analysts are not generic and that some will prefer rules whereas others will not, and the best way to settle such questions is not with rules at all but with adequate information about the context in which a specific question of technique is arising. My own clinical experience has repeatedly taught me that what appears to be a technical dilemma is merely the visible sign of an unrecognized transference–countertransference interaction. I also disagree that we should substitute the term *analytic* for *kosher.*[6]

The essential role of context with regard to breaking rules was illustrated in an anecdote told by Ed Weinshel, a very wise and tactful analyst and former chairman of the Board of Professional Standards of the American Psychoanalytic Association, who told of an experience of his own that he believed would shock us until or unless we knew the context. He told us that he once said to a patient, "Fuck you." He left the context to our imagination, and I will leave it to yours (see Stone, 1954).

I have chosen a clinical example of a minor disagreement with a psychoanalyst from my own theoretic school. I certainly hold basic psychoanalytic beliefs in common with him, more so in fact than with Dr. Kogan. So, the disagreement I discuss here is intended to illustrate a specimen example of a disagreement between two analysts who belong to the same theoretic school. We should not discuss disagreements of this kind in only a general way or at experience-distant levels. That is also true about our agreements. Viewing such experience-near disagreements in depth between colleagues from the same theoretic school should be the occasion for growth in our understanding of our differences that are far more fundamental than the case with inter-model disagreements. I can have a coherent disagreement with Dr. Brenner but not with an analyst who rejects the role of psychic determinism or the use of the associations of the patient to arrive at inferences of unconscious meaning. I think it is useful to speak of coherent and incoherent disagreements based on whether the disagreements at issue can be discussed by using the same criteria of evidence. That is the key difference between religious and scientific disagreements. Science adheres to belief in ideas that are the best currently available explanation for data that are consensually agreed to be the basis for discussion. It is just this last phrase that we have woefully neglected in our literature. Too often, we disagree without knowing what clinical data constituted our views. We have fatefully too often assumed that we all heard the same thing during the session even though we have known, theoretically, that this could not be true and even though we have countless examples of our failing to define what we thought we were disagreeing about. I suggest here that we will not be able to have a reliable methodology for comparative psychoanalysis until we clarify this problem in any one of our various theoretic models.

On another occasion during a discussion about this same Kogan paper, a colleague raised the following objection: "What difference does it make if the analyst does or does not link the two questions of this patient? Certainly an analyst of Dr. Brenner's stature will ultimately deal with all the relevant issues. He would simply take a different path to get there." This is known as the argument of equifinality.[7] It is a pragmatic argument rooted in the assumption that most analysts get good results one way or another and that it does not matter that much how they get there. This is an argument based on faith rather than evidence, and it is a slippery slope—slippery because it is adjacent to pragmatic views about simply defining truth in terms of what works.[8] We have numerous clinical examples of patients and analysts who agree that an analysis should be declared successful only to discover later that serious residual problems had not been resolved adequately. Before Freud, doctors got good results by advising patients to visit a spa. Norman Reider (1956) wrote a wonderful paper about patients who got much better with a few therapy sessions or without any treatment at all. Those were examples of a nothing that worked just as well as something. Long ago Glover (1931) spoke of the inexact interpretation that relieved anxiety because it enhanced repression. The de-emphasis of clinical evidence in much of our recent literature is parallel to the de-emphasis of the epistemological foundational significance of the associations of the patient.

Allow me to summarize certain agreements and disagreements. I agree with Kogan's willingness to answer the second question but not her omitting to contextualize her understanding of the link between the two questions that the patient asked her. Brenner disagrees with both Kogan and me only manifestly about the issue of technique. The less visible disagreement that I have with Kogan and Brenner regards their de-emphasis of the patient's first question. This is a disagreement about contextualizing criteria and the contextualizing horizons enabled by those criteria. Dr. Kogan and Dr. Brenner had a one-question contextualizing criterion, and I had a two-question contextualizing criterion. As a result, we each arrived at different contextual horizons. Her criterion and his was the manifest question later in the session: Is that a new plant? My contextualizing criteria linked both her first and second questions together: "Whose hair is on the pillow?" becomes contextually resonant with "Is that a new plant?" To paraphrase the controversy about one- versus two-person models, we might say that this is a disagreement about one- versus two-question contextual horizons. Therefore, in this sense, we have a disagreement similar to that about Casement's patient where the discussants differ about

technique without recognizing or agreeing that there is an important difference in contextualizing the associations of the patient before the technique
disagreement became visible (Boesky, 2005). Brenner (2004, personal communication) stated that since he and I both relied on psychic determinism
that we were really using the same methodology. I do not believe that that is
true, because it omits the question of contextualizing criteria altogether. Our
agreement about psychic determinism to which Brenner refers is at a much
higher level of abstraction. To say that the sequential patterning of associations is determined is not to say anything at all about how to contextualize
those associations.

The assumption of equifinality is fallacious (Abrams, 1971). I doubt that
the platitudinous consolation that all roads lead to Rome will settle the vexing
question of evaluating clinical evidence. This is the familiar argument of the
principle of equifinality in a different guise. Equifinality is a theoretical air-
brush that is used to claim that all analysts get good results no matter what
their theories might be. But different analysts in the same theoretic school can
help patients in different ways by dealing with different issues, and so can different analysts from different schools. The facts do not support the conclusion
that any time the analysis ends with the mutual approval of the patient and
the analyst, they have ended up where any other analyst and patient would
have ended. If one wishes to argue that all roads lead to Rome, it is necessary
to do two things. First, one would have to deal with the problem that on the
world map of psychoanalysis, there are a number of different cities called
Rome. If we are discussing York and New York, we have to be sure we are on
the same side of the Atlantic. Even within the boundaries of the modern conflict model (to use the phrase that Brenner has chosen to describe modern
structural theory), we have no consensually acceptable definition of what
home consists of. In this case, I would have preferred to remind the patient
about the similarity of her opening and later questions so that we could keep
our attention in this session on the transference where I believe the affective
urgency of the patient was being lived.

Perhaps, one reason for this disagreement is that Kogan, Brenner, and I are
using different contextual criteria. I am often inclined to give special attention
to the associations at the beginning of the session. In our oral tradition of supervision, it has long been common to compare the opening associations of
the session, the opening topics of the analysis, and the opening lines or opening chapter of a novel or poem. The patient or the author is privileging these
opening communications by granting them pride of place. But not all analysts
share that assumption.

There would be even more disagreement about keeping in mind the closing
associations of the prior session, but *pace* Bion, there are times when it is use-

ful to begin a session with a clear memory of the last session. Certainly, Brenner is more than aware of this oral tradition; in fact, he has written about it and taught it for years. There is another less obvious problem here. We analysts have a variety of contextualizing criteria, and we deploy these in a hierarchical manner. These hierarchies of contextualization form the terrain in which the subjectivity of the analyst determines shifts in the importance of conflicting hierarchical priorities. Examples of these shifts include the cases when we do and when we do not choose to depart from our general technical precepts. We need to clarify the fact that this is an important problem. Not only do we have disagreements between analysts about contextualizing priorities, we have shifts as well as contradictions within any given analyst's contextualizing priorities, and we simply cannot assume that we have that information when we discuss a case unless it is spelled out. Again the issue here is not who is right about such a difference of opinion, and it is certainly not the question of whether the analyst should or should not answer questions. I hope that everything that I have said will indicate that I would disagree even with the assumed premises of such a question solely based on technical rules. I prefer my own contextualizing criteria in this example. But the point at issue here is that in a disagreement such as this, we should have access to the contextualizing criteria that the analyst has employed. To paraphrase the French aphorism, to understand everything is to forgive everything.

Local Versus Broader Contextualization

Whether Brenner's intervention was unnecessarily depriving is a different question from that of whether his decision to abstain from answering her question was based on an optimum understanding of all the available data. In my view, his deflecting her question by directing her attention to her immediately preceding associations sprang from a "local" contextualization that determined his choice of intervention. As I noted, in my view, the better contextualizing alternative would have been to infer that there was a dynamic continuity between the patient's two questions. Recognizing this does not automatically indicate how to intervene, but it would provide a better range of choices for the analyst. This is related to a well-known but still insufficiently appreciated aspect of the methodology for contextualization that I discuss in chapter 7. Many individual sessions are thematically organized by a contextually prominent latent affective urgency that is pressing for disguised expression. This major contextual theme runs like a subterranean river throughout the session, rising at certain points to the surface and then disappearing from view. There is an important danger that the analyst may miss the possible presence of such organizing latent contextual themes and yield to the ever-present temptation to contextually disconnect one group of associations from what may be a larger and affectively more important contextual unity.[9] Such a "local," or partial, contextualization can be performed on any utterance of the patient and yield unlimited speculative inferences. This is the location of the Achilles' heel of psychoanalysis: Anything can mean anything.

To base our intervention on the authority of the analyst instead of the context of the patient's own associations is a most important distinction. If we discover that this is what our disagreement is about, then we have better opportunities for further discussion of which of two views accounts better for the available data. The reason is that at the higher level of abstraction, we do not explicitly know about which data the two analysts are debating. If certain data are included and even privileged and other data are not included within the contextual horizon of the two analysts who are disagreeing, it is impossible to arrive at coherent conclusions about the comparative advantages of the two different interventions. Ironically, if this is indeed the reason for Brenner's technical recommendation, then he and Kogan agreed at the clinical level because each of them responded to a question of the patient by distracting her from the transference—and each did it by pushing for more attention from her on her childhood history and away from the transference. Kogan did that when she responded to the opening question about the hair on the pillow by reminding the patient of the death of her sisters at the hands of the Nazis. Brenner did that when he advised replying to her question about the replacement plant with his own question about her talking just before that about her mother. Kogan and Brenner are miles apart theoretically but seem to have done something quite similar in their actual intervention. In practice, they elected to avoid the transference. Kogan did this out of her clinical concern for the safety of the patient and herself; Brenner, for his concern for maintaining what he believes to be the proper analytic attitude toward reacting to a patient's asking the analyst a question. So, here we see a theoretic disagreement between two analysts who actually agree to avoid a transference priority in practice. Another ironic agreement between Kogan and Brenner lies in their choice to narrow their contextualizing choice to a merely local event in the session by disconnecting or deracinating the second question from the context of the opening question. Here we have a concordance of technique that conceals a divergence of theory. This dissociation between theory and technique is widely recognized, but it is not yet sufficiently appreciated in our discussions of pluralism.

This is illustrated in the following statement by Brenner (2003):

> The way in which each analyst listens to patients is determined by that analyst's understanding of mental development and functioning in general and of psychopathology in particular, i.e., by that analyst's "general notion" (= theories) of

mental development and functioning. There is considerable variation from analyst to analyst on this matter, a feature of analytic theory that is often referred to
as pluralism. (p. 770)

I agree strongly with Brenner about that statement, but the problem is that we
cannot assume that we know the relationship between the guiding theory officially deployed by the analyst and the actual behavior of the analyst. Informed pluralism is the sign of an open mind, but uninformed pluralism simply conceals nihilistic relativism in which all ideas are equally useful.

In our current climate of exuberant pluralism, practice and theory are often
dichotomously opposed. Fonagy (2003)[10] has said—and I very much agree—
that the assumption of a close relation between practice and theory is illusory
and often politically motivated. But there are serious problems that will ensue
if we advocate divorcing theory and practice rather than trying as best we can
to remedy how loosely coupled they are.

The disagreement between Kogan, Brenner, and me cannot even begin to
lead to a meaningful comparison of views without comparing the different
contextual horizons chosen by two of us. The analyst employing Arlow's contextualizing criteria (1979) of repetition of a theme in the associations of the
patient would arrive at a different contextualizing horizon than would the analyst who at that moment privileged the information about the relationship
with the patient. We learned after 1492 that horizons can be illusory. An advantage to the term *contextual horizon* is its metaphoric insistence that what
lies beyond the horizon is not yet visible. The notion of horizon has an old
history in the hermeneutic literature,[11] and I want to emphasize a neglected
link between our use of the associations of the patient and hermeneutics.

Many of those who view psychoanalysis as a natural science have derisively
dismissed hermeneutics as an epistemological base for psychoanalysis and, in
so doing, ignored its heuristic advantages. After all, the argument goes, patients are not texts. Yet, the methods by which they give up their secrets to us
are the same as those that poets and authors have used for millennia. The two
questions asked by the patient that I discuss in the clinical example are powerfully linked if we view them in terms of the hermeneutic circle so that we
can see them as being situated in the same contextual horizon. Each question
is much like the other: Whose hair is this on your pillow? and Have you got a
new plant today? It does violence to the affective integrity of this patient's subjective experience to disconnect the two questions. Each question is in turn
dynamically linked to one of the most powerful themes in her life: whom has
she replaced, which child died so that she could live, and who will replace her.
All her life, she has waited for this ax to fall. So, we want to help her see the
continuity of what she feels about the analyst with her life history, and what
better way to do that than to contextualize these two questions as part of one

dynamic unity. Each of the two questions enhances the meaning of the other. The part can only be understood as an aspect of the whole, and certain of its parts enhance the meaning of the whole. It is this reciprocal enhancement of meaning in the dialectic between the part and the whole that constitutes the hermeneutic circle. This is an illustration of why hermeneutics does not define the scientific nature of an enterprise, only its methods of interpretation.

This additional information about contextual information allows us to see that what appears to be only a matter of differences in technique is, in this and many other instances, the consequence of a difference in contextualizing. Sometimes, such contextualizing differences are the direct outgrowth of theoretic differences but by no means always, as this discussion illustrates. At other times, the inability to perceive a contextual horizon is analogous to the inability to enjoy certain literature or get a joke. It all depends on the perceptive equilibrium and the defense organization of the analyst. Thus, contextual capacities are a sensitive gauge of countertransference. To summarize, it is my suggestion that when we make the contextual criteria that give meaning to an intervention explicit, it becomes possible to see what we are disagreeing about at a level closer to the original data. That is no small achievement.

Notes

1. Other versions of this chapter were delivered as the Freud Lecture, New York University Psychoanalytic Institute, May 21, 2007, and at a scientific meeting of the Michigan Psychoanalytic Society.

2. Kogan's paper (2003), with the three discussions by Brenner (2003), Ferro (2003), and Herzog (2003), was published in *Psychoanalytic Quarterly.* The issues considered by Ferro and Herzog are outside the scope of this discussion.

3. An idea that Dr. Brenner had suggested to Dr. Kogan earlier in a private communication.

4. Compare the discussion of the hermeneutic circle in chapter 8.

5. The pitfalls of using rules in psychoanalytic treatment are well known (e.g., see Goldberg, 2001).

6. The issue of abstinence was eloquently debated in papers by Dr. Brenner (1979) and Leo Stone (1961, 1967), and their debate was described in a *New Yorker* profile by Janet Malcolm (1980a, 1980b).

7. I discuss this further in chapter 6.

8. There is a tendency in our own literature about science and pragmatism to equate those who view analysis as a science with the views of naive realism. Compare Goldberg (2002) and Renik (1998) with Hanly (1999) and Hanly and Hanly (2001).

9. These organizing themes are what I call *contextual horizons* in other discussions of this topic (e.g., chapter 2 and 7).

10. Fonagy (2003) said,

This paper considers the current fragmentation of psychoanalytic theory as a result of the illusorily close association of practice and theory. The author argues that the politically motivated assertion of a direct connection between theory and practice should be set aside and that practice should be liberated from theory, permitting theory to evolve in the context of radically modified patterns of practice. If theory were decoupled from practice, technique might progress on purely pragmatic grounds, on the basis of what is seen to work. Psychoanalytic theory of mental function could then follow practice, integrating what is newly discovered through innovative methods of clinical work. Such a *pragmatic,* principally action-oriented use of theory would bring psychoanalysis more in line with modern, postempirical views of science. (p. 13; italics added)

11. For a discussion of horizons in the hermeneutic tradition, see Gadamer (1999). See also, chapter 8.

References

Abrams, S. (1971). Models of the psychic apparatus. *Journal of the American Psychoanalytic Association, 19,* 131–142.

Arlow, J. (1979). The genesis of interpretation. *Journal of the American Psychoanalytic Association, 27S,* 193–206.

Boesky, D. (2005). Analytic controversies contextualized. *Journal of the American Psychoanalytic Association, 53,* 835–863.

Brenner, C. (1979). Working alliance, therapeutic alliance, and transference. *Journal of the American Psychoanalytic Association, 27,* 137–157.

Brenner, C. (2003). Commentary on Ilany Kogan's "On being a dead, beloved child." *Psychoanalytic Quarterly, 72,* 767–776.

Ferro, A. (2003). Commentary on Ilany Kogan's "On being a dead, beloved child." *Psychoanalytic Quarterly, 72*(3), 777–783.

Fonagy, P. (2003). Some complexities in the relationship of psychoanalytic theory to technique. *Psychoanalytic Quarterly, 72,* 13–48.

Gadamer, H. G. (1999). *Truth and method* (2nd rev. ed.). New York: Continuum.

Glover, E. (1931). The therapeutic effect of inexact interpretation: A contribution to the theory of suggestion. *International Journal of Psychoanalysis, 12,* 397–411.

Goldberg, A. (2001). Postmodern psychoanalysis. *International Journal of Psychoanalysis, 82*(1), 123–128.

Goldberg, A. (2002). American pragmatism and American psychoanalysis. *Psychoanalytic Quarterly, 71*(2), 235–250.

Hanly, C. (1999). On subjectivity and objectivity in psychoanalysis. *Journal of the American Psychoanalytic Association, 47,* 427–444.

Hanly, C., & Hanly, M. (2001). Critical realism: Distinguishing the psychological subjectivity of the analyst from epistemological subjectivism. *Journal of the American Psychoanalytic Association, 49*(2), 515–532.

Herzog, J. (2003). Commentary on Ilany Kogan's "On being a dead, beloved child." *Psychoanalytic Quarterly, 72,* 785–796.

Kogan, I. (2003). On being a dead, beloved child. *Psychoanalytic Quarterly, 72,* 727–766.

Malcolm, J. (1980a, November 24). The impossible profession, Part I. *New Yorker.*

Malcolm, J. (1980b, December 1). The impossible profession, Part II. *New Yorker.*

Reider, N. (1956). *Bulletin of the Menninger Clinic,* XIX, 1955, "A type of psychotherapy based on psychoanalytic principles," pp. 111–128 [Abstract]. *Psychoanalytic Quarterly, 25,* 617–618.

Renik, O. (1998). The analyst's objectivity and the analyst's subjectivity. *International Journal of Psychoanalysis, 79,* 487–498.

Stone, L. (1954). On the principal obscene word of the English language—An inquiry, with hypothesis, regarding its origin and persistence. *International Journal of Psychoanalysis, 35,* 30–56.

Stone, L. (1961). *The psychoanalytic situation.* New York: International Universities Press.

Stone, L. (1967). The psychoanalytic situation and transference. *Journal of the American Psychoanalytic Association, 15,* 3–58.

II

ASSOCIATIONS, CONTEXTUALIZATION, AND HERMENEUTICS

6

Another Kind of Incompleteness: Associations and Interpretation

---

There is another kind of incompleteness which I myself have intentionally introduced. I have as a rule not reproduced the process of interpretation to which the patient's associations and communications had to be subjected, but only the result of that process.

—Freud (1905/1953, pp. 12–13)

OUR GRAND VIEW OF ABSTRACT THEORIES from lofty altitudes has not been earned by the hard and tedious work of mapping the paths and trails we took when we started our ascent to reach those heights. We have many bold claims by genuine pioneers and would-be pioneers that challenge and contradict each other, but the evidence provided to support these claims is too often unpersuasive. Comparative psychoanalysis is a discipline in its infancy, and it has not achieved a consensually accepted methodology to adjudicate these rival claims of superiority. One prevalent current attitude toward our defective methodology for evaluating clinical evidence is to congratulate ourselves on our pluralism. It is said that, for the most part, we all get as equally good results no matter what our theoretic banner, and this claim of equifinality has drowned out the sober question, what would it take to make any of us change our mind about our ideas? From a different source, the epistemology wars of the postmodern turn have mounted arguments about the logical impossibility of claiming that there could even be such a thing as evidence. The caustic rejection of the claim that psychoanalysis is a science that has traditionally sprung from the scientific and medical community has now been joined by many psychoanalytic colleagues on the grounds of the indeterminate flux of intersubjectivity at the heart of the psychoanalytic process.

Science and Evidence

Green (2000)[1] has argued that psychoanalysis is a science but that empiric research as an instrument for its evidential support is inherently irrelevant. The epistemological criticisms have reinforced the always prevalent attacks about psychoanalysis as an art rather than a science. The cumulative effect of this confluence of tributaries has been a flood of arguments proclaiming the death of clinical evidence. It is certainly true that we have gained a great deal from our finally accepting the fact that none of our theoretic models has the whole truth or necessarily even the most important part of the truth that it has staked out. My views about the role of associations of the patient are rooted in the conviction that psychoanalysis is indeed a science and that our progress as a science is threatened by some important confusion in our notions about clinical evidence arising in our "science wars." I am convinced that we will not continue to develop as a science if we do not do a better job about the issue of our unsatisfactory understanding of the problem of evaluating clinical evidence. This must be done to clarify the notorious weak links between our abstract theories and our actual practice. I suggest that one important reason for our polemics about whether it is even possible to speak logically about the very existence of "evidence" has to do with some difficult, tricky, and arcane philosophic ambiguities about the nature of "meaning." The serious error of perpetuating the either-or reductive polarized view that psychoanalysis must be either a science or a hermeneutic–constructive enterprise is one of the underlying reasons for our continued neglect of the foundational epistemological significance of the associations of the patient. I develop my reasons for saying this further in this chapter but also in chapters 7 and 8.

I discuss the problems of our methodology for arriving at conjectures about the unconscious meanings of the communications of our patients from a rather unusual angle. Rival explanations for the mysteries of the world have characterized every branch of science for millennia. Furthermore, challenges to whatever psychoanalytic theory at whatever time that theory was in ascendance have always been with us. Much of our attention has been drawn to these large and abstract disagreements. Think of Alfred Adler, Carl Jung, Karen Horney, Sandor Rado, Melanie Klein, Franz Alexander, Heinz Kohut, Donald Winnicott, and Jacques Lacan. Think also of the ongoing disputes about exactly what it is that is mutative about successful psychoanalytic treatment. Every candidate learns to recite the famous battles of our own civil wars: the corrective emotional experience as opposed to abstinence and neutrality; conflict versus deficit theory; pre-oedipal versus oedipal pathology; interpretations versus the relational authenticity of the analyst; the one-person versus the two-person model. Our libraries are the Gettysburg commemorating these battles.

It is not news to say that one of the contributing factors to our endless debates and confusion has been that the level of our disagreements has been far too removed from the data that presumably generated the abstract theory. But we have neglected an even less obvious factor. We have erroneously assumed that the agreements and disagreements among the partisans within a given theoretic school were of only minor interest or significance as compared to the differences between different models. I have come to the opposite conclusion. It is a big mistake to think that we can continue to study only the differences between competing theoretic models while we minimize the quieter differences among colleagues within any of our models. I refer to the fallacious notion that analysts need not worry too much about disagreements about experience-near clinical disagreements. The argument is that it does not matter that much if we disagree about single sessions because in the end, we agree with our main theoretical assumptions. The consoling assumption is that if we agree at the top of the ladder of abstractions, the bottom disagreements are not that important. We tend to overlook our disagreements about whether the information about single sessions is of any relevance in evaluating an entire analysis. That is another example of the disconnect between our theory and practice because in actual practice, many analysts would be reluctant to pass judgment about the outcome of an analysis without having information about the events of a sampling of individual sessions. We might compare this scenario to the wish of the surgeon to have microscopic as well as grossly visible inspection of biopsy material. We do not want to know only that the transference was dealt with extensively; we want to know the actual sounds and cries of the battles, the smell of the gun smoke, as well as the perfume and passions of the analysis that can only emerge in meaningful accounts of selected sessions. The argument that we cannot tell everything has become a justification for telling nothing. Goethe said that life was green and theory was gray. Our clinical reports are gray, and we behave as though it is impossible to restore their color and meet the rigorous demands of science. One place where the color and passion have been cut out is the single session. The reasons for the de-emphasis of the individual session are beyond the scope of this chapter, and the problems of devising a reliable method to sample them in reporting an entire case are daunting. However, I wish here to highlight what we have lost by throwing up our hands at this critical problem that underlies our evidence wars.

Attention to Associations Has Declined

Our consistent de-emphasis of the original raw material from which our theoretic generalizations are derived has meant the de-emphasis of our attention to the associations of our patients. Kris (1982) drew attention to our neglect of the role of associations in our theory and practice about 25 years ago and pursued the topic from a rather different direction than I do here. He said,

> We need to know more about the individual styles of conceptualizing and theorizing as they determine the analyst's participation in the free association method. *For it seems far from clear to me what makes one way of formulating appeal to one analyst but not to another.*[2] Such differences are hard to study when the analytic method and process are defined in terms of the very theoretical concepts in question. A more operational definition of psychoanalytic method and process . . . seems an essential prerequisite to resolving the present confusion of theoretical tongues. (p. 104; italics added)

Few authors have devoted such concentrated attention to the topic of free associations. Mahony (1979), Bollas (2002), and Hoffer (2004, 2006)[3] are notable exceptions. This neglect of the role of associations in our methodology of interpretation may be due to two problems. The first is the tendency in our literature to treat the topic of the associations of the patient as being wedded to the term *free associations*. This in turn has been fatally linked—earlier to the fundamental rule and later to the writings of Paul Gray and his followers. Kris (1982) also said that he had "not attempted to discuss how the analyst or even this analyst makes his selections and formulations. That important topic lies outside the scope of this book" (p. 13). That topic is, of course, the major focus of the present discussion. How does the analyst make selections from the ocean of associations to privilege certain samples, and then how does the analyst fashion conjectures and interpretations from those associations?

The term *free association* has been mostly viewed in recent times as an obsolete vestige of our history because it has been reductively equated with the obsolete exhortations of the fundamental rule. For instance, Hoffman (2006) said that free association is still one of the sacred cows of the psychoanalytic tradition. He challenged the traditional and still prevalent view of free association, arguing that it entails three forms of denial or myths: denial of the patient's free agency, denial of the patient's and the analyst's interpersonal influence, and denial of the patient's share of responsibility for co-constructing the analytic relationship. Fonagy (2002) described free association as a residue of an outmoded one-person psychoanalytic psychology.

If most analysts actually still commanded their patients today to obey the fundamental rule in this way, I would agree with Hoffman's criticism, but in view of the widespread better understanding of these issues in current practice, this seems to be a straw man argument. In fact, 20 years ago, Lichtenberg and Galler (1987), in their careful survey of more than 100 psychoanalysts about this topic, said the following about the fundamental rule:

> In summary, our respondents indicate that the fundamental rule has not become a matter of fact to be taken for granted. The initial guidelines are not regarded as a given in the analytic situation, like the color or contours of the couch. Instead, they are regarded as a dynamic influence on the analytic process, an influence potentially capable of modification by personal experience or by study. . . . Our findings confirm an impression of diversity of approaches to the fundamental rule and indicate that what is said and the reasons for it should be given greater attention in analytic education. (pp. 73–74)

Hoffman contrasts his own dialectical–constructivist model with the views of Gray (1994) and Busch (1994, 1997) as follows:

> When the emphasis is on free association itself, as in those with an ego psychological perspective such as Gray and Busch, aspects of the patient's self that have been shut out in one way or another are seen as finding their way into the flow of the patient's thoughts [and] consciousness . . . and can be communicated and accepted. Conversely, when the emphasis is on the interaction, multiple aspects of self are seen as distributed between the analyst and the patient. (Hoffman, 2006, p. 47)

Hoffman seems to believe that Gray and Busch have co-opted the use of free associations or that all analysts who give importance to the epistemological significance of associations are practitioners of outmoded authoritarian and one-person views of psychoanalysis or are in agreement with Gray and his followers. To further illustrate the diversity of views among analysts of the same school, consider the ringing endorsement of the value of careful attention to the associations by Aron (1990), who criticized the widespread tendency of his relational colleagues (e.g., Hoffman) to falsely link free associations to the one-person model of psychoanalysis. Hoffman wrongly implies that careful attention to the interaction of analyst and patient requires an exclusively constructivist epistemology and that careful attention to the associations of the patient requires exclusively a one-person epistemology. That is a category error conflating epistemology and outmoded rules of technique. In chapter 4, I illustrated that the exact opposite is true and that careful attention to the associations facilitated a two-person view of the transference.

In this connection Ogden (1996) said,

> Although the term "fundamental rule" was not introduced by Freud until 1912 (1913), the concept was already a central part of Freud's thinking about analytic

technique in *The Interpretation of Dreams* (1900). In his essay "On Beginning the Treatment (Further Recommendations on the Technique of Psychoanalysis," Freud made his most fully elaborated statement regarding "the fundamental rule of psychoanalytic technique which the patient has to observe." This must be imparted to [the analysand] at the very beginning: "One more thing before you start. What you tell me must differ in one respect from an ordinary conversation. . . . You will be tempted to say to yourself that this or that is irrelevant here, or quite unimportant, or nonsensical, so that there is no need to say it. You must never give in to these criticisms, but must say it in spite of them—indeed, you must say it precisely because you feel an aversion to doing so . . . So say whatever goes through your mind . . . Finally, never forget that you have promised to be absolutely honest, and never leave anything out because, for some reason or other, it is unpleasant to tell it (*SE* 12, pp. 134–135). (p. 888)

The argument is that this would interfere with Ogden's required definition of the psychoanalytic process as the interaction of the reveries of the patient and the analyst. But such criticisms about free associations are a reductive distortion in which the epistemological value of associations disappears and all that remains is the straw man of the authoritarian analyst that is assaulting the agency of the victimized patient. However, this kind of behavior by an analyst would also interfere or destroy the psychoanalytic process for modern conflict analysts as well as modern Kleinian or Bionian analysts. At the time that Ogden wrote that paper, 11 years ago, the analysts who persisted in the use of Freud's 1913 views of the fundamental rule were already by far in the minority, and there were no more of them than there were analysts who adhered to Freud's 1913 views of defense or pathogenesis. This argument thus again welds free associations to the fundamental rule as an aspect of technique rather than as an epistemic requirement in which the associations are the ore from which we arrive at inferences about what we can know.

To paraphrase LaPlanche and Pontalis (1973),[4] the word *free* enshrined ambiguities. First, the term *free* conflates the conscious objections of the patient with the unconscious anxiety that fueled the objections—that is, *free* meant free of *conscious* editing. That kind of freedom was assumed in an archaic version of topographic theory that was abandoned by many if not most analysts at varying periods over the decades after 1920. Viewed in the structural model, the associations of the patients were never free of the unseen, unconscious shaping influence of unconscious conflict and psychic determinism, regardless of the patient's conscious wish to cooperate with the instruction of the analyst. The second ambiguity derives from ancient confusion about free will versus determinism. The persistent debates in certain strong relational theories about the indeterminate associations of the patient contrasted with the views of traditional models of psychoanalysis are evidently another version of the philosophic conundrum of free will "versus determinism".[5] To infer causes for an event in no way excludes contingency or choice. The term *free associations* was like the term *hay fever*, an affliction not caused by hay that does not produce a fever.

By the 1950s and 1960s, many analysts knew that expecting the patient to associate "freely" was an impossible task. The value of the waning use of the fundamental rule was not only in freeing us of the consequences of literal compliance by the patient but in the opportunity for patient and analyst to investigate together the inevitable moments when it became impossible for the patient to fulfill such an expectation. Many analysts as long as 50 years ago tried to create a climate with their patients of predicting that the task could not be fulfilled and welcoming such opportunities as useful points for collaborative investigation. The description of the contemporary authoritarian analyst demanding such compliance is a straw man. The naïve view of commanding the patient to cease and desist from conscious editing was a time-bound rule that made no sense after Freud made radical changes in his theories of anxiety and defense. In this discussion, I use the word *associations* without the word *free*, and I suggest that we have neglected the vitally important epistemological role of the associations of our patients. This epistemological importance is the important baby that was thrown out with the bath of the fundamental rule. Psychoanalysis is an enterprise defined by the quest for hidden meanings. There is no meaning without context and no context without associations. Advances in understanding led the majority of analysts to abandon the technical use of the fundamental rule a long time ago.

Most of what I say about the use of associations to infer latent meanings from manifest content derives from a large literature on hermeneutics as the study of the nature of meaning.[6] The complex back story of epistemology and hermeneutics in the large psychoanalytic literature on these topics is beyond the scope of this discussion. Suffice it to say here that a common misuse of the term *hermeneutics* is illustrated in the strong constructivist view that the derivation of meaning in the psychoanalytic treatment situation is unique to each patient–analyst dyad. Such a view conflates hermeneutics as a branch of knowledge dealing with the methods of interpretation and philosophical issues concerning ontology.[7] Thus, there could never be any transcontextual realities that existed prior to the relationship of the psychoanalytic dyad (Hanly, 2007, personal communication). So none of what I say about the inference of meaning is original. What may strike the reader as being novel in the present discussion is the radical and relentless insistence that I propose for the attention that we should direct to the associations of the patient as the raw material for the rich yield of psychoanalytic inference.

The Integral Link of Associations and Psychic Determinism

I here remind you that the principle of psychic determinism, as I have employed that term in psychoanalysis, is inseparable from the associations of the patient. Every communication of the patient—every utterance, gesture, word, or deed—is an association, in the sense that it has been determined by the affective immediacy of the unconscious conflicts of the patient in the session. Furthermore, every such association has been just as much determined as the physical events in the world. To say that all of the associations of the patient have been shaped and influenced by psychic determinism in no way implies that we could have predicted these associations. The profoundly important fact is that if we examine the associations of the patient in a reasonably well-conducted psychoanalytic relationship, we can predict backward at certain points and establish conjectures about disguised meanings foreshadowed by the earlier associations. The associations of the patient are the observable facts. But the problem that has always vexed our best efforts is that too often, different analysts listening to the same facts might have differing views about whether or when to intervene and, if so, what that intervention should be. Thus, it is at the most basic level conceivable that we have always had a terribly important problem that we have neglected and that some of our most pressing problems as a science are the direct result of that neglect. This is what Freud called merely "another form of incompleteness."

I refer here to the notorious ambiguity of the relation of observation to inference, the unreliability of our inferences, and our inability to resolve the question of the relation between evidence and meaning. The winner of a debate about meaning in our literature and in our meetings is, to put it charitably, not always the person with the most persuasive clinical evidence. To put it another way, we have a purloined letter in our history. The actual associations of our patients are like the famous letter on the table, hidden from our view, precisely because they are so deceptively visible: How could the deepest secrets of our patients be revealed by viewing the associations of our patients as a disguised mine shaft down which we must descend to extract the ore we seek. The epistemological value of radical attention to the fact that the contextual flow of associations is dynamically determined is to force us to understand better our strategies for contextualizing priorities. Clinical and theoretic differences of opinion appear in a more coherent light when we can explicitly state why we privileged certain associations of the patient and de-emphasized others. Coherent disagreements are based on a mutual agreement about what data are under discussion. Since that is untrue of incoherent disagreements, those tend to be more like political and religious disputes.

Disagreement in psychoanalysis has too often centered on high levels of abstraction. Think of oedipal versus pre-oedipal or conflict versus deficit as examples of polarized and tendentious abstract debates in our history. Freud spoke of the incompleteness of his case reports in a manner suggesting that only the realities of confidentiality and practicality precluded the furnishing of such details. But in the Dora case, he said,

> There is another kind of incompleteness which I myself have intentionally introduced. I have as a rule not reproduced the process of interpretation to which the patient's associations and communications had to be subjected, but only the result of that process. Apart from the dreams, therefore, the *technique* of the analytic work has been revealed in only a very few places. My object in this case was to demonstrate the intimate structure of a neurotic disorder and the determination of its symptoms; and it would have led to nothing but hopeless confusion if I had tried to complete the other task at the same time. (1905/1953, pp. 12–13)[8]

Apart from this terse statement in the Dora case, Freud said little or nothing about his methodology of interpretation throughout his writings. He trivialized the importance of this omission by describing it as merely "another form of incompleteness," similar to the incompleteness forced on him by considerations of confidentiality and the inordinate length that would have been required to report a completed treatment. But our interpretations of latent meaning from the manifest associations of the patient have always been subject to the valid criticism of infinite overdetermination. Because anything can be said to mean anything, our complex abstract theories are an inverted pyramid resting on a fragile point: the actual associations of the patient.

Our empiric research efforts to date have not produced consensual agreement about exactly what information was the basis for the final reported conclusions of the analyst about why an analysis was successful. We have followed Freud in shrugging our shoulders about this omission to provide information about just what the patient said or did that led to what interpretation that led to which additional information except for highly selective excerpts from an entire case. We psychoanalysts have always implied that we could provide that evidence were it not for the practical obstacles. In that sense, one can say that we have taken out an IOU and continued to renew the original loan without paying off on the principal. I want to be clear that the data that have always been most omitted are the closest to the level of clinical observation: the associations of the patient and the interventions of the analyst. It may be immediately objected that I am suggesting naïve solutions, such as making audio recordings of the sessions of the patient. But that would, of course, not begin to deal with the problem of knowing how the analyst was listening; it would merely provide a differently selective record of what the patient said and what the analyst said over certain limited periods. It is well known that absent the essential information provided by the analyst about why she or he said or did not say something, such recordings are often quite opaque. As a group, we have collusively agreed to wage our disputes on much higher levels of abstraction, which has brought our further development to the unreliable if not treacherous shoals of our present pleas for mutual respect and humility. To put this in another way, we have barely begun to resolve our theoretic disputes in a coherent manner. Instead, we wage our abstract disagreements about intersubjectivity, constructivism, pluralism, and the promise of neuroscience at a level of abstraction safely immune from evidential challenge. In the blooming confusion of our theoretic controversies, we have continued to neglect a problem that is the central topic of my discussion: We have never had solid agreements within our putatively mainstream model about our methodology of inference.

Contextualizing Criteria

Originally, the associations of the patient were the foundation for a vague and implicit methodology of arriving at our inferences of latent meaning from manifest content. In a century of psychoanalytic experience, we have gradually created a written literature as well as an oral tradition that uses this methodology, but it has never really been codified. We do not have interpretation manuals and what literature there is about the actual methodology of interpretation is scattered in numerous articles about other topics. The oral tradition is most visible in the supervision of our candidates. It is illustrated when a supervisor asks a candidate, "What was the reason you said this to the patient?" The supervisor correctly assumes that there are often only unrecognized links between the observable associations and the student's intervention. The part of this oral tradition that I am discussing is the loosely organized contextualizing criteria that we employ when we listen to the associations of our patients. The listening to which I refer here is in no way welded to a one-person model of psychoanalysis in which the nonparticipating analyst is a mere observer. In fact, my own preference is to listen to my patients with the full awareness of my own participation in what I am also observing (Boesky, 1990). I cannot pursue here the problems of integrating the tendentious and polarized contrasts of the one- and two-person models, but to avoid misunderstanding, I indicate that the theoretic ability of the analyst to be an observer is neither technically nor theoretically forbidden in a two-person model.[9] Certainly by now, most analysts have abandoned the idea of a solitary meaning for any communication of the patient. It is useful to distinguish between the term *overdetermined* to connote the possibility of more than one meaning and the term *determined* to connote that the understanding of associations is enhanced by viewing them as being shaped and determined by antecedent associations (Waelder, 1963). The discussion of meaning in psychoanalysis has been exhaustively discussed in a large literature about psychoanalysis, philosophy, and science. I pursue these topics further in chapter 8. Readers unfamiliar with the relevant philosophic terms may consult the glossary in Appendix A for definitions.[10]   When the analyst listens to the patient, he or she is performing acts of contextualizing triage. That is to say, he or she is prioritizing the importance of the associations and revising priorities as the session proceeds. Arlow (1979) derived several important contextualizing criteria from Aristotle: repetition of themes or narratives, congruence of dynamic themes, context, and contiguity—for example, two narratives in the session that center on shame experiences are dynamically congruent as well as repetitive. Whether associations occur at the beginning or the end of a session or at the time of the analyst's vacation is an indication of context. It is crucially important here to understand that this way of listening to the associations of the patient depends on two basic theoretic assumptions: psychic determinism and unconscious defense. In the familiar high school physics demonstration of magnetic fields of force, the instructor displays a piece of paper sprinkled with randomly positioned iron filings. When the teacher then places a strong magnet beneath the paper and moves the magnet back and forth, the filings are no longer randomly distributed but are instead patterned in accordance with the force field produced by the moving magnet. In this way, the associations of the patient can be viewed as being analogous to the iron filings, and the dynamic emotional tensions of the patient can be viewed as the magnet that is shaping the patterning of the associations. This illustrates that I am speaking of the associations here as the epistemological basis for psychoanalytic observation and not as a method of technique. That explains why those theoretic models that do not adhere to an epistemology of psychic determinism give little attention to the contextualizing of the associations of the patient.

Experience teaches the analysts of various theoretic models to give special attention to conflicts and issues of separation at the time that the analyst cancels sessions. If, at such a time, the patient speaks of an unreliable worker who did not show up for a repair job, the analyst would likely, at least privately, contextualize that information in the light of his or her own pending vacation. Associations at the beginning or end of a session often take on special significance. The formal elements of associations are potentially important—for example, the same thing can be expressed in a question to the analyst or as a simple declarative statement. In my own view, the analyst's listening in this manner takes no association as being worthless, undetermined, or without meaning. Furthermore, the analyst first assumes that nothing that the patient says can be taken safely at face value and secondly assumes that the arrangement of the associations of the patient has been defensively altered by the unconscious conflicts of the patient. But not every analyst shares those assumptions. Theories about the causes and nature of these defensive alterations vary between models, but those models that share this epistemological view can be coherently compared and those that do not will be incommensurate.

If one shares these assumptions about the raw material of the patient's communications, then it is necessary to clarify how the analyst uses this information to contextualize them and formulate interpretations from them. Those topics are pursued in chapters 7 and 8.

Notes

1. See also, Torsti-Hagman (2003).

2. In the ensuing 25 years since Kris wrote this, few authors to my knowledge have responded to this observation.

3. Hoffer (2004) helpfully discussed the different meanings of the term *free associations* for various analysts: "Do self-psychologists, Kleinians, Bionians, Lacanians and others actually have the same concept in mind when they talk about 'free association'?" (p. 1489).

4. "The term *acting out* enshrines an ambiguity intrinsic to Freud's thinking here" (Laplanche & Pontalis, 1973, p. 4).

5. Compare the discussion of indeterminism in the earlier chapter concerning the work of the BCPSG (chapter 3).

6. There is a vast literature about the scientific status of psychoanalysis—for example, see the discussion of philosophical arguments about whether psychoanalysis should be regarded as a science by Wallerstein (1986), who commented on

the logical positivist, the Popperian, and the information-processing systems theory arguments . . . [and] the two current, most widespread philosophy-of-science assaults upon our credibility as science, that of the hermeneuticists (Ricoeur, Habermas, Gadamer, and others), and . . . of the philosopher, Adolf Grünbaum. (p. 414)

7. For example, from a netcast discussion of Paul Gray's work:

Each of us holds different opinions, some diametrically opposed, as to what we are doing, why we do it and how we account for the results. If what we are doing has a scientific basis, how can this be? Are we the blind men examining different parts of the elephant? Or is it as some claim that it is general factors of the relationship that matters and what we are doing is a fancy rationalization. Do we take a more hermeneutic view, that a unique meaning is constructed in each analytic pair? (*JAPA* PSA-Netcast, 2006)

8. I am indebted to Dr. M. Bornstein for this citation.

9. It is useful to recall that Freud first used the method of free association on his own dreams and that he was his own analyst. This was literally a one-person model in which analysis was born, and I suggest that this is our only instance of a truly one-person model.

10. See Opatow (1996) and Ahumada (1994).

References

Ahumada, J. (1994). Interpretation and creationism. *International Journal of Psychoanalysis, 75,* 695–707.

Arlow, J. (1979). The genesis of interpretation. *Journal of the American Psychoanalytic Association, 27S,* 193–206.

Aron, L. (1990). Free association and changing models of mind. *Journal of the American Academy of Psychoanalysis, 18,* 439–459.

Boesky, D. (1990). The psychoanalytic process and its components. *Psychoanalytic Quarterly, 59,* 550–584.

Bollas, C. (2002). *Free association: Ideas in psychoanalysis.* Cambridge, England: Totem.

Busch, F. (1994). Some ambiguities in the method of free association and their implications for technique. *Journal of the American Psychoanalytic Association, 42,* 363–384.

Busch, F. (1997). Understanding the patient's use of the method of free association: An ego psychological approach. *Journal of the American Psychoanalytic Association, 45,* 407–423.

Fonagy, P. (2002, May). *Discussion of case presentation by Lucy LaFarge.* Paper presented at the American Psychoanalytic Association spring meeting, Philadelphia.

Freud, S. (1953). *The standard edition of the complete psychological works of Sigmund Freud: Vol. 7. Fragment of an analysis of a case of hysteria* (J. Strachey, Trans.). London: Hogarth Press. (Original work published 1905)

Green, A. (2000). What kind of research for psychoanalysis? In J. Sandler, A. M. Sandler, & R. Davies (Eds.), *Clinical and observational psychoanalytic research: Roots of a controversy* (pp. 21–26). London: Karnac.

Gray, P. (1994). The ego and analysis of defense. Northvale, NJ: Aronson.

Hoffer, A. (2004). Is free association still at the core of psychoanalysis? *International Journal of Psychoanalysis, 86,* 1489–1492.

Hoffer, A. (2006). What does the analyst want? Free association in relation to the analyst's activity, ambition, and technical innovations. *American Journal of Psychoanalysis, 66*(1), 1–23.

Hoffman, I. (2006). The myth of free association and the potentials of the analytic relationship. *International Journal of Psychoanalysis, 87,* 43–61.

JAPA PSA-Netcast. (2006, November 9). *"Paul Gray's narrowing scope: A developmental lag in his theory and technique"* by Sidney Phillips [Online discussion]. Robert White, moderator. Archives available at http://www.psychoanalysis.net/JPN-Archive/FOVA-000192A6/

Kris, A. (1982). *Free association: Method and process.* New Haven, CT: Yale.

Laplanche, J., & Pontalis, J. (1973). *The language of psychoanalysis.* Norton: New York.

Lichtenberg, J., & Galler, F. (1987). The fundamental rule: A study of current usage. *Journal of the American Psychoanalytic Association, 35,* 47–76.

Mahony, P. (1979). The boundaries of free association. *Psychoanalysis and Contemporary Thought, 2,* 151–198.

Ogden, T. (1996). Reconsidering three aspects of psychoanalytic technique. *International Journal of Psychoanalysis, 77,* 883–899.

Opatow, B. (1996). Meaning in the clinical moment. *Journal of the American Psychoanalytic Association, 44,* 639–648.

Torsti-Hagman, M. (2003). *Harvesting free association.* London: Free Association Books.

Waelder, R. (1963). Psychic determinism and the possibility of predictions. *Psychoanalytic Quarterly, 32,* 15–42.

Wallerstein, R. (1986). Psychoanalysis as a science: A response to the new challenges. *Psychoanalytic Quarterly, 55,* 414–451.

7

Contextualization

The last association before the dream is the first association to the dream.

—Old psychoanalytic adage

A theoretic model is a context generator.

—Panel (2007)

IN THIS CHAPTER, I EXAMINE THE CONTEXTUALIZING ACTIVITIES of the analyst at work. It would not be an exaggeration to say that one of the major goals of psychoanalytic education is to teach the future analyst to contextualize.[1] Without some assurance about one's methodology of contextualization, an analyst would be unable to formulate inferences about hidden meanings, no matter what the theoretic model. Yet, we have few seminars, if any, devoted to the methodology of contextualization.

Our lowest level of formulating inferences about meaning has always been unclear. Many of the psychoanalytic partisans of science have insufficiently acknowledged a contradiction in our science wars. This group of analysts place far more emphasis on the mutative importance of interpretations than do the analysts in radical constructivist groups. The contradiction is this: Interpretation explains meaning. Meaning cannot exist outside of context. So, if we wish to view interpretation as worth preserving, we will have to include our methodology for contextualization within our definition of our science. But that is also a contradiction because the literature authored by advocates of psychoanalysis as a science gives little attention to the inseparable links between interpretation, meaning, and our crude methodology of contextualization. Of course, there are many definitions of science. Even though subjectivist–constructivist analysts place far less mutative importance on the role of interpretations, these analysts use interpretations in their work. Eventually, most psychoanalysts find it useful to explain something to their patients that the patients had kept out of their conscious awareness.

Here is where we arrive at the central premise of my discussion. If the inference of meaning is one of the bedrock processes in any psychoanalytic theory, we should address our confusion about how we infer meanings as the necessary foundation for a future discipline of comparative psychoanalysis. Meanings are inferred by organizing what the patient says into certain contexts. But after a century, we have yet to agree on how we do that.

In chapter 8, I demonstrate that our existing clinical methods of contextualization are strikingly similar to the methods of the hermeneutic circle. When we who view psychoanalysis as a scientific enterprise recognize that, we confront a problem. The polemics of our science wars argue that our use of ideas that derive from the hermeneutic tradition are incompatible with science. In that argument the use of hermeneutic methods mistakenly assumes commitment to the epistemology of radical constructivism and a coherence theory of truth in which there is (according to the argument) no transcontextual reality that exists outside of the analytic dyad. I am in agreement with Cavell (1999), if I understood her correctly, that this argument confuses what we know with how we know it. I pursue that at greater length in chapter 8.[2]

If interpretation is still to be included as an important part of what we do, then we must include our methodology for contextualization in our scientific views. What follows is a preliminary discussion of the constituent components of this highly important activity of the analyst at work: contextualizing. It is preliminary because we still know so little about it. I hope that the following will evoke a dialogue that can add to our understanding.

Context

Data selection is not often consciously recognized by the analyst until he or she has selected a contextual horizon. We must therefore begin by considering the too-often neglected meaning of the term *context*. It is useful to recall that the noun *context* derives from the Latin *contextus*, meaning "connection" or "coherence." Unrecognized confusion about context in a disagreement between two persons is the basis for incoherent disagreements. In addition, the dictionary gives explicit recognition to a fact often neglected by those analysts who de-emphasize the role of the associations of the patient. The Latin verb *contexere* means "to weave" or "to associate." The noun *context* in English means

> the part or parts of a written or spoken passage preceding or following a particular word or spoken passage preceding or following a particular word or group of words and so intimately *associated* with them as to throw light on their meaning. (*Webster's*, 1986, p. 492; italics added)

It is noteworthy that the dictionary welds the definition of meaning and context, furthermore, that it actually describes the intimate link between context and meaning when this recognition seems to have disappeared from our own psychoanalytic literature.[3]

Contextualizing Criteria

Contextualizing criteria, as I propose them, vary in content, scope, complexity, nearness to observation, and level of abstraction. Any intervention made by the analyst is based on simplified assumptions about the patient's communications because any intervention made by the analyst inevitably and artificially brings forward certain associations for emphasis and so pushes other associations into the background. It is the dialectic between foreground and background, between emphasis and de-emphasis, where many of our psychoanalytic controversies begin and where confusion flourishes. Contextualizing criteria govern the matter in which the analyst listens. Contextualizing criteria denote the simultaneous decision to emphasize something and de-emphasize something else. It is widely recognized that for any individual analyst, there is a fluctuating variation and inconsistency between his or her theoretic model and his or her actual method of listening and intervening. That is why inconsistent and contradictory uses of contextualizing criteria are a sign of a potential gap between theory and technique.

There is no definitive list of contextualizing criteria, and it is unlikely that there ever will be, because the nature of the complexities of our contextualizing processes defies such a possibility. But we can do better than what we have done in making explicit what little we know about these processes. The time has come for us to begin to map them explicitly, even though our efforts will prove crude and preliminary.

By *contextualizing criteria*, I mean any or all of those inferential assumptions employed by the analyst to infer meaning from the raw data. Sorting red and blue beads enables one to make a determination different from one made by sorting round and square beads. Contextualizing criteria allow the organization of the communications of the patient to privilege some of them and de-emphasize others. Contextualizing criteria are a small but vitally important neglected component of the totality of links between theory and practice. The analyst has used a contextualizing criterion whenever he or she considers whether things said by the patient should be linked and whether and how certain things said by the patient should be linked to the theoretic ideas of the analyst. We immediately confront an ambiguity in my use of this term *contextualizing criteria* because it is a Janus-faced conceptual hybrid. Contextualizing criteria are used to link selected aspects from any of the patient's communications, as opposed to only the patient's verbalized associations. For purposes of convenience, I use only the term *associations*. However, the analyst also uses contextualizing criteria to link one's contextualizing assumptions to one's theoretic assumptions. Thus, contextualizing criteria are bridges between associations and theories and so exist on widely diverse levels of abstraction. It is important to recognize this diversity of levels of abstraction in our contextualizing criteria, explicitly because it is precisely the ambiguities inherent in our understanding of how we contextualize our data that is the locus of our confusion about the loose links between theory and practice. Contextualizing criteria are like multilevel freeway intersections that bridge associations with each other as well as with our theories. They are the vast panoply of inductive and deductive functions that govern how the analyst listens; they govern these links that we use to bridge what we have heard with what we know or what we have chosen to hear with what we think we know. When we have not defined the contextualizing assumptions that are the basis of a dispute, we have lost a vital link between theory and practice. Failure to define our operative contextualizing criteria is one major reason for our weak link between theory and practice. When analysts disagree and think that the disagreement is theoretical, it is often the case that they have not clarified which contextualizing decisions defined their clinical disagreement. This is what I have characterized throughout this book as an incoherent disagreement.

Contextualizing criteria are often chosen preconsciously or unconsciously but not always. These contextualizing criteria represent a vastly diverse group of linking decisions made by the analyst that derive from many different frames of reference. Contextualizing criteria are all of the concepts, ideas, information, and theoretic assumptions that the analyst uses to link the raw data from the patient to other data about the patient and to other assumptions of the analyst. All contextualizing criteria are linking criteria.

The conviction that the analyst feels about the reliability of specific contextualizing choices varies, from mere assumptions or hunches to strong conviction (e.g., "I will do best to understand that this information should be joined with that piece of information, and for now I will put this third piece of information in the background for possible later retrieval"). If the listening of the analyst were to be compared to filing records, the decision of whether to use new folders or open new drawers, and whether to make the data active or inactive would illustrate the use of contextualizing criteria for sorting and placement of new information. But such a mechanical and linear description is invalid because, perhaps, the most important part of the contextualizing activities of the analyst at work occurs preconsciously or unconsciously. The analyst would be just as crippled by relying on only conscious contextualizing, as would a golfer in thinking about each element of the swing. The encroachment of the blind spots and personal conflicts of the analyst on contextualizing choices is another neglected area in our seminars and literature.[4] Contextualizing criteria are seldom consciously accessed as the analyst listens to the patient. Just as a musician, athlete, or automobile driver no longer thinks consciously about the sequence of bodily movements, so the analyst autonomously, preconsciously, and unconsciously references certain contextualizing criteria that guide his or her translation of the patient's associations into the language of his or her preferred theoretic model.

We know that anything that the patient says can be understood by the analyst to mean anything that the analyst prefers to hear. This is one of the major reasons that critics of psychoanalysis reject the scientific truth claims of psychoanalysis. All theoretic models are sufficiently complex and abstract that almost anything that the analyst chooses to hear in the patient's associations can be rationalized much easier than it can be proved. Arbitrary and inconsistent uses of contextualizing criteria facilitate this confusion. If a theoretic model such as conflict-defense theory, self-psychology, or relational theory is viewed as a language, then we can see that something is always lost in the translation from the communications of the patient into the theory of the analyst.

There are many reasons why there is a large gap between theory and technique. This gap causes striking differences in the way in which members of the same theoretic model listen to clinical material. Thus, it is a commonplace to observe that two colleagues from the same theoretic school will hear the same clinical material quite differently.[5] It is also not rare that colleagues from two different theoretic models might hear clinical material with quite a bit of agreement. But the problems of translation are usually exponentially more complicated when clinicians from differing theoretic models compare inferences about the same clinical material. Compounding the problem of contextualizing criteria in the latter case is the utter impossibility of successfully translating the data and concepts of some of our numerous psychoanalytic theoretic models into each other (Grossman, 1995a, 1995b). The facile eclectic analyst ignores this problem. Shifting models in midsession is a bit like shifting horses in mainstream. It is sometimes necessary, but you had better be a good swimmer. It is disquieting that to many analysts, such a shift seems to be no problem. I wish to be clear that this is not an argument against using more than one model. For example, I think that the modern Kleinian view is better able than conflict theory to account for certain events in the interaction between the patient and the analyst. What I am stressing is that it is necessary to be clear why one is shifting models and to be clear about how doing so affected the manner in which the analyst contextualized the communications of the patient.

Rubovits-Seitz

A promising place to improve our understanding of our evidence lies in the clarification of the criteria that we utilize to contextualize the associations of the patient. The diversity of these inferential processes was partially described by Rubovits-Seitz (1998) as *interpretive formulations* reflecting a pluralistic epistemology:

> The various types of interpretive formulations that clinicians construct in psychoanalysis . . . reflect the pluralistic epistemology of interpretive inquiry, for example:
>
> 1. some constructions are theoretical constructs, that is, causal-explanatory inferences regarding motivational determinants which are linked to the general theory of psychoanalysis;
> 2. other constructions have less connection with psychoanalytic theory per se than with the therapist's clinical experience with similar patients;
> 3. still other constructions deal primarily with latent meanings rather than determinants of patients' experiences;
> 4. some constructions attempt to explicate both latent meanings and determinants;
> 5. others focus on what a patient may be experiencing at a particular time, rather than on possible meanings or determinants of the experience; and
> 6. many constructions involve applications of common sense psychology rather than specifically psychoanalytic theory or previous clinical experience. (p. 40)

My term *contextualizing criteria,* like *interpretive formulations,* includes functions across many levels of abstraction but also many that are experience near— that is, the actual words and behavior of the patient. What I find most relevant for the purpose of the present discussion is that as Rubovits-Seitz continues, he links these views about interpretive formulations closer to the level of clinical observation. Here is where I believe that he and I are working in the same mine. The contextualizing criteria and the interpretive formulations of Rubovits-Seitz cross several levels of abstraction. Listening, observing, and formulating are vague and overlapping terms that mask our woefully incomplete knowledge about the numerous functions employed by an analyst to make inferential assumptions about the patient.

Rubovits-Seitz suggested that we distinguish the individual components of *interpretive inquiry*, a term that overlaps my suggested term *contextualizing criteria*. His term includes processes in the listening of the analyst that point toward ensuing interpretive activity and bridge or overlap the term *contextualizing criteria*. My reason for choosing the term *contextualizing criteria* is to highlight the fact that these criteria denote the private preliminary contextualizing processes in order to focus better on the methodology of listening and understanding that may or may not be followed by an overt intervention by the analyst. All of these subcomponents of interpretive inquiry are, of course, also a necessary part of the contextualizing processes. Contextualization processes are highly complex precursors of interpretation, and they have been a seriously neglected component of our understanding of psychoanalytic theory and practice. I do not have a simple way to reconcile the Rubovits-Seitz types of interpretive formulations that constitute his larger category of interpretive inquiry with my own term *contextualizing criteria*.[6] A logically tight integration of his vocabulary and mine is not intended, because they derive from two different frames of reference. I do not feel sufficiently clear about the daunting complexity of how the analyst contextualizes the associations of the patient to sort out the interrelationships of the precursors of contextualizing choices, the subjectivity of the analyst, the relationship between inductive and deductive inferences, and the interaction of data and conjectures derived from theory and past clinical experience. I have chosen terms that are not committed to information about how the analyst achieves the contextualization. Instead, I intend the terms to indicate that a contextualization has been attempted or completed and to point to what data constitute that contextualization. I next discuss three other terms that I find helpful for describing how the analyst contextualizes: *context markers*, *trial contextualization*, and *contextual horizon*.

Context Markers

To distinguish those visible experience-near elements of the data, I suggest the term *context marker*, which I discuss here. Context markers are the manifest communications selected for foregrounding because they seem to promise a contextualizing yield. They might be associations, behavior, or events that the analyst privileges as a consequence of deciding that these markers meet the requirements of his or her chosen contextualizing criteria.[7] The analyst chooses these as markers because he or she predicts that giving them more contextual attention will be useful. Past clinical experience teaches us that certain historical facts about the patient or certain events in the analysis are potentially more meaningful than other facts or that we will want to note or mark them for further inquiry or contextual linkage. In my theoretic model, the knowledge that Casement (chapter 2) had just returned from vacation before his patient reported her dream was a context marker. The fact that he had insisted on repeating his interpretation after she had asked him to stop saying this to her was also a context marker. The private thought of the listening analyst that a certain association of the patient has latent meaning worth further pursuit indicates that the analyst has marked this association for further contextual linkages. An unexplained late arrival for the session or the report of a dream are both context markers.

Clinical experience has taught us that associations during the ensuing hour may shed light on why the patient came late or that associations before or after the dream might lead to the latent content of the dream. Context markers are the entire visible or manifest panoply of communications that we employ to lead us to the latent contextual potentials of these associations. When I referred to the fact that many analysts privilege the first communication of the session, I marked that specific content as being more important than the second communication. The idea of a marker is useful in indexing or tagging certain contents in any session so that analysts who are discussing a clinical example can conveniently refer to what they have marked and what they have left unmarked. When analysts disagree about meaning, it would help to know if they agree about what context markers they were each using. Only then can we understand the important question of whether they have used different contextualizations to arrive at their manifestly different views of the clinical material. Because we usually lack this information, we are often surprised by how the analyst intervenes when we listen to a case presentation. *Context marker* is the most concrete, most experience near of the terms I am proposing. It connotes the manifest content, or the actual associations or behavior, of the patient that the analyst has decided in a provisional or committed manner to view as a reference point for a decision to link this content to contextually associated material earlier in the analysis, whether earlier or later in the session. Comparing context markers would be a rational basis for a comparative psychoanalytic methodology for evaluating supportive evidence in a clinical disagreement. The job would only have commenced because we would then have to compare the related contextualizations; but we could not even commence such comparisons without at least agreeing on our criteria for privileging some information and de-emphasizing other information with regard to contextualizing.

Trial Contextualization

Trial contextualizations by the analyst are the counterpart of trial identifications by the analyst that are the core of empathy. Just as the analyst must be able to establish a mobile, transient identification with the patient to know what the patient is feeling, so also the analyst must form trial and private contextualizations of what the patient is communicating—for example, the analyst may privately ponder whether the first and second narrative in the hour are thematically related; then, if they are manifestly related, the question will arise about how are they latently linked or dynamically congruent. The analyst may establish a conjecture based on this contextualization that was in turn related to contextualizing criteria linking this dynamic link to others only to hear a third narrative that is dissonant, thereby requiring the rejection of the first conjecture. In many sessions that too rarely end up as papers in our literature, the analyst concludes the session with a confused feeling that none of the several contextualizing conjectures that had at first seemed plausible were timely to share with the patient. In my experience, the continuing absence of such confusion signals a smug analyst, and the extended and repetitive presence of sessions in which there are no evident contextual horizons is a danger signal of a disorganized analysis under strain.

Missing in many of our theoretic disagreements is just such information about what the analyst chose not to say and why it was deemed better not to say it. I am thinking here of the judgment by the analyst that certain conjectures are too thinly substantiated. Equally and perhaps more important are the instances in which a contextualization is clear to one analyst and not to another, regardless of their adherence to any theoretic model. Experience repeatedly shows that the avoidance of certain topics is profoundly important in determining what data are generated. It is well known that there is only a loose connection between theory and technique. This anomaly would be easier to clarify if the author's contextualizing criteria were explicit in such instances where theory diverges from technique.

Contextual Horizon

By the term *contextual horizon*, I mean a group of associations that are dynamically linked by the contextualizing criteria utilized by the analyst to capture the major dynamic urgency in a given session.

A contextual horizon, like its metaphorical analogue, defines the perimeter of visibility by selectively directing the view of the observer. This horizon has the advantage of emphasizing certain particulars in the foreground, but at the same time, it blurs our view of anything beyond this horizon. Additional travel may well change that view, but for now, this is all that can be seen at the edge of the visual field. Another analogy to illustrate what I have in mind with the notion of a contextual horizon is the selection of a string of beads based on sharing the same color from a box full of beads of various colors. Which colors deserve inclusion, and which colors should not matter for now? So, the contextual horizon is a prioritizing inference about data selection; it is a hunch or a conjecture, and it can only be achieved by selecting certain data for emphasis and de-emphasizing other data. Even that statement is too simple. Data selection has to occur for the analyst to be able to assume the existence of a contextual horizon. But when the horizon is assumed, additional data selection occurs, by exclusion of some data and by special privileging for the data included in the contextual horizon. All of this may happen in complex ensembles of conscious, preconscious, and unconscious functioning in the mind of the analyst.

The term *horizon* has a venerable history in the hermeneutic literature.[8] I propose its use here to facilitate our understanding of the contextualizing processes of the analyst at work. I think that a careful consideration of the hermeneutic tradition clearly indicates that since the time of Freud, we psychoanalysts have used a methodology of interpretation that is often similar to the ideas used in the hermeneutic tradition. We analysts have done that often without knowledge that we were independently rediscovering a methodology of interpretation quite similar to that of hermeneutics. Our neglect of the fact that we have "rediscovered America" is an important problem in perpetuating the science wars in our literature between the advocates of coherence versus correspondence theories of truth (e.g., Spence and Schafer versus modern conflict theorists). Gadamer (1999) spoke of the horizon of understanding as follows:

> The horizon is the range of vision that includes everything that can be seen from a particular vantage point. Applying this to the thinking mind, we speak of narrowness of horizon, of the possible expansion of horizon, of the opening up of new horizons, and so forth. Since Nietzsche and Husserl, the word has been used in philosophy to characterize the way in which thought is tied to its finite determinacy, and the way one's range of vision is gradually expanded. A person who has no horizon does not see far enough and hence over-values what is nearest to him. On the other hand, "to have a horizon" means not being limited to what is nearby but being able to see beyond it. A person who has a horizon knows the relative significance of everything within this horizon; whether it is near or far, great or small. Similarly, working out the hermeneutical situation means acquiring the right horizon of inquiry for the questions evoked by the encounter with tradition. . . .

The concept of "horizon" suggests itself because it expresses the superior breadth of vision that the person who is trying to understand must have. To acquire a horizon means that one learns to look beyond what is close at hand—not in order to look way from it but to see it better, within a larger whole and in truer proportion. (pp. 302, 305)

Epistemology and Ontology

It is important to be mindful of the numerous levels of abstraction at which we try to understand our patients. In our attention to subjectivism versus objectivism[9] and in our futile debates about one-person versus two-person models, we need to redirect our attention to the fact that our methodology of observing, listening, and understanding continues to be neglected. The continuing polemic about one- versus two-person models arose over the best way to account for the interactional, interpersonal, or intersubjective domain in our theoretic mapping. These three *inter*'s are too often confusingly treated as though they were categorical synonyms when in fact they are in different frames of reference. In the controversies about this issue of one- versus two-person models, most of the attention in our literature has been about what should be understood and much less on our methodology of inferences about how to understand it. To put this another way, the question of what we are trying to explain is anchored in epistemology and ontology.

Interpretive Inquiry

Let us then return to the views of Rubovits-Seitz (1998). Every one of these items, except no. 10, is a component of the contextualizing processes of the analyst at work:

Interpretive inquiry is an exceedingly complex and incompletely understood process which involves conscious, preconscious and presumably also unconscious operations[10]

1. Various types of *prerequisite knowledge*, including "competences," which are preliminary to but necessary for interpretive work (what Gombrich referred to as the need for a "very well stocked mind").
2. A set of *basic methodologic (core) concepts*, general background assumptions (in contrast to specific clinical theories) that orient, guide, and inform interpretive inquiry ...
3. Data-generating methods, some applicable to the patient and others to the [analyst]. The goal of both is to produce as extensive, diverse, and relevant a database as possible for interpretive inquiry. ...

4. Data gathering methods, for observing and collecting as large a number and as wide a variety of clinical data as possible from both patient and therapist.

5. Data-selection methods and *criteria*, to reduce the voluminous clinical data to a workable but adequate sample of highly relevant information.[11]

6. Data-processing methods, for cognitive transformation of selected clinical data and information into unique personal meanings and determinants that are specific to the individual patient.

7. Construction of tentative, alternative interpretive hypotheses.

8. Methods of checking, revising, and rechecking alternative constructions in order to determine the most plausible hypotheses.

9. Methods of justifying the most plausible interpretive hypothesis employing multiple criteria of evidence and truth.

10. Reformulating the hypothesis verbally so that it may be conveyed to and understood by the patient—the technique of interpretation.

11. Progressive modification of the interpretation in response to feedback from and "negotiation" . . . with the patient, as well as from further information as it accrues during the therapeutic process

12. Reflection on one's interpretive understanding of individual patients. (pp. xii–xiii; italics added)

Contextualizing Triage

The term *triage* facilitates understanding of the complex process of data selection that is an essential contextualizing tool for the analyst at work. In the heat of the fray, the analyst, like the medic tending the wounded, must make rapid decisions. Which associations need to be taken behind the lines for immediate attention, and which can be returned quickly to the frontline? The metaphor of triage is useful to shed light on an old fallacy that is all too prevalent. We cannot assume that any two analysts are listening to the same patient or to the same material. True, we are well aware that no two analysts are alike and that subjectivity divides us all. But I am referring more here to the manner in which the communications or the associations of the patient are contextualized and not only to the individuality of the analysts themselves or to the more widely discussed variations in the attitudes or perceptions of the same patient by two analysts. The instant that the session begins, we begin to foreground and background what the patient is communicating, and the instant we do, we introduce important variations. So much so that after varying lengths of time, we can no longer assume that any two analysts are hearing the same material anymore. We have long known that patients of Jungian analysts have Jungian dreams, but that has to do with the disputed role of suggestion. But what is at issue here is the variation introduced by the powerful indirect influence of the contextualizing activities of the analyst. Those express a group of triage decisions shaped by the links (too complex and variable to define) between the associations of the patient and the totality of the understanding efforts of the analyst. These contextual triage decisions have the immediate effect of privileging (by foregrounding)[12] certain associations of the patient and deemphasizing others. I wish to emphasize that the seemingly subtle contextualizing choices by the analyst have a strong shaping influence on the flow of the ensuing material.

A related question about the uncertainties of truth is whether either of two disagreeing analysts would be free to use the contextualizing strategies of the other. To a profound extent, the use of theory is the consequence of the personal conflicts of the analyst. The inadvertent intrusion of the subjectivity or conflicts of the analyst—the so-called dumb spots or blind spots of the analyst—are often later offered as the rationalized reason for applying various theoretic choices to explain clinical events. The method that we use to make these poor choices is a suboptimal contextualization. But this is a neglected reason for why analysts apply their theories inconsistently. Here I can only say that it would be seriously misleading to suggest that I could listen in the same way that any other analyst does, given that our listening expresses our entire personality. We are not all equally free to benefit from the influence of experienced colleagues, just as we are not all equally free with all patients to be able to understand what they are experiencing. The limitation here, sometimes simplistically designated as our subjectivity, is not absolute. Most of us do learn something from experience, and many analysts change over the course of their careers because of what patients teach them. We simply do not yet know enough about how we learn and change. It is in this area that a better understanding of our methods for contextualizing could teach us so much.

Finally, I wish to be clear about the direction of contextualizing in the listening process. It is not true that the objective analyst simply employs his or her preferred theoretic model as a map. In that reductive view, the analyst is thought to be driving through unfamiliar countryside and referring first to the map and then to the visible landmarks that match context markers in the visible terrain with their iconic representations on the map. Such a reductive model illustrates the analyst's use of deductive reasoning. It corresponds to the familiar danger of the analyst who attempts to impose a theoretic agenda on the patient.[13]

Arlow's description (1979) of how the analyst formulates an interpretation is derived from Aristotle. It is a brilliant pioneering contribution to this problem, and it is closely related to my suggesting the idea of contextualizing criteria:

> In general there are certain *criteria* that transform what would seem to be random associations or disconnected thoughts into supportable hypotheses that

can be entertained with conviction and buttressed by fact. . . . Most important is
the context in which the specific material appears. Contiguity usually suggests
dynamic relevance. The configuration of the material, the form and sequence in
which the associations appear. Other criteria are to be seen in the repetition and
the convergence of certain themes within the organized body of associations.
The repetition of similarities or opposites is always striking and suggestive. Material in context appearing in related sequence, multiple representations of the
same theme, repetition in similarity, and a convergence of the data into one com-
prehensible hypothesis constitute the specific methodological approach in psychoanalysis used to validate insights obtained in an immediate, intuitive fashion
in the analytic interchange. (p. 202; italics added)

This is, to my knowledge, the first explicit list of contextualizing criteria. It includes contiguity, the form and sequence in which the associations appear,
repetitions, and convergence of certain themes. An analogy to contextualization is the staining technique of the pathologist whose chemical treatment of
human tissue vividly exposes contrasting shades of red and blue patterns
under the microscope, instead of the confusing shadows of colorless natural
tissues. Depending on which stain is used, certain structures are more visible,
and others are less so (Cheshire & Thoma, 1991).[14]

Theories of Truth

It would be helpful to articulate the relationship of the notion of contextualizing criteria to the notion of correspondence criteria. The former points toward context, and the latter to external reality and the justification of truth
claims. But such a clarification would plunge us into complex issues concerning epistemology and the philosophy of science because the term *correspondence* is linked to a series of polarized views of science predating Freud: the
Naturwissenschaften, or sciences of nature, of which the model is physics, versus interpretive or ideographic sciences, the *Geisteswissenschaften,* or cultural
or human sciences. The term *correspondence* is deeply entrenched in the literature of philosophy (the correspondence theory of truth) and in psychoanalysis as a component of the justification of truth claims. There are strong
connotational linkages via the bridge of the correspondence theory of truth to
a well-known series of polarized disagreements about the definition of psychoanalysis as a science. Merely to indicate what I have in mind, I refer to explaining versus understanding, narrative truth versus historic truth, nomothetic versus ideographic sciences, and the relation of inductive and deductive
inference (see, e.g., Ahumada, 1994, 1997, 2001). These issues in turn under-

lie an important attack over recent years about the idea of an observing analyst as a logical fallacy deriving from the tendentious view that this is a relic of positivism (Wallerstein, 1986)—and this is merely an arbitrary and selective list.

Contextualizing criteria and correspondence criteria are radically different in content and frames of reference. The term *contextualizing criterion* faces inward to the analytic dyad and the assumed gain achieved by linking certain pieces of information to each other and then, in some instances, by linking those links to a variety of the assumptions and knowledge of the analyst. Correspondence criteria face outside of the dyad and refer to evidence adduced to support the assumed link between all of the above contextualizing assumptions with things as they actually are in external reality. That includes the existing scientific literature and the past clinical experience of the analyst. Correspondence criteria are in the frame of reference of justifying truth claims, and contextualizing criteria are in the frame of reference of justifying contextual eligibility.

But in our literature, the terms *correspondence* and *contextualizing* derive from their related stem theories of truth, the correspondence and coherence theories of truth, respectively. These two theories of truth have been at the center of the philosophic debate that has defied resolution by the best philosophic minds of the past three millennia. In classical Greek philosophy, these two rival theories of truth divide idealism from realism.

This has been the origin of serious confusion. I suggest that it is time for us to separate our heuristic methods of contextualizing from the epistemological task of justification of truth claims. There has been unnecessary confusion caused by erroneously assuming that psychoanalysis cannot be a science if it relies for its observable facts on the contextualization of its data. That tendentious idea derives from conflating the coherence theory of truth with the role of coherence in the methodology of contextualization. This is a confusion of epistemology and methodology. I pursue this at greater length in chapter 8, on hermeneutics.[15]

We have a substantial literature about the correspondence theory of truth and the correspondence of our theories to actual external realities. We have very little written about the manner in which the coherence of our contextualizations is a vital underpinning of the actual correspondence between the raw data and the relevant assumptions of the analyst in single sessions. Without this information about contextualization, truth claims become less reliable.

It is at this point that one can see the conflation of two frames of reference in our epistemology polemics about the coherence (falsely equated with hermeneutics) theory of truth and the correspondence theory of truth. When we wrongly assume a link between the coherence theory of truth with our methodology of contextualizing, the following argument has an illusory credibility. If there is no transcontextual reality that you can base your claims on, then you have only an internal coherence of your data and no correspondence with reality; therefore, you are practicing a hermeneutic art instead of a psychoanalytic science. What I suggest is that the coherence of the manner in which the analyst contextualizes the available data is merely an expression of the comparative advantages of the various possible contextualizations that could be achieved. There are always numerous contextualizing alternatives, as illustrated in all of my clinical discussions in the earlier chapters. The coherence of contextualizations describes the fit between the raw data and the entire panoply of understandings brought to this data by the analyst. Whether this contextualizing choice corresponds to verifiable facts about the patient's life and to verifiable facts about other patients is a matter of evidential support on a different level of abstraction. The polarized, dichotomous, and schematic opposition of coherence and correspondence theories of truth derives from the literature of philosophy and does violence to the complexity of the dialectics of inductive and deductive reasoning of the analyst.[16]

One of the major purposes of this book is to call attention to the fact that our contextualizing criteria have too often remained tacit, implicit, and in the oral tradition and have not become a regularly explicit evidential obligation of psychoanalytic authors. When we justify[17] an interpretation by demonstrating the basis for it in the patient's associations, we are using contextualizing criteria. When we use the ensuing or preceding associations of the patient to justify the interpretation, we are using both contextualizing criteria and correspondence criteria, the former by linking a group of associations together contextually and the latter by asserting that this response is congruent with the view that it supports the interpretation. Empirical research based on outcome studies devoid of process information is therefore unreliable.[18] At issue is whether the assertion of the treating or research analyst corresponds to certain facts about the patient.[19] In the constraints of the views that I am expressing here, contextualizing criteria are a necessary antecedent to the application of correspondence criteria, not the other way around. I use the term *correspondence criteria* to connote currently held views by an analytic group— this is never totally consensual—about the reliability of inferring that certain elements in its theory correspond to conflicts in the patient. The use of these correspondence criteria assumes that these conflicts are transcontextual. That means that they predate the treatment and were not co-created in the treatment or that they might not have existed in reality before the treatment (for a similar definition see Garza-Guerrero, 2000).[20]

Contextualizing Criteria and Levels of Abstraction

How do we formulate these contextualizing criteria deployed by the analyst that govern the decision to include or omit information from a provisional contextual assumption? Clarification of that question is an essential task of improving our methods for comparative psychoanalysis. All of the dozen components of interpretive inquiry described by Rubovits-Seitz are variously operative in decisions for or against any contextualizing assumptions by the analyst. We can illustrate the diverse levels of abstraction of our contextualizing criteria by reviewing the eight items that I list in my discussion of Casement's patient (chapter 2, pp. 34–39). Recall how diverse these contextualizing criteria were. They included information about the vacation of the analyst, the absence of her father when she was a small child, the complex history of prior disagreements between patient and analyst about issues of power and control belonging to him or permissible to her, the shared assumption by analyst and patient that she had access to accurate memories from her infancy, the role of the birth of her baby 10 months prior and the age of that baby coinciding at the time of her dream with her own age as an infant when she had been scalded, the manifest dream element of the androgynous appearance of the baby in her dream, and the barrier nursing of the patient after the scalding. In that discussion, I introduce an eighth criterion precisely because it was absent from the discussions of the case: There was no available information about the sexual conflicts of the patient. The clinical disagreement among the discussants centered on whether the analyst should have granted her request to hold his hand. This desexualization of the contextualization of the controversy was an additional determinant that rendered this controversy incoherent, at least for those analysts who would have required sexual information to reach further conclusions. And it was certainly contextually consequential that each of these items in turn had meaning for the analyst in terms of his theoretic preferences and assumptions. In my use of the term, each of these eight items deserved consideration as a contextual criterion. The most important point is the wide diversity of contextualizing criteria used by the authors of all the discussions of Casement's clinical report. It is not the diversity but the failure to recognize the diversity of contextualizing criteria that renders this controversy incoherent.

If certain communications, events in the life of the patient, or details of the analysis itself are not explicitly considered as contextualizing criteria, then they will not be present in the important contextual horizons or contextualizing decisions made by the analyst. This is analogous to the medical diagnosis that cannot be made if it is not considered as a possibility. That is why this is the area that is so promising for our further mining in comparative psychoanalysis.

The assumption of a context is only that: an assumption. The associations of the patient are always overdetermined, and the list of possible meanings is inexhaustible because our methodology for contextualizing is so undeveloped that this overdetermination is potentially infinite. We began the discussion with that problem (recall the Achilles' heel of psychoanalysis). My suggestion is to direct our attention to the embedded, assumed, and yet-to-be-defined linkages between these interpretive inquiries defined by Rubovits-Seitz and the so-called raw data of the patient's communications. I would therefore prefer the term *interpretive-contextualizing inquiries.* I use the term *communications* to establish more general applicability to those models that omit or de-emphasize the associations of the patient. It is my suggestion that if we can think of contextualizing criteria as bridges between the communications of the patient with each of the interpretive–contextualizing inquiries suggested by Rubovits-Seitz, then we would have a better understanding of how contextualizing was achieved both in a model and across models.

Contextualization

Whether the model is conflict-defense, relational, self-psychology, intersubjective, or Kleinian, it is an a priori assumption that the communications of the patient express a meaning in altered form. No matter how minimal the role of interpretation might be as the agent for therapeutic change in any of these models, the analyst eventually feels it necessary for that model to explain something to the patient that the patient did not know. These explanations, no matter how diverse their frames of reference, depend on contextualizing the communications of the patient in a manner that the patient had not previously understood.

Whatever their disagreements, all of our competing theoretic models share certain assumptions. Our literature has frequently referred to the question of these commonalities between the numerous theoretic models.[21] The list of these commonalities is familiar and would have formerly included infantile sexuality and the dynamic unconscious. One bedrock consensus that appears intact is the view that psychoanalysis is an enterprise that attempts to find latent meaning in manifest content. If so, it follows that the communications of our patients are not to be taken only at face value.

Spence (1994) has made a useful distinction in this regard between the manifest and the latent clinical facts in our clinical work:

A ten-minute silence in the middle of the hour is not a psychoanalytic fact but merely a matter of record; it changes its stripes when the patient tells a story about the silence, gives associations to it, or in some other way brings it into the hour. In similar fashion, a bounced check, a missed appointment or a midnight phone call are not facts for the analyst, even though they could easily become (if verified) facts for an attorney or a scientist. What about the analyst's unspoken thoughts about a particular clinical moment—are these facts? . . . Many of the more standard clinical facts cannot be understood without some awareness of these private musings, and they may belong more properly to what might be called contextual facts (as opposed to clinical facts).

The point I wish to emphasize is that there may be a class of latent facts that have the potential for both greater reliability and greater falsifiability than the average clinical fact. As clinical accounts are supplemented with this new kind of information, it then becomes possible to have arguments over fact as much as over theory. (pp. 915, 922)

In my view, the contextualization of the manifest associations of the patient is the core of these latent facts that we have too long ignored. The distinction between manifest and latent clinical facts and that between contextual and clinical facts represent the same area of confusion that Spence and I wish to clarify, but his epistemology is rooted in a coherence theory of truth, and mine is in critical realism.[22]

We lack not only understanding about the qualitative aspects of contextualization. We have much to learn about the quantitative questions that are relevant. In practice, we evaluate single sessions but also runs of material across several sessions, and when we make our all-important determinations about therapeutic change, we select and contextualize large numbers of sessions across large time intervals. In fact, we have yet to codify what differences there are in our methods for evaluating micro and macro aspects of our total information about our patients. There has been substantial attention to the question of demanding more information from the authors of clinical papers about the countertransference, about tape recording sessions so that important data will not be lost, and about what the analyst was thinking during the time reported in the published vignette. Self-disclosure has recently been a widely discussed topic, but there is a special paradox in this issue about what should be disclosed and to whom. A number of analysts feel it necessary to disclose all kinds of information to their patients about themselves and to their readers what they have so candidly shared with their patients. Yet, it is the rare analyst who volunteers to tell the reader how the analyst contextualized the information. These contextualizing criteria are usually left implicit or omitted altogether. The lack of information about contextualizing criteria represents still another form of incompleteness in our clinical literature about the problems of selectively reporting clinical experiences. It is a rarity for authors to discuss alternative contextualizations to demonstrate why they preferred one trial contextualization to another. The chapter about Casement's patient vividly illustrates this problem. One (only one) promising instrument for the clarification of our disagreements about clinical evidence is the development of explicit descriptions of how the analyst has contextualized the associations of the patient. This could some day lead to developing a more clear understanding of the contextualizing criteria that determine the choices that govern the entire range of decisions about the organization of the associations that supposedly correspond to the theory and technique of the analyst. Even in the criticisms of conventional case reports by Galatzer-Levy (see Panel, 1991), Klumpner and Frank (1991), Michels (2000), and Spence (1982), emphasis was placed on incompleteness of content rather than about contextualizing information.

To contextualize is not only to begin to assign meaning; it is always a selective meaning. Every contextualization made by the analyst is a choice that is profoundly consequential. Darwin said that every observation is for or against something; so is every contextualizing choice that the analyst makes. The very act of contextualizing privileges only a part of what the patient has communicated and thereby relegates all else into the background of inattention. Therefore, the complex problem of understanding how we arrive at meaning when we listen to our patients underlies the entire issue of clinical evidence. I have suggested that we name the diverse theoretic assumptions used by the analyst to connect what the patient communicates with the analyst's preferred theory as *contextualizing criteria*. The most visible (not final) bridge between theory and data is the act of contextualizing the communications of the patient. I say "not final" to remind us that the path from raw uncontextualized information to the organization and selection of data achieved by contextualizing consists of a large number of trials contextualizations. These are part of the antecedent subcontextualizing processes in the mind of the analyst. I say "most visible" to convey that the achievement of contextualizing presupposes a myriad of antecedent implicit, embedded, and often never articulated contextualizing criteria that are deployed up and down the ladder of levels of abstraction. I am suggesting that there are actually many bridges between the theory of the analyst and the information from the patient and that it is useful to think of these contextualizing criteria as the multiple components of the process of contextualizing. In actuality, there is no simple linear process of assembling a context from individual blocks of contextualizing criteria.

Considerations of exposition to this point have required me to give an artificial description that implies a separation of these cognitive aspects of contextualizing from the intuitive, affective, and conflicted elements that shape the manner in which the analyst listens. I do not want to ignore the "third ear" of the analyst so much as to consider our neglect of the other two ears of the analyst. In our necessary and unavoidable emphasis on the intuition, subjectivity, countertransference, and the heart of the analyst, we have some catching up to do with the head, the experience, the training, clinical experience, and the judgment of the analyst. I speak here in the spirit of Arlow's observation that the analyst must have both a soft heart and a tough mind. So, contextualizing criteria are the ideas and organizing principles that the analyst uses to contextualize the associations of the patient by grouping them into a gestalt that supports the theoretic preferences of that analyst. But contextualizing can only be the final result of the totality of the analytic functioning that we reductively describe as listening. Without the subjectivity of the analyst, the contextualizations of the analyst will be shallow; without the integrated objectivity of the analyst, the contextualizations will be unreliable. The enormously complex dialectics of subjectivity and objectivity in the analyst at work form a powerful component of the contextualizing precursors of our interpretive activity.

Conclusion

Contextualizing criteria are the diverse integrating, linking organizing concepts that bridge three domains: first, the raw, uncontextualized associations of the patient; second, the way that the analyst interacts with the patient while participating and observing; and, third, the explicit theoretic model favored by the analyst. I suggest here that the choice of contextualizing criteria by the analyst is a neglected aspect of the so-called subjectivity of the analyst in the enormously complex group of processes that constitute the interaction of the analyst and the patient. The choice of contextualizing criteria made by the analyst is fateful because it at once forces certain information from the patient into the foreground of attention and so pushes other information into the background. The optimum choice of contextualizing criteria is the least settled and most confusing part of any theoretic model. The advantage of the choice of better contextualizing criteria involves enhanced understanding, and the use of not-as-good contextualizing criteria will have a detracting influence on the forward movement of the treatment process. That is not at all the same thing as saying that there is only one contextualizing choice—quite the contrary, because the problem that we are trying to clarify is the legitimate diversity of contextual choices. At issue is the fact that there is a price to pay for choosing the not-so-good contextual choices and an advantage for choosing the better.[23]

Contextualizing is the sum total of all the mental processes used by the analyst to assign meaning to what the patient is experiencing and communicating. Contextualizing also expresses the subjectivity as well as the objectivity of the analyst at all levels of his or her mental functioning, and it comprises a complicated hierarchy of component sub-functions, which badly need further clarification. Psychoanalytic contextualization links ideational and affective elements that are not manifestly unified. It is a mistake to reduce the richness of hermeneutic contributions to our contextualizing processes by erroneously thinking that this would mean treating the associations of our patients as a simple text to be deciphered. Simple literal, narrative, or textual context is only one of many contextualizing criteria. The integration of that kind of preliminary contextualizing is but a preparation for the dynamic contextualizing with all that we have learned about unconscious conflict. Contextualizing as a process is the supraordinate goal for all of the contextualizing criteria that are utilized in any theoretic model. My interest here is not in context as a noun but in contextualizing as a process.

The noun *context* denotes the visible achievement of the contextualizing process that depends on all of the myriad contextualizing assumptions or criteria used by the analyst. Contextualizing as a process expresses the orchestrated polyphonic inference of meaning derived from using all relevant contextualizing criteria to arrive at a dynamic inference of meaning. To note that the associations were the first of the hour and then to link the dynamic theme of those first associations to its repetitive elaboration later in the hour is an example of the diversity of contextualizing criteria. Contextualizing criteria thus operate as provisional hypotheses. A trial contextualization is a beacon and a filter: The beacon tells us where to look, but the filter puts other areas in a dimmer light.

It is the need for context that leads the experienced analyst to be always alert to the question "Why now?" It is the decision to assign contextual significance to any event that endows the event with meaning. Many of our clinical disagreements hinge on the unrecognized utilization of different contextual organizing assumptions employed to understand the same clinical material. This is true in disagreements across competing models, but it is also true of analysts who are adherents of the same theoretic model. No postulated context would have organizing value unless the analyst had made a number of prior theoretic assumptions. Contextualizing criteria are least likely to be shared by analysts from different theoretic models and are most likely to be left tacit and unstated in most polemic disagreements.

The mere fact that the patient suddenly recalls a dream or an important memory following an intervention is not in itself proof that the intervention was valid or accurate.[24] Clinical experience indicates that incorrect interventions or countertransference enactments can lead to dreams and memories. It is well known that poor interpretations can have instructive consequences and that seemingly correct interpretations can have little immediate observable effect. There is potential value in the idea of a group of analysts evaluating an intervention by examining the contextualizing criteria used to make the intervention and then carefully considering the data neglected in favor of the intervention. Won't we then need different concepts and data to evaluate the individual intervention, then the individual hour, and, finally, the total outcome of the case?

A point that I want to emphasize here is that it is well known that the clinical information in our literature is merely illustrative, in part because what is published has been chosen arbitrarily. The problem is not only that we do not know enough. We have yet to define what we want to know.

I propose that we begin to report in our case presentations what contextualizing criteria the author utilized in arriving at his or her conclusions. The discovery of context is a decision more often arrived at with only partly conscious awareness in the mind of the analyst. The decision that a context has been established constitutes a late stage in each cycle of the listening process. Often, the analyst feels unclear about what is happening in the session. That is another way of saying that he or she is unable to arrive at a convincing decision that a meaningful context has been discovered. Meaning and context are inseparable notions. It would be useful to publish more papers about clinical material that the author did not understand instead of papers that cast the analyst in the role of hero.[25] If the clinical data were sufficiently detailed, we could then agree or disagree more sensibly about the contextualizing criteria that determined knowing or not knowing the meaning of the material.

Change

There is an entire series of local and minor therapeutic changes that take place during psychoanalysis. They are heterogeneous, composite, and multiply layered. We have confused matters by speaking of change at a level too far up the scale of all the antecedent changes that have to occur. We have asked questions that are too big (Edelson, 1984, 1988) and too vague about events that are too complex for us in our present level of developing a methodology for the evaluation of evidence. The clarification of the manner in which psychoanalytic data have been contextualized offers the promise of improving our ability to describe how we think we are supporting our truth claims. Ideally, our confusion of tongues can be ameliorated with the invention of a lingua franca of contextualizing criteria that will at least allow us to talk to each other rather than past each other.

Clarifying our contextualizing criteria would be a rational basis for a comparative psychoanalytic methodology for evaluating supportive evidence in a clinical disagreement. We have perpetuated Freud's silence on the topic of how we formulate our interpretations, and a concerted effort to begin to devote attention to this problem is overdue. A promising place to begin this investigation lies in our long neglected uncertainty about our methods for contextualizing the communications of our patients. We will be better able to teach our students how to contextualize when we can understand our areas of agreement, disagreement, and persistent confusion about this final common pathway to explanations and interpretations. We would be well advised to understand better our long-standing controversy about acknowledging our indebtedness to the hermeneutic tradition.

Notes

1. This chapter extends the discussion of the topics of trial contextualization and contextualizing criteria introduced in chapter 2.

2. For this reason we do not have to ratify the well-known definitional solution proposed by Gill (1988)—namely, that we call psychoanalysis a hermeneutic science. As I will discuss in chapter 8, that was a definitional solution to what is actually a conceptual confusion in two different frames of reference.

3. The link between meaning and context has been known for millennia and dates back at least to the writings of Aristotle.

4. The distinction between ignorance and defensive exclusion was described by McLaughlin (1991) as the difference between blind spots and dumb spots.

5. See chapter 5 for a discussion of the differences between Kogan, Brenner, and Boesky.

6. Detailed in chapter 2 about Casement's patient.

7. Spence (1994) used the term *marker* differently: "It turns out that pronoun co-occurrence is a marker of an underlying lawfulness in the analytic situation, which has implications for the understanding of more conventional clinical facts and a bearing on how they are reported" (p. 922).

8. I discuss hermeneutics and psychoanalysis in chapter 8.

9. See the glossary (Appendix A).

10. To which I add that all of this diversity occurs on many levels of theoretic abstraction at each level of consciousness of the analyst.

11. This use of *criteria* includes my term *contextualizing criteria* throughout the book but at a higher level of abstraction. It is this item (no. 5) on the list of items compiled by Rubovits-Seitz that I have been highlighting as being previously neglected in our literature.

12. For a more detailed discussion of Gadamer's views about foregrounding, see Gadamer, 1999, pp. 305–306.

13. See Appendix A, "Covering Law Model."

14. For a discussion of inductive and deductive reasoning in psychoanalysis, see Ahumada (1994, 1997a, 1997b, 2001). See also, note 15.

15. Ahumada (1994) drew my attention to this analogy, first introduced by Cheshire and Thoma (1991; see also, Bachrach, 2002, p. 46).

15. Cavell (1999) warned against conflating what we know with how we know. I return to a further discussion of this common error in chapter 8.

16. For a discussion of inductive and deductive reasoning in psychoanalysis, see Ahumada (1994, 1997a, 1997b, 2001).

17. The term *justify* here is used in its special philosophic sense to denote supportive evidence rather than proof (see Appendix A).

18. There is a tendency in some of our literature to stress the unreliability of process notes or summaries because of the unreliability of the memory of the analyst but not to consider the distorting effect of the omission of process notes on the probative evaluation of the therapeutic outcome claims (see, e.g., Galatzer-Levy, Bachrach, Skolnikoff, & Waldron, 2000).

19. The work of Waldron (1997) is a notable exception to this omission in much of the empiric research on efficacy.

20. Adjacent issues in philosophy were considered in the Casement chapter (see chapter 2).

21. See Wallerstein (1986, 1988, 1990).

22. Spence (1994) also uses the term *latent facts* differently:

Psychoanalytic facts are almost always capable of being put into words and they include things the patient tells us, things we tell the patient, and things we tell our colleagues. They include various combinations of observation and theory, evidence and hearsay, dream and reality. In contrast to the more usual facts of the everyday world, a psychoanalytic fact is almost never based on pure observation and it is partly for this reason that a dispute over facts frequently conceals a dispute over theory. It also follows that bare facts are almost never presented by themselves; when they are presented (as in a publication), they are almost never quite the same as when experienced in the session. Some meanings are lost in publication; others are inadvertently added by the reader, as he tries to fill in the gaps of a vague report. "Clinical" facts (which have just been described) should be distinguished from "contextual" facts, which color the way we hear the patient's reports, and from "latent" facts, which cannot be detected by the analyst in the session but must be measured by other techniques. Because the proportion of theory to observation is probably greater in clinical facts than in latent facts, the latter may provide more reliable measures of a clinical happening. Greater reliance on latent facts may also reduce our dependence on metaphor and smooth the transition from clinical moment to published account. (p. 915)

23. This is relevant to the claims of equifinality in which all roads lead to Rome. I discuss that topic in chapter 5 in relation to the case of Kogan.

24. For an extensive consideration of the issues of inference of meaning, see Rubovits-Seitz (1998). For a relevant discussion of the validation of interpretations, see Wisdom (1967).

25. See Weinshel (1984).

References

Ahumada, J. (1994). What is a clinical fact? Clinical psychoanalysis as inductive method. *International Journal of Psychoanalysis, 75,* 949–962.

Ahumada, J. (1997a). Disclosures and refutations: Clinical psychoanalysis as a logic of inquiry. *International Journal of Psychoanalysis, 78*, 1105–1118.

Ahumada, J. (1997b). Toward an epistemology of clinical psychoanalysis. *Journal of the American Psychoanalytic Association, 45*, 507–530.

Ahumada, J. (2001). The rebirth of the idols: The Freudian unconscious and the Nietzschean unconscious. *International Journal of Psychoanalysis, 82*(2), 219–234.

Arlow, J. (1979). The genesis of interpretation. *Journal of the American Psychoanalytic Association, 27S*, 193–206.

Bachrach, H. (2002). Discussion of Brenner. *Journal of Clinical Psychoanalysis, 11*, 38–47.

Cavell, M. (1999). Knowledge, consensus, and uncertainty. *International Journal of Psychoanalysis, 80*(6), 1227–1235.

Cheshire, N., & Thoma, H. (1991). Metaphor, neologism and "open texture." *International Review of Psychoanalysis, 18*, 429–455.

Edelson, M. (1984). *Hypothesis and evidence in psychoanalysis.* Chicago: University of Chicago Press.

Edelson, M. (1988). *Psychoanalysis: A theory in crisis.* Chicago: University of Chicago Press.

Gadamer, H. G. (1999). *Truth and method* (2nd rev. ed.). New York: Continuum.

Galatzer-Levy, R., Bachrach, H., Skolnikoff, A., & Waldron, S. (2000). *Does psychoanalysis work?* New Haven, CT: Yale.

Garza-Guerrero, C. (2000). Idealization and mourning in love relationships. *Psychoanalytic Quarterly, 69*, 121–150.

Gill, M. (1988). Metapsychology revisited. *Annual of Psychoanalysis, 16*, 35–48.

Grossman, W. (1995a). Psychoanalysis as science: Discussion. *Journal of the American Psychoanalytic Association, 4*, 1004–1014.

Grossman, W. (1995b). Psychological vicissitudes of theory in psychoanalysis. *International Journal of Psychoanalysis, 76*, 885–900.

Klumpner, G., & Frank, A. (1991). On methods of reporting clinical material. *Journal of the American Psychoanalytic Association, 39*, 537–551.

McLaughlin, J. (1991). Clinical and theoretical aspects of enactment. *Journal of the American Psychoanalytic Association, 39*, 595–614.

Michels, R. (2000). The case history. *Journal of the American Psychoanalytic Association, 48*, 355–375.

Panel. (1991). Presentation of clinical experience. *Journal of the American Psychoanalytic Association, 39*, 727–741.

Panel. (2007, January). *The role of nonverbal interventions.* Panel conducted by J. Chused, D. Boesky, J. Davies, and A. Harrison at the winter meeting of the American Psychoanalytic Association.

Rubovits-Seitz, P. F. (1998). *Depth psychological understanding: The methodological grounding of clinical interpretation.* Hillsdale, NJ: Analytic Press.

Spence, D. (1982). *Narrative truth and historical truth.* New York: Norton.

Spence, D. (1994). *The rhetorical voice of psychoanalysis: Displacement of evidence by theory.* Cambridge, MA: Harvard University Press.

Waldron, W. (1997). How can we study the efficacy of psychoanalysis? *Psychoanalytic Quarterly, 66*, 283–322.

Wallerstein, R. (1986). Psychoanalysis as a science: A response to the new challenges. *Psychoanalytic Quarterly, 55,* 414–451.

Wallerstein, R. (1988). Psychoanalysis, psychoanalytic science, and psychoanalytic research—1986. *Journal of the American Psychoanalytic Association, 36,* 3–30.

Wallerstein, R. (1990). Psychoanalysis: The common ground. *International Journal of Psycho-Analysis, 71,* 3–20.

Webster's third new international dictionary, unabridged. (1986). Springfield, MA: Merriam-Webster.

Weinshel, E. (1984). Some observations on the psychoanalytic process. *Psychoanalytic Quarterly, 53,* 63–92.

Wisdom, J. (1967). Testing an interpretation within a session. *International Journal of Psychoanalysis, 48,* 44–52.

8

Contextualization and Hermeneutics

Beauty is truth, truth beauty,—that is all Ye know on earth, and all ye need to know.

—John Keats

Truth is objective in the sense that the truth of a sentence or belief is independent of us; what is true about a particular matter may be different not only from anybody and everybody's opinion about its truth, but also from its utility: a belief that works for me, even for us, may turn out to be false. (Cavell, 1998b, p. 451)

REVOLUTIONARY CHANGES IN PSYCHOANALYTIC EPISTEMOLOGY in recent decades have brought progress and peril. That is true in all revolutions, but in this case, the revolution has endangered the notion of clinical evidence in psychoanalysis. This is why I became interested in the topic of epistemology and, then, in hermeneutics. There has been a spread of attacks in our literature against the logical possibility of claiming that we could ever generate clinical evidence, because we would destroy the essence of the psychoanalytic process with our efforts to justify our truth claims or we would be attempting to capture Niagara Falls in a bucket. To clarify what exactly we mean by *evidence*, I gradually became much more interested in the contextualizing processes of the analyst at work, given that the inference of latent meaning, which is the heart of psychoanalysis, is everywhere the consequence of contextualizing. When I realized that our methods of contextualizing were strikingly similar to those in the hermeneutic tradition, I concluded that a paradox existed. On one hand, the future of psychoanalysis depends on clarifying our problems about defining *evidence*, and that places me in the camp of those who define psychoanalysis as a science. On the other hand, my use of hermeneutic methods seems to require adherence to an anti-scientific subjectivist–coherence or constructivist perspective. This chapter clarifies why I think that this is a pseudocontradiction, one of a series of antinomian errors in our psychoanalytic history.

Science Wars

Does the psychoanalyst discover truth by observation and inductive inference, or does the psychoanalyst create truth by constructing it? I do not raise these questions because of a primary interest in philosophy but because misunderstandings about them are endangering the idea that it is important or even possible to clarify our methodology for evaluating clinical evidence. We confront here the nodal point of complex issues. Neither justification[1] nor evidence is a synonym for truth. Evidence, as I use the term, merely means what data one can provide to support hypotheses. It is my conviction that psychoanalysis is indeed a science. Of course, the status of psychoanalysis as a science has been vigorously challenged for decades, and this is the topic of a large literature (see, e.g., Wallerstein, 1986, 1988, 1990). My focus is the perfect storm of converging attacks against the idea that our evidence is in any way probative or even that such a thing as evidence can exist. These attacks have come from outside of psychoanalysis by philosophers of science (e.g., Grunbaum, 1984; Hook, 1959) from a variety of scientific disciplines (psychology, psychiatry, and some of the neurosciences) but also by the hermeneuticists Ricouer (less), Gadamer (1975, 1999; intermediate), and Habermas (1971; most), as well as from many in the academic community with the ascendance of the postmodern turn. From within psychoanalysis, the criticisms of metapsychology preceded the emergence of hermeneutic arguments by analysts about the deficiencies of psychoanalytic epistemology. With the emergence of relational theory in the United States, with its often associated epistemology of intersubjectivity and constructivism, the idea of striving to justify our interpretations—let alone view the analyst as a good-enough, albeit subjectively influenced, observer— was challenged further.

This precarious status of clinical evidence and a methodology for its evaluation simultaneously endangers the pursuit of latent meaning in psychoanalysis. This does not mean that psychoanalysis can or should attempt to adapt the laboratory methods of empiric research and statistics.

There is a widespread assumption that the view of psychoanalysis as a science is fatally flawed because it assumes the validity of discredited positivistic and scientistic views of reality. Consider the following: The concept of neutrality is revealed to be an illusion; hence, interpretations are always suggestions, transference is always contaminated, and analysts are never objective (Stolorow & Atwood, 1997).

I believe that such an argument is misleading. It is essentially an argument that repudiates the use of observation by the analyst, which equates the use of observation with the outmoded one-person model and scientistic positivism. For example, hermeneutic criticisms include the question of the logical possibility of a Popperian epistemology based on knowledge without a knowing subject (Haack, 1993). It is relevant at this point to clarify that this is a misunderstanding of what positivism actually means.

Benjamin (1991) raised this useful question about the proposals that constructivism should replace the previous positivist epistemology. She questioned, and I agree, whether

> the great changes occurring in our field can be articulated in terms of one epistemological principle, in this case from positivist to social–constructivist. To begin with, this premise raises a question as to the adequacy of any one epistemological or metapsychological principle to grasp these changes. (p. 525)

She also questioned if it was not

> only partly accurate to characterize the heretofore dominant position in psychoanalysis as positivist. Freud's self-understanding as a scientist included both German idealism and contemporary neo-Kantian scientific theory, which, strictly speaking, was not positivist since conceptualized causes could be seen in their effects, not in themselves. (p. 526)

Cavell (1998a), a professional philosopher as well as an analyst, echoed this important correction about positivism:

> I don't think labeling a position "positivist," as psychoanalysts so often do these days, is helpful. The word means too many different things, variously invoking August Comte, the Principle of Verification, scientism, or whatever going theory one wants to reject. (p. 1196)

Given the radical–constructivist argument, a number of analysts today believe that the methodology for evaluating clinical evidence that they have used for a century would have to be discarded. At the furthest fringe of this group are those who maintain a radical relativism and a nihilistic view of the use of any kind of evidential claims. But, as we shall see, that is not true of many constructivist–hermeneutic authors who reject the perspectivism in which all interpretations or perspectives are equally valid and so deny the possibility of mediating between them (Rubovits-Seitz, 1998). It is the confusion about the nature of evidence and the consequently precarious state of the status of clinical truth claims that is at stake in this debate

What Is Hermeneutics?

> In order to deliver the messages of the Gods, Hermes had to be conversant in their idiom as well as in that of the mortals for whom the message was destined. He had to understand and interpret for himself what the Gods wanted to convey before he could proceed to translate, articulate and explicate their intentions to mortals. (Steiner, 1995, p. 440)

With this link between the task of the god Hermes (see also, Steele, 1979)[2] to interpret the wishes of the gods for mortals, the task of theologians to interpret the scriptures, and the task of the analyst to interpret the unconscious feelings of the patient, Steiner mordantly illustrated the line of continuity between theological exegesis, classical hermeneutics, and modern psychoanalysis. Does the central role of interpretation in the history of psychoanalysis necessarily make hermeneutics a conceptual anchor for psychoanalysis that the scientists in this polemic are denying? Does the application of hermeneutic methods of interpretation—especially, the hermeneutic circle—necessarily bond psychoanalysis to a constructivist view with epistemological grounding in a coherence theory of truth with no necessary link between truth and external reality?

In part, this opposition of hermeneutics and science can be attributed to the profound influence of Heidegger and his student Gadamer upon the U.S. academic community:

> Twentieth-century hermeneutics advanced by Heidegger and Gadamer radicalize this notion of the hermeneutic circle, seeing it as a feature of all knowledge and activity. Hermeneutics is then no longer the method of the human sciences but "universal," and interpretation is part of the finite and situated character of all human knowing . . . [thus] *seeing science as a cultural practice.* (Audi, 1999, p. 378; italics added).[3]

Will adherence to hermeneutic methods deprive psychoanalysis of the right to claim knowledge about any realities about the origins and nature of the suffering of our patients that existed before what was co-created by that particular analyst and patient? The physicist Weinberg (1998) recalled that a fellow physicist once said that in facing death, he drew some consolation from the reflection that he would never again have to look up the word *hermeneutics* in the dictionary. Many an analyst would agree, given that the term has so many different connotations. In fact, one view of hermeneutics lies at the center of the psychoanalytic science wars in which psychoanalysis is erroneously claimed to be either a science or a branch of hermeneutics without epistemological bonds to an external reality.[4]

Steiner (1995) ably captured my own feelings about discussing hermeneutics as well as my own motives for doing so:

> The task of condensing into a few paragraphs what is in fact a large portion of Western thought with a substantial literature, mainly in German, dating back four or five hundred years, would be quite beyond me. Even a review of the main strands in the work of psychoanalysts such as Thomä, Kaechele, Schafer and Spence, among many others, and their use of the hermeneutical tradition in the work of Schleiermacher, Dilthey, Heidegger, Gadamer, Habermas, Ricoeur and others, is much beyond my scope. . . . I want to raise the question of the use of sources and the implications of applying ideas developed in one context in one discipline to the understanding of another context in another discipline, as for example in the application of hermeneutics to psychoanalysis. (p. 435)

This chapter represents a provisional attempt to trace the history of the hermeneutic tradition insofar as it is relevant to psychoanalysis and then to discuss the fate of the adaptation of hermeneutics by a number of authors in the tendentious controversy that is still unresolved about the either–or view of science and hermeneutics. But must we actually choose between them? The assumption that such a forced choice is necessary reflects our confusion about both science and hermeneutics. It is rooted in symmetrical distortions. Science, contrary to the views of radical constructivist analysts, is not a pursuit of ultimate or absolute truth. Science is an effort to arrive at the best available explanation of the observable data. I suggest in my later discussion that the welding of hermeneutics with a coherence–subjectivist epistemology is only one view of hermeneutics, no matter how prevalent at this time. I view hermeneutics in a different way. Later in this discussion, I suggest defining the use of hermeneutics in psychoanalysis in the heuristic sense, as a method of interpretation.

A reciprocal synergy of contextual enhancement results from applying the tradition known as the *hermeneutic circle*,[5] which originally arose in the study of textual exegesis. But this origin, the DNA of this interpretive parenthood, has been one reason for the continuation of polemics about the application of hermeneutic ideas to psychoanalytic data. Our scientists claim that hermeneutic methods mean abandoning a scientific epistemology. In addition, there are numerous examples of my use of the hermeneutic circle to contextualize the clinical data in chapters 2–5, none more clear than in my discussion of the case reported by Kogan (2003) and the comments about that case by Brenner (2003). The first and second questions that Kogan's patient asked are reciprocally meaningful when viewed in the same contextual horizon. Each of these questions was understood in the context of the entire session, and the session in its entirety was better contextualized by viewing the relation of each question to the other, as well as the relation of the two questions to the entire hour. This illustrates the use of a hermeneutic method, which does not require epistemic or ontological commitments.

We do not have the option of ignoring the hermeneutic tradition, because we who arrive at interpretations of latent meaning from manifest content are using ideas that, if not derived directly from this tradition, are parallel to it. The mutual ambivalence between psychoanalysts and philosophers dates to Freud himself, of course. But the hermeneutic philosophy of Heidegger, Gadamer, and Habermas and Derrida's views of deconstruction, as well as Spence and Schafer's hermeneutic views, attracted widespread following in North American psychoanalysis. A growing number of psychoanalysts have sought validation for their psychoanalytic views from the literature of philosophy. This has produced a densely complicated and tricky "postmodern" literature.

Over the years that I have struggled with the problems of understanding the very difficult problems that confuse our understanding of clinical evidence, it became increasingly clear that my ignorance of epistemology and ontology, my rudimentary college elementary philosophy, my puzzlement about the relevance of theories of truth to clinical psychoanalysis were not mine alone. In fact, we are long overdue in our institutes for the inclusion of seminars on philosophy of science and psychoanalysis. Only a better informed understanding of these philosophic issues will allow psychoanalytic clinicians to link the arcane issues of realism, idealism, constructivism, and intersubjectivity with detailed clinical material.[6] I am not equipped to discuss that primary literature, but I do have the impression that philosophers themselves are divided in their views about the epistemology of psychoanalysis and that there is not a consensual position among them about the topics of this chapter. Further complicating the problem is the fact that few professional philosophers are also psychoanalysts; Hanly (1983, 1990) and Cavell (1998a, 1998b, 1999) are among them. Cavell has set forth some relevant issues, and I am indebted to her for making the following distinction about intersubjectivity (but the responsibility for any misunderstanding of her intent in applying this distinction to our science wars is my own):

Subjectivity, in a certain key sense of the word to be defined later, goes hand in hand with intersubjectivity; but also, a concept of intersubjectivity that floats free from the ideas of objectivity and truth is no intersubjectivity at all. This is because of what I see as necessary conditions for the mental. Many psychoanalysts [I return later to some of these authors] have been saying in different ways that the "space" within which thinking can occur is triangular in character. So I say also; but the space I see is triangulated by one mind, other minds, and the objective world, discoverable by each of them, existing independently of their beliefs and will, a world they share in fact, and which they know they share. The argument I am going to work out is that two minds can know each other as minds only on the same condition. Take away this third point of the triangle, the objective world, and we are left with no minds at all. Give up the idea of an objective reality, "out there" between analyst and patient that we can be more-or-less objective about, and what we are left with is "the one-person psychology paradigm." (1998b, p. 451)

The idea of knowledge has been seminal to psychoanalysis from the beginning, first of all in Freud's claim that it is a science (*scire*, "to know"). It is at the heart of theories like Bion's about the nature of thought and belief; it surfaces in debates about the relations between subjectivity, objectivity and intersubjectivity; about whether the analyst's discoveries of another's mind are less "discoveries" than joint creations; about the legitimacy of the analyst's claim to some special authority; about the connection between the supposed truth of a psychoanalytic theory and what "works" in clinical practice; and about how, indeed, we know what works. Perhaps the fundamental anxiety in contemporary theorizing is this: we in the modern world take ourselves to be time-bound; limited, each of us, not only by culture and period but also by unconscious motivations and biases; and always subject to error. How is such limitation, such fallibility, compatible with claims to any knowledge at all? (1999, p. 1227)

One of our most important neglected problems with the application of hermeneutic ideas is that not all analysts share the a priori theoretic assumption that all of the associations of the patient have at least the potential to be understood as the expression of latent meaning. This variation in valuing the importance of the associations of the patient cannot be neatly allocated between one-person and two-person models or between classical and relational or interpersonal models. For example, Levenson (as cited in Hirsch & Iannuzzi, 2005),[7] who is often referred to as an interpersonalist, is a strong advocate of the importance of free associations. Also neglected is the confusing variation between analysts in the modern Freudian or Kleinian models about how carefully they attend to the meaning potential in all of the patient's associations. Actual commitment to the importance of free[8] associations is more often now viewed as a sign of adherence to an obsolete orthodoxy.

There is a vast disconnect between large portions of our literature about hermeneutics as an aspect of the philosophy of science and our daily clinical work in which so many analysts unknowingly use hermeneutic methods to formulate their interpretations. The psychoanalyst who utilizes interpretation is actually using ideas that derive from the hermeneutic tradition, knowingly or not. But this is not a sign of epistemological commitment so much as it is the indicator of the heuristic use by the analyst of certain methods that are not theory linked. I am indebted to Rubovits-Seitz (1998)[9] for this view of hermeneutics as a heuristic methodology. By the term *heuristics*, he means a "loosely systematic procedure for investigation or inquiry that gives good results on the whole, but does not guarantee them in any particular instance" (while not relying on a specific epistemology; Diesing, as quoted by Rubovits-Seitz, p. 295). I am in strong agreement with his view of a heuristic employment of hermeneutics rather than an epistemological definition of the hermeneutic tradition. However, I assume responsibility for extending his views to claim that the heuristic application of hermeneutics is not linked to either the coherence or the correspondence theories of truth.[10] Rubovits-Seitz said,

> One of the basic reasons that systematic methods of justifying interpretations are essential scientifically is because interpretations are the first-level inferences, the lowest level of theoretical statements of psychoanalysis . . . and as such they are the only propositions that can be tested by direct empirical evidence, that is, evidence from the case being studied. Higher level theories are tested in other ways. The evidential base of clinical interpretations is a major source of controversy in debates about the scientific status of psychoanalysis. . . . *Without generally accepted criteria of evidence for interpretations, every clinical finding and scientific claim of psychoanalysis . . . must be questioned.* (p. 212; italics added)

He also said the following:

> Rather than relying upon specific clinical theories to interpret latent mental contents, psychoanalysis . . . [has] a wide variety of *heuristics* available to guide interpretive inquiries. . . . Unlike algorithms, heuristics are methods of inquiry and search. The fundamental rule of psychoanalysis, for example, and the basic methodologic [core] concepts of psychoanalysis and interpretive methodology are heuristic strategies that both guide interpretive inquiry and serve as constraints to reduce unfruitful searches. Heuristic strategies collect and organize relevant information, reduce complexity and ambiguity, and increase understanding of what is important at a particular time. (p. 295)

He defined *hermeneutic criteria of evidence* as follows:

> Hermeneutic criteria of evidence to justify clinical interpretations include:
>
> 1. Evidence that helps to define and narrow the whole meaning of the data;
> 2. Evidence that increases the number of data accounted for by the whole (thematic) meaning and

3. "Small-scale" evidence, that is, coherence of interrelations among part meanings associated with individual elements of the data, and between part and whole meanings. (p. 106)

Hermeneutics is a term used differently by various authors, and it has connotations on a diverse number of levels of abstraction, some much closer to clinical detail than others. I am using this term *heuristics* to clarify the distinction between the uses of hermeneutics as a heuristic contextualizing strategy, from *hermeneutics* as an epistemological system with entangled roots in a coherence theory of truth.

The manner in which psychoanalysts listen and understand, always an enterprise of daunting complexity, has become exponentially more opaque with the emergence of the pluralism of our diverse theoretic models. It was my increasing interest in contextualization that forced me to become acquainted with the literature about the interface of psychoanalysis and hermeneutics. My discussion of contextualization is an artificial isolation of just one component of the ensemble of listening–understanding functions of the analyst at work. Nor is it a feature employed in all of our numerous theoretic models. But the methods of contextualizing that I learned as a candidate 50 years ago and that continue to be used by many analysts are parallel to interpretive methods in the hermeneutic tradition, at least over the past century. Really, one could say that the hermeneutic tradition represents the efforts over many centuries to codify the processes of contextualization that underlie interpretation. It remains a strangely unappreciated fact that we psychoanalysts who have argued so heatedly about the differences in our interpretations have directed so little attention to the methodology for the formulation of our interpretations. Because hermeneutic principles are only relevant to those theoretic models that include the associations of the patient as the raw data of their epistemology, what I have to say is not applicable to models that deemphasize the associations of the patient. Because of the complexity of the manner in which the analyst listens in the models that do adhere to psychic determinism and the use of the associations of the patient, what I say about hermeneutics describes only the more visible components of the manner in which the analyst listens. If one were to hypostasize this exquisitely complex group of components of listening with its attendant levels of awareness and ineffably obscure linkages, the relevance of hermeneutic views would be detectable quite late in the sequence of functions that we call listening that build toward the formation of a conjecture about the patient. It is this part of the listening of the analyst that is strikingly similar in my own experience to the ideas that embody the hermeneutic circle. In that sense, like Molière's Mr. Jourdain, who has been speaking prose all his life without knowing it, I came to realize that I had in part been thinking in the hermeneutic circle without

knowing it. Well, then, why not just say that and get on with it? The answer
lies in my prior unwitting acceptance of the one-sided bias in the psychoanalytic literature surrounding our science wars. I am strongly committed to the
idea that the future of psychoanalysis is linked to improving our methodology
for evaluating clinical evidence and that this in turn requires me to view psychoanalysis as a scientific enterprise. But what kind of science is it? Enter our
science versus hermeneutics polemics. At the stronger end of the extremes in
this literature, it was held that science was sensible and could be based on the
reliable enough observations of the analyst in a one-person model. And in the
view of those analysts, hermeneutics should be left relegated to the interpretation of literary, legal, or biblical texts. People who advocated hermeneutic
ideas were confusing art and science. In the hermeneutics camp, such scientists were the soon-to-be-dead European white males suffering from the rot of
positivism and scientism. Those scientists refused to admit that they could
never logically prove that any interpretation was correct and that they were
blind to this because of their naïve realism. These reductive stereotyped accusations pitted the one-person–naïve–realist–scientist against the two-person–nihilistic–relativist–postmodern–constructivist. This often meant pitting
the conflict theory against relational theory.

It is important to know that at least since the contributions of Gadamer
(1975, 1999), the notion of a hermeneutic method to be applied by psychoanalysts would be oxymoronic. There was no *the* hermeneutic methodology as
such because of the complexities of hermeneutic views about interpretation.
That was in part because Gadamer[11] insisted that there was no logical possibility of finding a method for validating interpretations because "the interpretation cannot be measured relative to some external, absolute standard"
(Strenger, 1991, p. 33). A growing number of analysts then argued against the
logical impossibility of speaking of evidence to support psychoanalytic interpretations. There were no correct interpretations and the confrontation of subjectivism and relativism against a spurious objectivity has hardened ever since
in our science wars. Better interpretations were often called "exact" interpretations in this argument to link them disparagingly with the inexact interpretations described by Glover (1931). This was a caricature of Glover's idea. He intended to emphasize that certain interventions of the analyst foster defenses
and resistance by providing defensive substitution for dangerous affects that
had been omitted from those interventions. And our scientists often speak of
hermeneuticists as scoffing at the belief in the very possibility of such a thing
as evidence and adhering to a silly total relativism in which no interpretation
can even be better than any other. That reveals an ignorance of the large
hermeneutic literature on justification. The equivalent straw man argument by
the hermeneuticists is to view the scientists as naïve realists who delude them-

selves into thinking that they can make exact interpretations based on observations untainted by their irreducible subjectivity. The flaw in that view is to equate "correct" interpretations with absolute truth, the final and preexisting truth that has been awaiting "discovery." In my view of the definition of science, that is a serious misunderstanding. But part of what I do every day with patients involves an application of some of the hermeneutic ideas, especially, the hermeneutic circle, as we shall see. If I wished to maintain my adherence to the definition of psychoanalysis as a science, would I be self-contradicting if I were to apply the methods of my opponents in the hermeneutic camp? But if I owned up to being a covert hermeneutician, could I ever again maintain that there was such a thing as clinical evidence that was transcontextual? So, if some are born for hermeneutics and others achieve hermeneutics, I had hermeneutics thrust upon me when I came to realize the gravity of the consequences of failing to understand that this polarized view of the incompatibility of science and hermeneutics is an unwarranted and misleading false controversy.

For clarification of these questions in the domain of psychoanalysis, I argue for the advantages of a descent into detail.[12] Only with copious detailed clinical material can we hope to illustrate the central importance of integrating our hermeneutic methodology of interpretation with a clarification of our methods for contextualizing the associations of our patients. I regard the scientific status of psychoanalysis as a definitional matter[13] and the opposition of hermeneutics and science in our literature as the result of a category error. That error is the one defined by Cavell (1999), when we conflate what we know with how we know. I return to this important distinction later in the discussion. In this regard, Cavell (2002) also stated,

> An unspoken theme of some of the best philosophical work over the past century is that questions in epistemology, philosophy of language, the theory of meaning, philosophy of mind, the interpretation of the words and doings of others, and the explanation of action are all interdependent. Of course, psychoanalysts can recognize this complexity without taking on all of it. Philosophy and psychoanalysis have to divide up the enterprise they share in common. (p. 324)

The application of modern hermeneutic ideas to psychoanalysis has entangled us in the connotation of hermeneutics as a system of epistemology. Hermeneutics as a philosophic tradition has deep roots in philosophic controversies about truth, knowledge, objectivism, subjectivism, and reality dating to Aristotle and Plato, through Kant and Schleiermacher, Nietzsche and Dilthey, to Gadamer, Habermas, Heidegger, and Kuhn. The fraction of the very large topic of hermeneutics that I discuss is the hermeneutic circle, in the sense of its heuristic application to contextualizing and not the total hermeneutics tradition, which would also have to include philosophy of science and epistemology.

To be clear, I should state explicitly that our methodology of inference is constituted of far more than the contextualization of the associations of our patients. I address here the visible part of that iceberg that has to do with these
methods of contextualization.[14] For the epistemological, ontological, and
philosophic ramifications of contextualization, I suggest authors who were especially helpful to me in Appendix B. (The analyst who wishes to make a
philosopher smile need only speak of "truth.") For the psychoanalytic clinician
the main question is how to apply many of these arcane philosophical discussions about epistemology and ontology to the evaluation of clinical evidence at
the experience-near level.[15] The book by Rubovits-Seitz (1998) is an exhaustive
and invaluable source for a deep understanding of the philosophic and clinical
issues that concern the justification of our interpretations. It is to my knowledge the most comprehensive reference to date about these problems. Thoma
and Kachele (1975) were among the first authors to explain the hermeneutic
tradition for psychoanalysts. Wallerstein (1986) has provided good surveys of
the emergence of the science wars in our literature:

> The overall hermeneutic argument has taken a number of forms. It has tried (as
> in the writings of Ricoeur [1977] and of Steele [1979]) to cope with the question
> of how psychoanalytic propositions are validated and proved. Alternatively, it
> has sought to reject these very questions of evidence and proof as reflecting un-
> acceptable distortions of the essential nature of the psychoanalytic endeavor (as
> in the work of Schafer [1981] and Spence [1982]. (p. 421; see also, Wallerstein,
> 1988, 1990)

The basic introductory writings on hermeneutics in psychoanalysis are the
milestone contributions by Ricouer (1970, 1977) and the discussion of the
topic by Steele (1979). But quickly after those publications, the problems of
validating truth claims became broader and deeper:

> Others within the hermeneutic camp have tried to eschew the language of proof
> and truth altogether as itself a miscasting of the essential issues of the psychoan-
> alytic dialogue. The distinction posed by them is of the quest for narrative fit
> rather than for so-called historical truth. In this view, psychoanalysis becomes
> the telling and retelling of stories, stories of a particular life, until analyst and
> analysand finally come to a consensus on a better story or on their best possible
> story. This would be the one that more widely encompasses the previously re-
> pressed and disavowed, one that makes better sense of the puzzling motley of
> symptoms, behaviors, and dysfunctions with which the analysand had initially
> presented himself for treatment. (Wallerstein, 1986, p. 422)

This was a reference, of course, to the work of Schafer (1976, 1981) and
Spence (1982).[16] And by now the battle lines about truth, objectivism, reality,

and science on the one side and pluralism, subjectivism, relativistic ontology, and epistemology on the other were sharply drawn and have continued ever since. However, the majority of U.S. psychoanalysts were unacquainted in the early 1980s with the philosophic subtext of European philosophy that had prepared the soil for this controversy.

Antinomian Struggles

The necessity to discuss hermeneutics hinges on two points. The first is the importance of hermeneutics for clarifying our methods of interpretation. The second is to challenge the widespread view that hermeneutics is, of necessity, linked to the coherence theory of truth and to constructivism. Attacks against the scientific claims of Freud from critics outside of psychoanalysis began at the outset of his work. Almost at the same time and from the beginning, there were always challenges to Freud's views from within psychoanalysis. But with the mounting criticisms of metapsychology that became prominent in the seventies, there was a joining of the critics from outside of psychoanalysis with the analysts from within who mounted articulate and influential attacks on the foundational elements of Freud's metapsychology. George Klein, Roy Schafer, and Donald Spence in differing ways challenged prior epistemic assumptions, and Schafer (1976, 1981, 1983) especially found support in the European hermeneutic tradition of Dilthey (1976) and Gadamer (1975, 1999). Schafer argued that psychoanalysis was based on personal meaning rather than positivistic fact; therefore, it was not to be viewed as a science but to be located in its proper place in hermeneutics and philosophy. This was an early explicit statement of the antinomian contradiction between psychoanalysis as a science and psychoanalysis as philosophy, hermeneutics, art, or a humanities type of enterprise incompatible with science. In the 1990s, the emergence of the relational literature and constructivism, together with the academic ascendance of the postmodern turn, reshaped the graduate education of the emerging generation of psychologists as they became eligible for full training in the institutes of the American Psychoanalytic Association. The confluence of forces, opposed to the prior claimed hegemony of the classical model of psychoanalysis, emerged most visibly by then in the form of an antinomian struggle between psychoanalysis as a science versus psychoanalysis as a form of hermeneutics.

This polarized view of psychoanalysis as either science or hermeneutics in our literature resonates with vivid contrasts between the two factions such as Rorem's observation: "Everything and everyone falls into either French or German aesthetic camps. The French aesthetic favors lightness, texture and surface beauty; the German is concerned with rigor, depth and structure."[17]

And this polemic of science versus hermeneutics ultimately became a rally-
ing cry for the later formation of the battle lines that could be too easily carica-
tured. On the one side, from the cold wastes of the Baltic, we find the Freudian,
positivist, Apollonian, scientistic, detached analyst who deluded himself into
thinking that he could be an objective observer of absolute truth, who deprived
and frustrated his patients as a matter of theoretic principle. This unempathic
analyst imposes his theoretic agenda on patients and then claims to have discovered support for his theoretic bias. On the other side, from the Mediter-
ranean, are the forces of the Ferenczian, warm, interacting, intersubjective,
spontaneous, and authentic constructivists who fly by the seat of their technical pants and love their patients. This merchant of empathy ignores the unconscious conflicts of his patients and naïvely assumes that he is providing a corrective emotional experience. Like all caricatures or national stereotypes, there
is a certain wildly exaggerated accuracy in both views.

In our science wars,[18] at their loudest volume, the scientists speak of
hermeneuticists as philosophical crackpots who ignore the existence of real
problems in the lives of patients. Furthermore, hermeneuticists think of scientists as stamping around the perfumed garden of the human soul in Pruss-
ian boots with measuring instruments. Our scientists wrongly insist they can
discover objective truth while omitting full consideration of the influence of
the behavior of the analyst on the interaction that she or he wishes to think
that she or he is merely observing. Our hermeneuticists, at least our radical
constructivists, want to get rid of the idea that we can ever get outside of our
subjectivity enough to grasp any kind of truth that exists independent of the
constructions of the analytic dyad.[19] There is more than a little merit to both
criticisms.

History of the Concept of Hermeneutics in Psychoanalysis

Friedrich Schleiermacher (1768–1834) demonstrated that the exegesis of biblical texts in classical hermeneutics was founded on the same principles as the
interpretation of modern texts (Strenger, 1991).[20] Our present confusion
about the role of hermeneutics in psychoanalysis lies in the outgrowth of a
venerable dispute in the hermeneutic tradition within European (especially
German) philosophy between two competing positions. The first followed
Dilthey (1833–1911) and saw interpretation as understanding, or *verstehen*. In
Dilthey's view,[21]

> interpretation was an imaginative but publicly verifiable reenactment of the sub-
> jective experiences of others. Such a method of interpretation reveals the possi-

bility of an objective knowledge of human beings not accessible to empiricist inquiry and thus of a distinct methodology for the human sciences. (as quoted in
Audi, 1999, pp. 377–378)

Verstehen (understanding) was contrasted with *verklarung* (explaining). *Verklarung* discovered causes in light of general laws and took an external perspective, but *verstehen* aimed at explicating the meaning that an action has for the
actor from an internal perspective.[22] We can discern here in shadowy outline
the prodromal phase of the controversy in the United States a century later between the views of psychoanalysis as either a science or a form of hermeneutics. This distinction between understanding and explaining paved the way for
a further methodological and ontological distinction in German philosophy
between the natural and human sciences, the *Naturwissenschaften* and the
Geisteswissenschaften. This schism has come to represent the subtext for the
split in the psychoanalytic community in our own culture war about whether
or not psychoanalysis should be viewed as a science or as an art. These are the
roots of the contemporary debates about meaning. Is meaning discovered or
constructed in the psychoanalytic process? What is the relationship of compatibility between the understanding of a meaning and an explanation by a cause?
Are these commensurable? Can subjectivity be rendered in objective terms
(Opatow, 1996)? Or is psychoanalysis something in between science and
hermeneutics (Gill, 1976, 1994c; Strenger, 1991). It is also the subtext for divi-
sions within various theoretic models about the view of what is mutative: the
ontological events of intersubjectivity a la Heidegger in two-person models or
the observational phenomena viewed by an observer in one-person models.

Dilthey lived from 1833 to 1911, but Freud seemed never to have read
Dilthey, and although Freud's work required him to immerse himself deeply
in the methods of interpretation,

> he did not seek or use some highly relevant knowledge of interpretation that
> would have been available to him in Dilthey's writings.[23] He remained self-
> taught in the theory, methodology, and practice of clinical interpretation. . . .
> Dilthey saw in hermeneutics the possibility of a methodologic foundation for
> the human and social sciences—disciplines which, like psychoanalysis but unlike
> the natural sciences, attempt to interpret the manifold expressions of the inner
> life of human beings. (Rubovits-Seitz, 1998, pp. 16–17)

Both men tried to recognize the need for a genetic and historical approach to
psychology. Most important for our present purpose is that Dilthey's use of
the part–whole concept was so similar to Freud's interpretive methodology:

> Another parallel between the two men was Freud's use of a part-whole concept
> similar to that of hermeneutic methodology, e.g. his insistence that the meaning

of any fragment depends upon the meaning of the whole. . . . Both Freudian and hermeneutic approaches to interpretation require the ability to perceive the multiplicities of part meanings in the material while simultaneously recognizing the central theme or whole meaning that runs like an undercurrent through all of the data. (p. 17)[24]

But it was Martin Heidegger (1899–1976) who is credited with promulgating the conceptual framework for philosophic hermeneutics as it evolved in the twentieth century (as well as discredited for his Nazi affiliation in World War II). The most often-quoted philosopher–authority on this topic in the psychoanalytic literature is Gadamer, who was Heidegger's pupil.

The Hermeneutic Circle

Wallerstein (1986) summarized the views of Ricouer and Steele about the hermeneutic circle as follows:

> In essence, explanations in psychoanalysis are offered in terms of the framework of the "hermeneutic circle." In this conception, knowledge of the parts is required to understand the whole, but the parts in turn can only be understood as aspects of the whole which envelopes them with meaning. Nine key postulates are stated by Steele as constitutive of this hermeneutic circle, all being variants or implications of the constant circular or dialectical movement between the parts and the whole. What is sought is again the harmony of the parts with the whole in terms of *coherence*, consistency, and configuration. This, to Ricoeur, is constitutive of "proof" in psychoanalysis; Steele declares it to be the distinctive "hermeneutic method." As the natural sciences are defined by their use of the scientific method so the cultural sciences are defined by their use of the hermeneutic method. (pp. 421–422; italics added)

The key element in this excerpt is the term *coherence*, which is the pivotal epistemological distinction in the antinomian opposition of hermeneutics and science views. The hermeneutics tradition as it was deployed in these polemics was allied with the coherence theory of truth, and the scientific theory of truth was allied with the correspondence theory of truth.[25] But there are various definitions of the term *hermeneutics*, and it is by no means consensually accepted among philosophers that a theory of truth is a connotational anchor for the term *hermeneutics*.

Here we confront a rather frequent misreading of the hermeneutic literature in which the views of some authors, such as Schafer, are reduced and exaggerated to mean that the coherence theory of truth means that we need not be concerned with evidence at all. In that view, we are only able with psychoanalytic treatment to arrive at aesthetically pleasing narratives about a patient's life, and thus we can stop worrying about evidence altogether. Although that seems to be a correct inference in the case of some of the radical constructivist authors, it is by no means the case for Ricouer and others.

Rubovits-Seitz (1998), who is generally sympathetic with the value of the hermeneutic tradition for enriching psychoanalysis, said of the hermeneutic circle that it produced

> an unwarranted over-confidence in interpreters, that is, the interrelations of part and whole meanings in the interpretive process. The interpreter infers part meanings from individual elements of the clinical data, but also must construct a whole meaning that both specifies and ties together all of the part meanings. The whole is derived from the parts, but the parts are delineated and integrated by the whole—an intrinsically circular process. (p. 63)

Ricouer (1977) said the following about critics who said that

> validation in psychoanalysis is condemned to remain circular since everything is verified at once. It is all the more important to consider this argument since the notion of a circle is not foreign to all the historico-interpretive disciplines, in which a "case" is not only an example to be placed under a law, but something which possesses its own dramatic structure which makes it a "case history." The problem, Heidegger says with reference to the hermeneutic circle, is not avoiding the circle but properly entering into it. This means: taking measures so that the circle is not a vicious circle. Now a circle is vicious if it takes the form of begging the question, that is, if the verification in each of the areas considered is the condition for verification in another area. The circle of verification will not be vicious, however, if validation proceeds in a cumulative fashion through the mutual reinforcement of criteria which taken in isolation would not be decisive, but whose convergence makes them plausible and, in the best cases, probable and even convincing. I will say, therefore, that the validation apt to confirm the truth claim belonging to the domain of psychoanalytic facts is an extremely complex process which is based on the synergy of partial and heterogeneous criteria. (p. 866)

As is so often the case in psychoanalysis, the same terms have different meanings for different authors. For example, Goldberg (1994) described the hermeneutic circle as follows:

> The process of interpretation is defined as that of the hermeneutic circle wherein an observer or interpreter views an object or text or another person and thereby brings his or her prejudice to bear upon the studied phenomena. A to-and-fro process then takes place as the interpreter aims to fill out and complete his circle of expectations from the perception or study of the object, which subsequently

demands a feedback and correction procedure until the circle is complete, and he arrives at what is felt to be a correct interpretation. Since such a conclusion of correctness is so dependent upon the initial bias or viewpoint of the observer, it is naturally felt that there is unlikely to be a single correct interpretation that will be arrived at by a number of observers. (pp. 23–24)

Strenger's valuable monograph (1991) about hermeneutics gives a different account of the hermeneutic circle:

A reader setting out to interpret a text must assume that there is something to be understood there, that he is not faced with a meaningless jumble of sounds or of ink stains. Also, the interpreter must have preconceptions about what it is to communicate something through a text, what types of text there are, etc. understanding a text is to integrate it into the horizons of intelligibility by which we structure our world. The result is in a sense circular: the interpreter sets out to understand by presuming, to begin with, what kind of meanings there are to be found. If he does not succeed in fitting the text into his frame of intelligibility, he has failed to understand the text; the text remains literally meaningless to him. The process of interpretation seems to be caught up in itself: if the interpreter can only find meanings of the type he reads into the text, he cannot correct his own understanding. *Gadamer's view on this is that the process of correcting one's presuppositions must always be partial.* Only if we succeed in partially integrating the text into our preexisting frames of meaning can we notice that we fail to understand it in part. This failure will manifest itself by the text's recalcitrance to bend completely to our previous frame, which we can then try to enlarge in a way allowing us to accommodate the unintelligible parts. (pp. 31–32; italics added)

The most authoritative philosophic reference for an explication of modern views of hermeneutics remains Gadamer (1975, 1999). Strenger quotes Gadamer with apparent approval and, at the same time, raises issues in the science wars in a manner with which I disagree:

The title of Gadamer's book *Truth and Method* is misleading since the thesis is precisely that *there is no such thing as a method for arriving at and validating an interpretation of texts.* That follows from two things: 1. understanding is the activity of placing texts into the structure of what we previously take to be meaningful. The interpreter's task cannot be to objectify the text completely. . . . A dialogue is an interaction and is not completely detached. . . . Texts do not have eternally fixed meanings independent of the reader. *But unlike Dilthey, Gadamer says the interpreter cannot step out of his own horizon of intelligibility and adopt the author's.* . . . he can only try to assimilate the author's text into his own horizon, by widening his own conceptions of meaningfulness. Gadamer does not take this to mean, though, that the very act of interpretation distorts the text; the opposite is true. Since the interpreter can see more than the author, he can often understand the author better than the author himself does or did. The interaction between text and reader can therefore be one of mutual enrichment. But this also means that there cannot be a *hermeneutic method.* The criterion of successful interpretation must ultimately remain the interpreter's experience of truly having appropriated the text. *The interpretation cannot be measured relative to some external, absolute standard.* Only the fact that the text has become transparent within the horizon of intelligibility of the interpreter (or interpretive community) can serve as the hallmark of appropriation. *The question then arises of how interpretive practice can be salvaged from falling into subjectivity.* If the criterion for successful understanding is the experience of having understood the text, every interpreter can only rely on his own intuitions, which would make objectivity and rational discussion of interpretations impossible. The answer of Gadamer is that trying to understand is an essential activity of human existence and is shared by all members of the culture, so that every one of us is a member of an interpretive community. This growing into an interpretive community can attain more specific manifestations if he goes through training in some hermeneutic discipline in the humanities or some of the social sciences (e.g. psychoanalysis). His initiation into the discipline occurs less by the learning of explicit rules than by participation in the interpretive practice of the respective community. Correspondingly, interpretive practice allows for objectivity despite the impossibility of providing algorithmlike rules for the correctness of interpretations. . . . The crucial step taken in this approach is to drop the picture of objectivity as the mirroring of an unconceptualized reality. Instead objectivity is understood, in a Kantian way, as intersubjectivity. (pp. 33–35; italics added)

In this sense, the term *intersubjectivity* is a synonym for *social constructivism* (see Appendix A) and not only the name of one of our numerous psychoanalytic theoretic models. I agree with Strenger's understanding of what Gadamer intended.[26] But I disagree with Strenger's approval of some of these views for application to psychoanalysis. I repeat the points that I believe have weakened the hermeneutic arguments in our literature.

The key issues include the following (all quotes from the aforementioned extract): "The interpretation cannot be measured relative to some external, absolute standard."[27] It is one thing to measure, and it is quite another to claim exclusivity of proof. With just this one assumption in which measuring is equated with proving absolute truth, we seem to lose the right to use probative evidence, the claim that one explanation is better than another. Would we not then fall into the crazy depths of total relativism and equivalence of all claims? Would that not prove the critics of constructivism correct? Would we not have to admit that the mathematical constant of pi was socially constructed or that it doesn't matter if the islands in the Pacific were created by angry gods or by volcanic upheavals? Not so, say the strong–constructivist advocates. "The answer of Gadamer is that trying to understand is an essential activity of human existence and is shared by all members of the culture, so that every one of us is a member of an interpretive community."[28] "The crucial step taken in this approach is to drop the picture of objectivity as the mirroring of an unconceptualized reality. Instead objectivity is understood, in a Kantian way, as intersubjectivity." By this slight of hand, the more radical hermeneuticist can evade the charge of endless equivalence and relativism and claim a certain objectivity of consensus, but an objectivity of consensus is disquieting—whose consensus about what issues? The consensus of 1491 rendered the earth as being flat. Strong or radical constructivism permits justification for the claim that an interpretation is plausible, but it implies relativism regarding comparisons.

The following is a version of the constructivist argument directly related to the views of Gadamer[29] from a constructivist colleague who took exception to the aforementioned questions:

You make the, to my mind, indefensible claim to be able to determine which knowledge claim is a closer approximation to "reality." Such a claim begs the epistemological question. We have our perceptions, which we refer to at times as observations, and we have reason, or inference. Both of these constitute the evidence that one must use to support the adequacy of one's theory of reality. But neither observation nor inference (theory) is reality itself. I know you realize this. What you do not acknowledge, it seems to me, is that you never have "reality" as a third term to compare the adequacy of any knowledge claims to in order to see which is a better approximation to it. All you have are various versions of observation and inference, and epistemology is the study of the adequacy (persuasiveness) of various models for judging the adequacy of knowledge claims, none of which can rely on direct access to "the thing in itself" to support its claims.

Let me ask you this: How do you compare your knowledge claims with "reality" (the thing in itself)? First, you have to have an incontestable, direct version of what "reality" is. If you already have that, why do you need science? Beyond observation (which, as you know, is not "the thing in itself") and reason (inference, theory, which is not "the thing in itself), on what grounds do you think you know what the "reality" that you are trying to describe and explain through your theories is?

Critical realism,[30] as I understand it, assumes that there is a reality beyond our construction of it. But the critical realist acknowledges that we have no direct (not "correct") access to any single facet, or fact, that represents "the thing in itself." All knowledge claims must rely on theories and observations to construct versions of reality that are consistent with what they, at another level entirely, abstractly contend are defensible and persuasive criteria (never legitimately relying on direct comparison to "reality"; only naive realists believe such direct contact with "reality" is possible) for judging what are better or worse constructions of "truth." Empiricist epistemology places more emphasis on observations, while constructivist epistemology places more emphasis on rational coherence, but all epistemological positions value some combination of both. (anonymous, personal communication, 2004)

The Science Wars

The lines of disagreement are clearly demarcated by the opposing views of Brenner (2000)[31] and Habermas (1971). Brenner stated, "I suggest that any objection to the idea that psychoanalysis is part of natural science is specious" (p. 601).[32] Habermas (1971) referred to "the self-misunderstanding of psychoanalysis as a science" (p. 247). Each of the two camps rejected the deceptive plausibility of the opposing view. The polarized view of our forced choice between psychoanalysis as a science or psychoanalysis as a hermeneutic discipline has been long overdue for correction. Among those who championed the view of hermeneutics as a corrective for the allegedly positivist criticisms based on an epistemology without a knowing subject, Modell (1978) praised the hermeneutic views of Habermas and Ricouer. Goldberg (1984, 1994) agreed that hermeneutics offered an alternative to the erroneous views of positivist analysts who assumed that interpretations could be validated.

Hermeneutics Is Not Linked to a Specific Epistemology

In my own view, psychoanalytic hermeneutics is a methodology of interpretation of disguised meanings that is not afloat in a relativistic disconnect from reality. To be sure, I want to say at this point that I am carving out one connotation of hermeneutics from its broader definition in psychoanalytic polemics. This is, to put it mildly, not a consensually accepted view, but I hope that it will clarify some of the distinctions I wish to suggest. I am questioning the misleading common view that traditional hermeneutic guides to interpretation are linked to the coherence theory of truth with its attendant skepticism about the possibility of a gradually improving approximation of an actually existing reality. Cavell (1999) has made a valuable distinction in this regard:

> It is important to distinguish how we learn or come to know something from what it is we then know. The distinction between how we know and what we know, which is particularly easy to lose track of in the complex examples of psychoanalysis. (p. 1234; italics added)

As we shall see in the later discussion of Gill's contributions to this topic, there is a prevalent tendency to reduce the hermeneutic literature to only one definition of hermeneutics and only one view of its relevance for psychoanalysis. The view of hermeneutics as a synonym for the coherence theory of truth or as being inseparably linked to the constructivist models is misleading. In this erroneous view, there has been a co-opting of the hermeneutic tradition by constructivist or coherence epistemology.

I apply Cavell's distinction between what we know and how we know to distinguish hermeneutics from its philosophical and exegetic origins. I do not expect that the deeply entrenched connotation of hermeneutics as a polar opposite to science will then be abandoned, although I wish it could be. Psychoanalytic history has taught us that analogous polarized battles fought by battalions under the banners of slogans and stereotyped labels will run their course and then be replaced by newer polarized controversies. Think of the oedipal–preoedipal, the conflict–deficit, and the verbal–relational as mutative factors or the transference–extra-transference as illustrative examples. Many of our great controversies in psychoanalysis have never been resolved. In a like vein, Bertrand Russell once observed that witchcraft was never really disproved; it merely stopped being of interest. Analogously, what has happened is that the interest of the psychoanalytic community gradually shifts away from its polarized controversies and moves on to others. Kuhn (1970) was, of course, aware of such shifts of interest, but they were not the central focus of his widely influential book where he discussed his famous views of paradigm shifts.

Kuhn and Paradigm Shifts

The literature about our science wars has made much of Kuhn's views about paradigm shifts. Many authors have wrongly assumed that Kuhn's views are an authoritative basis for psychoanalysis to shift from the prior objectivist, positivist one-person paradigm to the new subjectivist, intersubjective paradigm. Kuhn is often cited as the authority for the latter, and Karl Popper repudiated (e.g., 1959) for the former. So what did Kuhn (1970) say? A central concept in his views of scientific revolutions (e.g., Copernican versus Ptolemaic astronomy) is the paradigm:

> [Paradigms are] universally recognized *scientific* achievements that for a time provide model problems and solutions to a community of practitioners. (p. viii)

> Paradigms gain their status because they are more successful than their competitor's in solving a few problems that the group of practitioners has come to recognize as acute. (p. 23)

> Normal science does not aim at novelties of fact or theory and, when successful, finds none. . . . *Then research under a paradigm must be a particularly effective way*

of inducing paradigm change. That is what fundamental novelties of fact and theory do. Produced inadvertently by a game played under one set of rules, their assimilation requires the elaboration of another set. After they have become parts of science, the enterprise, at least of those specialists in whose particular field the novelties lie, is never quite the same again. . . . . Discovery commences with the awareness of anomaly, i.e., with the recognition that nature has somehow violated the paradigm-induced expectations that govern normal science. (pp. 52–53; italics added)

When . . . an anomaly comes to seem more than just another puzzle of normal science, the transition to crisis and to extraordinary science has begun. The anomaly itself now comes to be more generally recognized as such by the profession. More and more attention is devoted to it by more and more of the field's most eminent men. (p. 82)

All crises begin with the blurring of a paradigm, and the consequent loosening of the rules for normal research. . . . Sometimes normal science ultimately proves able to handle the crisis-provoking problem . . . (or the problem defies present solution). . . . A crisis ends with the emergence of a new paradigm. (p. 84)

Like the choice between competing political institutions that between competing paradigms proves to be a choice between incompatible modes of community life. Because it has that character, *the choice is not and cannot be determined merely by the evaluative procedures characteristic of normal science, for these depend in part upon a particular paradigm, and that paradigm is at issue. When paradigms enter, as they must, into a debate about paradigm choice, their role is necessarily circular. Each group uses its own paradigm to argue in that paradigm's defense.* (p. 94; italics added)

Next, Kuhn examined the question of how one paradigm replaces another: "The proponents of competing paradigms must fail to make complete contact with each other's viewpoints" (this relates to the incommensurability of the pre- and postrevolutionary normal–scientific traditions). "In the first place, the proponents of competing paradigms will often disagree about the list of problems that any candidate for paradigm must resolve. Their standards or their definitions of science are not the same" (p. 148).[33]

But what follows seems to be the most telling reflection of Kuhn's views about how and why scientists change their minds, because it is formulated more in terms of a social process rather than in terms of the evolving criteria of evidence:

I would argue, rather, that in these matters *neither proof nor error is at issue.* The transfer of allegiance from paradigm to paradigm is a *conversion* experience that cannot be forced. . . . Still to say that resistance is inevitable and legitimate, that *paradigm change cannot be justified by proof,* is not to say that no arguments are relevant or that scientists cannot be persuaded to change their minds. We must . . . ask how conversion is induced and how resisted . . . because [this question] is a new one in a situation in which *there can be no proof,* our question is a new one, demanding a sort of study that has not previously been undertaken. (p. 151)

The phrases in italics are examples of Kuhn's views that echo the adversarial views that Kuhn himself described in such disagreements. Among those analysts whose epistemology paradigm is strongly constructivist, Kuhn's views are taken as authoritative support for their epistemic relativism. But there are certainly those who disagree. Kuhn's ideas were criticized by the Nobelist Steven Weinberg (1998), first because of the tendentious nature of his views about how science changes but also because of his epistemological views:

What does bother me on rereading *Structure* and some of Kuhn's later writings is his radically skeptical conclusions about what is accomplished in the work of science. And it is just these conclusions that have made Kuhn a hero to the philosophers, historians, sociologists, and cultural critics who question the objective character of scientific knowledge, and who prefer to describe scientific theories as social constructions, not so different from democracy or baseball. (n.p.)

Friedman (1977)[34] made a similar observation about Kuhn's views:

[Kuhn's] essential point is that observations are not epistemologically independent of the theories held by the investigator who is making the observations to test the theory. Consequently, the truth of the theory is made to rest upon the agreement of experts working with the theory rather than upon the agreement of the theory with fact.

What psychoanalysts who draw upon this philosophical view often seem to fail to appreciate is that the view is itself philosophically controversial because it has some inherent difficulties. Usually reference is limited to the more familiar and popular statement of it by Kuhn. (p. 633)

And Hanly (1983), a psychoanalyst as well as a professional philosopher, said, "It is misleading for psychoanalysts to rely upon the anti-objectivist thesis of Kuhn as though it were uncontroversial in philosophy" (pp. 394–395).[35]

Spruiell (1983) illustrated the misuse of Kuhn's ideas in the psychoanalytic literature by authors who attempted to use Kuhn's ideas to justify their advocacy of theories from a new paradigm. Spruiell made the important point that a number of these authors who insisted that psychoanalysis was a nonscientific, constructivist, or hermeneutic–narrative discipline were self-contradictory in using Kuhn's views to support their arguments, because Kuhn had made it clear that paradigms shifted in sciences. Because there had been so much confusion about the various ways that the term *paradigm* had been used, Kuhn (1977) suggested its replacement with the term *disciplinary matrix.*

Merton Gill

Merton Gill (1914–1994) discussed hermeneutics extensively over a span of many years. He is most commonly understood in our literature to have pioneered and championed the idea that psychoanalysis is a hermeneutic science. That is usually taken to mean that in the controversies over recent decades as to whether or not psychoanalysis should be viewed as a natural science or a branch of hermeneutics, he favored a both–and, rather than an either–or, view of this dichotomy.[36] As I understand this thoughtful and careful theoretician, his view is only partially correct because it infers that he proposed a merely definitional solution to problems that actually resulted from conceptual ambiguities. Gill's interest in hermeneutics arose as a response to his conviction that it was necessary to eliminate metapsychology from psychoanalytic theory. It is important to note that Gill is unusual in the hermeneutic literature for his careful carving of the numerous hermeneutic authors into three distinct groups, instead of lumping them all together, as was typically the case before and after Gill's papers appeared.

> The psychoanalyst who espouses the conception of psychoanalysis as a hermeneutic science emphasizes that the patient does much more than speak and, even more important, that *he responds in an interpersonal dialogic exchange to the analyst's interventions as a text cannot.*
>
> Those who believe a hermeneutic discipline cannot be a science point to the fact that hermeneuticists use the concept of reasons in their explanations rather than causes, as in natural science. They point to the distinction advanced by hermeneuticists between understanding and explanation (*verstehen* in the Geisteswissenschaften and *erklären* in Naturwissenschaften . . .) as implying that a hermeneutic discipline cannot employ the canons of natural science. Those who believe there can be a hermeneutic science, even if the major extant systems of philosophical hermeneutics reject that possibility, argue on the contrary that a hermeneutic investigation in psychoanalysis can employ such canons, albeit in dimensions other than those of the natural sciences. Yet a third group argues that hermeneutic data require canons of investigation which differ from those of natural science, and which are admittedly only in the process of development. They argue that hermeneutic thought has so far been primarily philosophical and applied only to theological, juridical, and literary productions essentially in the interpretation of texts but that they need be no less empirical and oriented toward explicating the nature of reality than the canons of natural science. . . . *The debate involves strong emotional currents so that each side has a tendency to view the other as a global, undifferentiated position. Individual hermeneuticists espouse particular*

theories which are unthinkingly considered by others to be inevitable concomitants of any hermeneutic position, so that an argument against one contention is considered to be an argument against the entire hermeneutic position. (Gill, 1988, pp. 37–39; italics added)

I am in strong agreement with that last statement, but I do have a question about the next one:

The psychoanalyst who espouses the conception of psychoanalysis as a *hermeneutic* science emphasizes that the patient does much more than speak and, even more important, that he responds in an *interpersonal* dialogic exchange to the analyst's interventions as a text cannot.

Yes and no. He seems to be defending his views from the scientists who criticized him for treating patients as though they were texts, by highlighting the manner in which the analyst and the live patient interact in contrast to the defenseless text. I agree. But here Gill departs from his usual fair-mindedness and insists that the use of hermeneutic ideas also means the use of an exclusively interactional two-person model that excludes the possibility of also employing observation of the intrapsychic domain. This is an erroneous assumption that is widely shared by constructivists who use an exclusively subjectivist–intersubjective epistemological model. But it is by no means a consensually shared opinion that using the mode of observation cannot be coupled with the perspective of the two-person model.[37]

I agree with Gill's view that both terms, *hermeneutics* and *science*, are deeply ambiguous because of their multiple accretions of connotation. I also agree with his caution to avoid homogenizing the diverse views of various hermeneutic authors. I also agree with Michels's useful summary (1996) of Gill's views:

Psychoanalysis can be, for Gill, psychological, interpretive, scientific, and constructivist all at the same time, without concern about possible contradictions among these. He is careful to point out, however, that his brand of constructivism recognizes that 'the constraints of reality' cannot be ignored, that it is possible to uncover things in the patient that pre-existed the analysis—with the constructive aspect relating to the context and meaning of the recovered memory, but not to some core aspects of the memory itself. (p. 621)

But Gill, like Freud, was not always consistent. Two years after he published the book reviewed by Michels, he said the following:

Although we can reach consensual agreement in our view of reality, we must always allow for the plausibility and usefulness of other views of that reality. *As the issue is often expressed, the criterion of validity of a particular view of reality is not correspondence with an unknowable reality as such but only of comprehensiveness and consistency.* (Gill, 1994a, pp. 763–764; italics added)[38]

Subjectivity and Intersubjectivity

With that last statement, I disagree. Here Gill seems to equate the necessary imperfection of any scientific hypothesis (because all hypotheses are underdetermined by data) with the relativistic equivalence of the explanations in the strong constructivist view of reality. Did he or did he not view constructivism as being consistent with a transcontextual reality? Science requires a correspondence theory of truth that, in turn, requires a reality that is transcontextual. Therefore, Gill seems here to contradict himself. Cavell (1998b) helpfully put this issue as such:

> Some psychoanalysts now hold that an intersubjective model of the mind and of the analytic situation renders the ideas of truth, reality and objectivity obsolete. Arguing from a position of sympathy with the view that we are overdue for including the role of the analyst as a participant, I believe the "irreducible subjectivity" of the analyst does not disqualify the analyst as a good-enough observer or condemn the analyst to the caricature accusation of being infected unknowingly with the rot of positivism. I maintain that both a real, shared, external world and the concept of such a world are indispensable to propositional thought, and to the capacity to know one's own thoughts as thoughts, as a subjective perspective on the world. Without the idea of an objective world with which we are in touch and which we attempt to be more-or-less objective about, any so-called intersubjectivist model collapses into a new one-person paradigm of radical Cartesian doubt and solipsism. (p. 449)

The key issue here is that the epistemology of various hermeneutic authors is quite diverse. We would do well here to recognize that the term *hermeneutics* has been co-opted in much of the psychoanalytic literature as an erroneous synonym for *subjectivist* or *constructivist*. With regard to the relation of interpretation to an actual external reality, there are important differences between Ricouer and Dilthey, on one hand, versus Schafer and Spence on the other. There never has been an actual welded link between using hermeneutic methods and adhering to a coherence theory of truth. I here designate the authors who speak of psychoanalysis as exegesis (as though the patient were a text) as radical hermeneuticists, to distinguish them from Ricouer and others whose hermeneutic epistemology is contingent upon an actual reality.

We often cannot reach agreement on our view of reality. It is good, even essential, that we allow for the plausibility and usefulness of other views of that reality. But are there no limits to the equivalence of value? And if there are limits,

who defines them and how? How do we balance the perils of meaningless relativism and total equivalence against the necessary inclusiveness that must follow
when we know the contingency of our opinions? How do we distinguish our
opinions from knowledge, and does that matter? The incorrectness of the inferences of the analyst as corrected by later and better understanding as the treatment progresses is not the same as the relative equivalence of a variety of inferences about the same events in the treatment. The crucial ambiguity here lies in
the conflation of imperfection of inference (there is no such thing as eternal absolute truth) with radical–constructivist equifinality.

But there is another important omission in Gill's views of hermeneutics, as
well as in the bulk of our own literature about hermeneutics. Ricoeur pointed
out that psychoanalysis requires theories of meaning but also theories of force.[39]
In addition to offering his valuable distinctions between the old and the modern hermeneutic literature and the important differences between several
prominent hermeneutic authors, Friedman (2000) pointed out that hermeneutics insufficiently describes barriers to meaning. I assume that Gill knew about
this but did not deal with that problem when he attempted a definitional solution to reconcile hermeneutics and science. Perhaps, he felt more concerned
about ridding psychoanalytic theory of its metapsychological encumbrances
about psychic energy, but that is mere conjecture. To accept that psychoanalysis
entails both meanings and causes requires accepting a different kind of duality
than what Gill discussed in his hybrid definition of science and hermeneutics.
Another problem is this. To say that psychoanalysis must be either science or
hermeneutics is false because it conflates hermeneutics as heuristics with
hermeneutics as an epistemology anchored in a coherence theory of truth. To
say that it is "both" preserves the erroneous view that there is some kind of ram-
ming together or compression of two different categories or frames of reference
when that was never actually the case and need not be now.

I believe that there is a subtle but evident ambiguity in Gill's views about
hermeneutics in relation to science in the excerpt that I quote next. Gill
(1994b) said,

> Kohut's thesis that psychoanalytic observation comprises introspection and em-
> pathy can also be described as defining psychoanalysis as hermeneutic, that is, as
> an interpretive discipline dealing with meanings. I believe, contrary to the view
> of many and in agreement with Goldberg (1985), that psychoanalysis can and
> should be *not only hermeneutic but also a science.* I agree with Kohut's rejection
> of Freud's metapsychology and, in particular, his metapsychology of instinctual
> drive. (p. 203; italics added)

This is, again, in my reading, a statement of uniting two incommensurate categories, such as purple–patriotism.[40] To say that psychoanalysis can be both

hermeneutic and scientific clearly implies a need to reconcile two *opposing* categories that are wrongly viewed as being irreconcilable because they are viewed as rival epistemologies. I think this perpetuates the ambiguity of our views of science. Science is an enterprise constituted by many methodologies of which hermeneutics is but one. A hyphen between hermeneutics and science is a conceptual slight of hand masking a confusion of parts and wholes.

Where Gill wanted to preserve the view of psychoanalysis as a science by freeing psychoanalysis from metapsychology, I wish to preserve the view of psychoanalysis as a science by freeing hermeneutics from the coherence theory of truth (the distinction noted earlier between how we know and what we know). This widespread assumption that hermeneutic methods are inseparable from a coherence theory of truth confuses methods of justification with how we formulate our interpretations. If we view hermeneutics as a methodology of interpretation free of ontological commitments, the contradiction appears in a different perspective. All of science ultimately depends on interpretation of data, albeit in highly complex dialectical interaction of inductive and deductive inferences.

The confusion about reality, science, intersubjectivity, metapsychology, and causes versus meanings, materialism, and idealism is a heady brew. I make no claim for resolving philosophic conundrums that have defied resolution by our best philosophic minds for three millennia. For instance, the issues of subjectivism and relativism continue to generate vigorous debates among professional philosophers.[41]

I wish to be clear that I have not based my views on the epistemological assumption that the associations of the patient are the only raw material from which the analyst arrives at conjectures about latent meaning. It would certainly be incorrect to say that, and I explicitly note that everywhere that I have said *associations*, I have intended to include all of the patients' communications as associations, not only their verbalized statements.[42] In that looser sense, the patient who is unnecessarily late for an appointment is communicating something that should be included in the contextualizing activities of the analyst. However, that clarification alone would be insufficient. Many things that happen in an analysis transcend the complexity of simple dichotomous, verbal-versus-nonverbal distinctions. The daunting complexity of enactments[43] illustrated in the clinical examples of my own and other analysts in the earlier chapters illustrate that repeatedly.

Is There Only One Two-Person Perspective?

I have argued elsewhere (e.g., Boesky, 1990) in favor of employing a one-person as well as a two-person model in which the analyst is a participating observer. But this analyst is not a Sullivanian participant observer. That description emerged in an interpersonal epistemology. In my own view, the analyst knows full well sooner or later that what she or he observes is inevitably subjectively influenced. But the ensuing inferences of the analyst in this view are established in the intrapsychic domain as a consequence of the oscillating attention of the analyst to the associations of the patient and to the analyst's own participation in the interaction in which she or he is observing. The analyst participates knowingly or—commonly and necessarily—inadvertently in this two-person model. Then, when conditions allow, the analyst observes his or her own participation as well as the associations of the patient in the one-person intrapsychic domain. This was illustrated in my clinical example in chapter 4. Thus, I suggest that there is more than just one two-person model. I suggest that this enactment participation of the analyst is not only inevitable but also mutatively necessary. Certainly, this is a two-person model, and equally certain, it is also a model that oscillates between one- and two-person perspectives. Moreover, it is constituted by a critical realist rather than by a constructivist epistemology.

A number of authors from more than one school clearly advocate a two-person perspective combined with the traditional methods of contextualizing (see Boesky, 1990; Chused, 1991; Chused & Raphling, 1992; Hirsch, 2003; Jacobs, 1986; McLaughlin, 1991; Poland, 1992). Chodorow (2007) has designated this trend to use observation and interaction perspectives among certain conflict theorists, such as McLaughlin, Poland, and Jacobs, as "intersubjective ego psychology." That has the advantage of directing our attention to the fact that there are big differences between two-person models. Gill (1983) foresaw this possibility:

> It may be that one can agree that any psychological observation is influenced by the position of the observer without necessarily agreeing that all psychological observations must have interpersonal relations as their basic organizing framework. (p. 201)

In other words, a classical analyst could use a two-person model but remain in the intrapsychic domain in the contextualization of enactments in which the analyst had been a participant—even though the literature on enactments would be a decade away. In fact, he stated,

> An adherent of the interpersonal paradigm need not ascribe a major participant role to the analyst and that an adherent of the drive discharge pattern may ascribe a major participant role to the analyst. The term two-person model is treated by some authors as requiring only an intersubjective, constructivist epistemology and that is misleading. (p. 202)[44]

Even among those analysts who believe that unconscious conflicts are a key source of pathogenesis, there is substantial variation about whether and how much to use the associations of the patient to arrive at inferences about latent content. Usually, our literature considers only the intermodel variations in this regard but not the intramodel variations. This in turn relates to the contrasting views in our literature about discovery versus creation of understanding. Cavell (1999) has made some trenchant observations in this regard:

> Ogden writes about a particular kind of experience in which the analyst draws on his own musings, feelings, fantasies and apparent wanderings of the mind to understand what is going on at that moment in the mind of the other, and to communicate that understanding in the most effective way. The empathic activity is something to which both persons contribute and which may transform them both (Ogden, 1994). . . . The route to discovering anything, at least anything interesting, is seldom a matter of impersonally following some standard procedure. Granted, knowing the mind of another may involve a kind of give and take between "subject" and "object" that is not in play in discoveries of other kinds. Yet the process by which Holmes discovered that Moriarty had committed the crime, or Einstein the general theory of relativity, or Watson and Crick together the structure of DNA, was unique to each person, or pair; in each case it called for creativity; in each case the discovery could have been made and verified by others; and they were discoveries, not creations or inventions. This is not to say that psychoanalytic interpretation is always a discovery. I don't think it is. Nor is it to deny that a mind is a very peculiar entity, to some extent always in the process of coming-to-be. (p. 1234)

More About the Science Wars

Certainly, I am not saying that we could have avoided much confusion if only Freud had read Dilthey. Consider the following about Dilthey's views of science:

> Coming from the philosophy of history, Dilthey and his followers put up a straw-man idea of science built to the measure of Galilean mechanics—notwithstanding that, under the influence of geology, botany and Darwinian biology, science had by Dilthey's time already acquired a strong historical bent (see Kermode, 1985). . . . The Diltheyan duality is dichotomous in that every discipline falls to either one side of the division or the other, and on it rests the dichotomy between causes and motives (or meanings). Their straw-man "natural" sciences they assume to be nomothetic, ahistorical and context-free, and hence linear and univocal; on the basis of such an assumed univocity of empirical science, Spence (1993) questions

what he calls the "psychoanalytic right" not to find a home for the "Rashomon effect," i.e. the fact that almost everything worth looking at has at least two sides to it—forgetting that under the impact of quantum theory even twentieth-century physics is a mammoth case of the "Rashomon effect." Once empirical science is made, as stated, nomothetic, context-free, ahistorical, linear and univocal, hermeneutists feel free to co-opt for purely "cultural" disciplines the study of the singular fact. In this way, Habermas (1971, p. 271) invokes the opposition of the invariance of natural laws and the spontaneity of life history as grounds enough for putting "causes" and "motives" apart. But this basic hermeneutic tenet ignores the fact that from Baconian *interpretatio naturae* onwards interpretation has been part and parcel of empirical science, be it "exact" or "observational"; a point Grünbaum (1984) argues with his usual vigour. On such a false assumption of univocity of empirical science, Steele forcefully alleges: "Interpretation is hermeneutics" (1979, p. 398). (quoted in Ahumada, 1994, p. 697–698)

Given that anything that the patient says can be interpreted to mean anything, there is no boundary to the limits of overdetermination other than the ingenuity and imagination of the analysts in any disagreement. Waelder (1963) described this as the central problem in the methodology for validating interpretations:

Overdetermination encounters a practical difficulty in psychoanalysis: in the psychoanalytic method of interpretation the introduction of the concept of overdetermination offers neither a guideline nor a boundary for the required overinterpretations. *Overdetermination is, as it were, open to infinity.* No principle of psychoanalytic interpretation can give any guidelines as to how far overdetermination extends or when it should be considered exhausted. (pp. 73–74; italics added)

There are, of course, laments in our literature about our lack of a methodology for forming, let alone justifying, interpretations. Ramzy and Shevrin (1976) said,

Unbelievable as it may sound, in the whole vast library of psychoanalysis—clinical, theoretical, technical or applied—there are hardly any references which outline the logical guidelines or the methodological rules which the analyst follows in order to understand his patient. (p. 151)

But this remarkable gap in our understanding is merely noted in most cases without a responsive outcry of assent in the psychoanalytic community. Wallerstein (1976, 1986), in his discussions of the challenges to the scientific status of psychoanalysis, noted that our leading theorists have long been aware of the absence of a consensually accepted methodology for the justification of our interpretations:

Though psychoanalysis is centrally dependent upon such interpretations, as Rapaport (1960) stated, "There is [as yet] no established canon [in psychoanalysis] for the interpretation of clinical observations" (p. 113). And Glover (1952), in his role as a polemicist on the shortcomings of psychoanalytic research, even earlier had declared that there is "no effective control of conclusions based on interpretation, [and this fact] is the Achilles heel of psycho-analytical research" (p. 405). (1986, pp. 415–416)

The scientists among us who make interpretations because they are methodologically or heuristically coherent also rely on a correspondence theory of truth for justification of their claims. One cannot enter the hermeneutic circle through any but an observational door, and one cannot leave without acknowledging that new knowledge about an actual existing external reality may be improved by better explanations in the future. The conflation by hermeneuticists of contextual contingency and subjectivism with the absence of absolute truth is erroneous.

How do we gain knowledge, and how do we claim knowledge? Here is the locus of our disagreement. The antiscientists say that we can never claim to have observed reality absolutely correctly, but that is true of any science. The anti-hermeneuticists claim that constructivists believe that no theory or interpretation is better than any other. But that is not true either. The future refinement of our justification of interpretations, in my view, lies in our adherence to some form of correspondence theory of truth about what we claim to know that is transcontextual, even though our methods for interpreting our data are context bound. The question of which metaphor is preferred, the staining of microscope slides or the use of poetic tropes to make interpretations is not the important divider. The important distinction is how both sides define the difference between opinions and knowledge.

If a philosopher correctly complained that I have simplified complex philosophic issues related to the hermeneutic tradition and to the problems of epistemology and ontology, I would readily agree. But I suggest here that philosophers will have to resolve those issues by themselves, and in any event, we can be grateful that they have not asked us to do so for them. We psychoanalysts seem to think that we will find the solution to validating our ideas in some domain other than our own hard-won clinical knowledge. But that will not come from philosophy or from neuroscience or from literature. Therefore, I have in no way provided a resolution to this debate. Instead, I repeat my proposal: I think it would be best if our authors in both camps would provide us with persuasive detailed clinical examples supporting their views. Explicit statements describing how these details were contextualized should accompany those reports. The debate is too often waged at the level of lofty theoretic abstractions that foster labeling and misrepresentation and misreading. Too many authors hide behind the excuse that their examples are intended only to illustrate but not prove their views. That is a hedge because too many clinical examples in the literature about this debate are not at all self-evidently illustrative. The claim that an example merely illustrates a theoretic view is often a sham. The claim even to "illustrate" a theoretic view with a clinical example is still actually an ambitious claim. It is time for editors to require far more rigorous vetting of such claims prior to publication in our journals. Raising our editorial standards is not a plea for elitism. It is not a form of censorship. Even the requirement that an author explicitly state the ambiguities of how justifiable his or her claims are to have illustrated certain views would be a good first step.

Some of us seek gravitas in neuroscience, others in philosophy, but too few of us direct our attention to refining our understanding of the vast mysteries of clinical evidence in psychoanalysis at the first and lowest level of inference. The incompleteness of our map of the methodology of interpretation and the reasons for our continuing inability to account for why we so often disagree about our interpretations continues to elude us. That clarification will not come from philosophy or from neuroscience or from literature. It will only come from our gradually increasing better understanding of how to know when we have been wrong or right. One of the many problems that have beset us in our history has been our difficulty in dealing constructively with our disagreements. One can still hope that an enterprise dedicated to the enhancement of the rationality of humanity will find better ways to disagree in the future. If we stop disagreeing, our psychoanalysis will die. If we do not get better at disagreeing, we will slow our growth. I hope this book will stimulate discussion about exactly what is it that causes us to disagree so vigorously when we are really talking past each other. When evidential support proves ultimately illusory, we shall not be surprised. After all, we are not expecting to have one theory of everything. But we will be better able to follow Beckett's famous advice: "Fail again, fail better."

Notes

1. See glossary (Appendix A).
2. Steele (1979) wrote,

Hermeios referred to the priest at the Delphic oracle. The roots of the word hermeneutics lie in the Greek verb *hermeneuein*, to interpret, and the noun *hermeneia*, interpretations. These words all point to Hermes the messenger god, who is associated with transmuting what is beyond human understanding into a form amenable to human comprehension. The forms of the word suggest a general process of bringing the unintelligible to understanding. (p. 389)

But for a different view of the etymology of the term see Thoma and Kachele (1975):

> Hermeneuo = I denote my thoughts by words, I interpret, I explain, I expound, I translate. We assume that there was an etymological relation between hermeneutics and Hermes because Hermes, the god of commerce, messenger of the gods, had the duty of an interpreter: he had to translate their messages. Prof. K. Gaiser of Tübingen University, whose help in this and other matters we gratefully acknowledge, has given us the philological opinion that the coupling of Hermes and hermeneutics is based on popular etymology, i.e., on the fortuitous resemblance of these words. *Hermeneuo* actually derives from a root with a meaning of identical to "speaking." (p. 51)

3. This may be the authority for Kuhn's views of science as a cultural practice. See discussion of Kuhn later in the chapter.

4. This is the psychoanalytic branch of the culture wars famously described by Snow (1993).

5. See glossary (Appendix A).

6. See Appendix A for a glossary of these terms. See Appendix B for a suggested reading list.

7. Specifically, Levenson (2005, pp. 605, 618, 621, as cited in Hirsch & Iannuzzi, 2005).

8. See Chapter 6 for a discussion of the technical connotation of the Fundamental Rule and "free" associations versus the epistemological connotation of the foundational significance of associations and meaning.

9. See Paniagua (1985) for some of the pitfalls of heuristics.

10. See glossary (Appendix A).

11. Gadamer lived until the age of 102 (1900–2002).

12. See Geertz (1966).

13. This is in agreement with the view of Grossman (1995).

14. For example, the complexities of the empathic attunement of the analyst are not captured in these views about contextualization, but I believe the understanding of such attunement will eventually require better understanding of our methods of contextualization.

15. See note 1.

16. For relevant later articles, see Spence (1989, 1993, 1994, 1996).

17. Quoted by Tommasini in *New York Times* (February 14, 2007, p. B1).

18. This is the psychoanalytic branch of the culture wars described by Snow (1993). The relation between hermeneutics and science is neither simple nor antithetical. Both terms, *science* and *hermeneutics*, are defined in diverse ways by different authors, but the term *hermeneutics* has become co-opted in recent times by the polemics in our own culture wars. It is a term of opprobrium by our scientists and a badge of honor by our antiscientists.

19. From Nagel (1998),

> This discussion will be concerned with an issue that runs through practically every area of inquiry and that has even invaded the general culture—the issue of where understanding and justification come to an end. Do they come to an end with objective principles whose

validity is independent of our point of view, or do they come to an end within our point of view—individual or shared—so that ultimately, even the most apparently objective and universal principles derive their validity or authority from the perspective and practice of those who follow them? (as cited in Williams, 1998)

20. For the history of hermeneutics in philosophy, there are useful summaries by Steele (1979), Strenger (1991), Audi (1999), and Rubovits-Seitz (1998). Ricouer's contributions (1970, 1977) remain an unsurpassed discussion of the integration of hermeneutics and psychoanalysis.

21. See Dilthey (1976).

22. This resonates with the analogous controversy in the psychoanalytic literature about meanings versus causes.

23. Freud's avoidance of philosophy, including his own highly influential earlier mentor, Brentano, is well known.

24. Kermode (1985) also noted Freud's avoidance of Dilthey's work.

25. For definitions of these theories of truth, see Appendix A, and for discussions, see Hanly (1983, 1990, 1992, 1995; see also, Hanly & Hanly, 2001). It would be helpful to articulate the relationship of the notion of contextualizing criteria to the notion of correspondence criteria. The former points toward the associations of the patient and the latter to external reality and the justification of truth claims. But such a clarification would require discussion of complex issues concerning epistemology and the philosophy of science that are beyond my competence and the scope of this discussion. The *correspondence* theory of truth is linked to views of science predating Freud: the *Naturwissenschaften*, or sciences of nature, of which the model is physics, versus interpretive or ideographic sciences, the *Geisteswissenschaften*, or cultural or human sciences. The term *correspondence* is deeply entrenched in the literature of philosophy (the correspondence theory of truth) and in psychoanalysis as a component of the rules or canon of evidence. There are also strong connotational linkages via the bridge of the correspondence theory of truth to a well-known series of polarized disagreements about the definitions of psychoanalysis and science. Merely to indicate what I have in mind, I refer to explaining versus understanding, narrative truth versus historic truth, nomothetic versus ideographic sciences, and the relation of inductive and deductive inference (see, e.g., Ahumada, 1994). These issues in turn underlie an important attack over recent years about the idea that an observing analyst is a logical fallacy deriving from the tendentious view that this is a relic of positivism (Wallerstein, 1986). And this is merely an arbitrary and selective list.

26. See my discussion of Gadamer's clarifying discussion of horizons and foregrounding in chapter 2.

27. This is practically verbatim the argument of the constructivist colleague (later in this chapter).

28. See later discussion of Kuhn.

29. See Strenger (1991).

30. See glossary (Appendix A) and Hanly and Hanly (2001).

31. See Boesky (1994).

32. See Boesky (2002).

33. Compare my discussion in chapter 3 of the BCPSG as being incommensurate with the prior paradigm or preradical constructivist epistemologies. For a different view of incommensurate theoretic models, see Goldberg (1984).

34. See also Friedman's valuable article (2000) about modern hermeneutics.

35. Hanly (1983) then went on to tabulate the votes of the objectivists against the anti-objectivists as follows:

> The arguments of Kuhn and Feyerabend have been extensively analyzed and found want-ing as a theory of knowledge in the social sciences (Cunningham, 1973). I shall limit my remarks on it to only a few points. *It is the case that philosophical opinion on the subject is divided roughly equally.* The objectivist thesis has been defended by Alexander (1963), Bergmann (1957), Bohm (1957), Braithwaite (1960), Butts (1966), Cunningham (1973), Gibson (1960), Hempel (1965), Kaufmann (1944), Mason (1962), Nagel (1961), Rudner (1966), Scheffer (1967), Shapere (1966), Smart (1963), Werkmeister (1959).
>
> Anti-objectivist arguments have been advanced by Berlin (1954), Burtt (1932), Butter-field (1962), Collingwood (1956), Hanson (1958), Leach (1968), Maciver (1931), Mannheim (1936), Von Mises (1958), Myrdal (1958), (1969), Nadel (1951), Parsons (1949), Polanyi (1946), (1958), Quine (1960), Toulmin (1961), Weber (1949), Winch (1958). (pp. 394–395; italics added)

36. Rubovits-Seitz (1998) suggested a rather different hybrid compromise:

> One of the unanswered questions regarding the postpositivist paradigm is how to interpret and implement its concept of relativism. The misguided notion that "anything goes" methodologically, that one interpretation is as good as another, and the "truth is only what is experienced as true" . . . goes to the opposite extreme from the previous positivist view that only absolutely certain knowledge is valid. A more balanced, middle ground between the extremes of absolute certainty and absolute relativism recognizes that science builds upon the best beliefs which are available, but leaves all aspects of those beliefs open to re-vision or rejection. Since both positivist and completely relativist arguments have been found to be inadequate, the task is to develop a theory and methodology of interpretive in-quiry that avoids absolutism, on the one hand, but does not collapse into complete rela-tivism, on the other. (p. 41)

37. See note 35.

38. Gill (1988, 1995) touched on this problem in two other papers (see also, Gill, 1983, 1994b, 1994c).

39. Ricouer (1977) continues

> What does this mean for our epistemological inquiry? Essentially the following: the pair formed by the investigatory procedure and the method of treatment takes exactly the same place as the operative procedures in the observational sciences which connect the level of theoretical entities to that of observable data. This pair constitutes the specific mediation between theory and fact in psychoanalysis. And this mediation operates in the following manner: by coordinating interpretation and the handling of resistances, analytic praxis calls for a theory in which the psyche will be represented *both as a text to be interpreted and as a system of forces to be manipulated.* In other words, it is the complex character of actual practice which requires the theory to overcome the apparent contradiction between the

metaphor of the text to be interpreted and that of the forces to be regulated; in short, practice forces us to think of meaning and force together in a comprehensive theory. It is through the practical coordination of interpretation and the handling of resistances that the theory is given the task of forming a model capable of articulating the facts acknowledged as relevant in analytic experience. It is in this way that the relation between the investigatory procedure and the method of treatment constitutes the necessary mediation between theory and facts. (pp. 848–849; italics added)

Gill may have neglected this important observation of Ricouer because of his wish to rid psychoanalytic theory of any vestige of metapsychology.

40. This also contradicts Gill's own earlier careful distinction of three groups of hermeneutic authors in which one group does not adhere to the coherence theory of truth (see Gill, 1988).

41. See note 1.

42. For the role of nonverbal communications, see Panel (2007).

43. Hernandez directs us to

the limitations of language with regard to affective movements that barely attain the condition of thinkability and thereby to the important and confusing topic of enactments, which are the lingua franca for the communication of dangerous and repudiated affects. Enactments bridge the interface between what is expressible and inexpressible, between what is forgotten and what is pressing for revival, between reality and fantasy and also between one-person and two-person psychologies. Conceptually the term enactment facilitates the integration of the concepts of fantasy, projective identification and countertransference. (as quoted in Boesky, 2000, p. 257)

44. See note 25.

References

Ahumada, J. (1994). Interpretation and creationism. *International Journal of Psychoanalysis, 75,* 695–707.

Audi, R. (1999). *Cambridge dictionary of philosophy* (2nd ed.). Cambridge, England: Cambridge University Press.

Benjamin, J. (1991). Commentary on Irwin Z. Hoffman's discussion: "Toward a social–constructivist view of the psychoanalytic situation." *Psychoanalytic Dialogues, 1*(4), 525–533.

Boesky, D. (1990). The psychoanalytic process and its components. *Psychoanalytic Quarterly, 59,* 550–584.

Boesky, D. (1994). Dialogue between C. Brenner and D. Boesky. *Journal of Clinical Psychoanalysis, 3,* 509–542.

Boesky, D. (2000). Affect, language, and communication: 41st IPA Congress Plenary Session. *International Journal of Psychoanalysis, 81*(2), 257–262.

Boesky, D. (2002). "Reflections on psychoanalysis": Observations on some aspects of current psychoanalytic theories by Charles Brenner. *Journal of Clinical Psychoanalysis, 11,* 55–68.

Brenner, C. (2000). Observations on some aspects of current psychoanalytic theories. *Psychoanalytic Quarterly, 69*(4), 597–632.

Brenner, C. (2003). Commentary on Ilany Kogan's "On being a dead, beloved child." *Psychoanalytic Quarterly, 72,* 767–776.

Cavell, M. (1998a). In response to Owen Renik's "The analyst's subjectivity and the analyst's objectivity." *International Journal of Psychoanalysis, 79,* 1195–1202.

Cavell, M. (1998b). Triangulation, one's own mind, and objectivity. *International Journal of Psychoanalysis, 79,* 449–467.

Cavell, M. (1999). Knowledge, consensus, and uncertainty. *International Journal of Psychoanalysis, 80*(6), 1227–1235.

Cavell, M. (2002). On reality and objectivity. *Journal of the American Psychoanalytic Association, 50*(1), 319–324.

Chodorow, N. (2007). McLaughlin's *The healer's bent: Solitude and dialogue in the clinical encounter. Psychoanalytic Quarterly, 76,* 617–630.

Chused, J. (1991). The evocative power of enactments. *Journal of the American Psychoanalytic Association, 39,* 615–639.

Chused, J., & Raphling, D. (1992). The analyst's mistakes. *Journal of the American Psychoanalytic Association, 40,* 89–116.

Dilthey, W. (1976). *Dilthey: Selected writings* (H. Rickman, Ed.). Cambridge, England: Cambridge University Press.

Friedman, L. (1977). Reasons for the Freudian revolution. *Psychoanalytic Quarterly, 46,* 623–649.

Friedman, L. (2000). Modern hermeneutics and psychoanalysis. *Psychoanalytic Quarterly, 69*(2), 225–264.

Gadamer, H. G. (1975). *Truth and method.* New York: Seabury Press.

Gadamer, H. G. (1999). *Truth and method* (2nd rev. ed.). New York: Continuum.

Geertz, C. (1966). The impact of the concept of culture on the concept of man. *Reflections, 2,* 42–55.

Gill, M. (1976). Metapsychology is not psychology. In M. Gill & P. Holzman (Eds.), *Psychology vs. metapsychology* (pp. 71–105). New York: International Universities Press.

Gill, M. (1983). The interpersonal paradigm and the degree of the therapist's involvement. *Contemporary Psychoanalysis, 19,* 200–237.

Gill, M. (1988). Metapsychology revisited. *Annual of Psychoanalysis, 16,* 35–48.

Gill, M. (1994a). Conflict and deficit. Book review essay on *Conflict and compromise: Therapeutic implications. Psychoanalytic Quarterly, 63,* 756–778.

Gill, M. (1994b). Heinz Kohut's self psychology. *Progress in Self Psychology, 10,* 197–211.

Gill, M. (1994c). *Psychoanalysis in transition.* Hillsdale, NJ: Analytic Press.

Gill, M. (1995). Classical and relational psychoanalysis. *Psychoanalytic Psychology, 12*(1), 89–107.

Glover, E. (1931). The therapeutic effect of inexact interpretation: A contribution to the theory of suggestion. *International Journal of Psychoanalysis, 12,* 397–411.

Goldberg, A. (1984). Translation between psychoanalytic theories. *Annual of Psychoanalysis, 12,* 121–135.

Goldberg, A. (1985). The definition and role of interpretation. *Progress in Self Psychology, 1,* 62–65.

Goldberg, A. (1994). Farewell to the objective analyst. *International Journal of Psychoanalysis, 75,* 21–30.

Grossman, W. (1995). Psychoanalysis as science: Discussion. *Journal of the American Psychoanalytic Association, 4,* 1004–1014.

Grunbaum, A. (1984). *The foundations of psychoanalysis.* Berkeley: University of California Press.

Haack, S. (1993). *Evidence and inquiry: Toward reconstruction in epistemology.* Oxford, England: Blackwell.

Habermas, J. (1971). *Knowledge and human interests.* Boston: Beacon.

Hanly, C. (1983). A problem of theory testing. *International Review of Psychoanalysis, 10,* 393–405.

Hanly, C. (1990). The concept of truth in psychoanalysis. *International Journal of Psychoanalysis, 71,* 375–383.

Hanly, C. (1992). *The problem of truth in applied psychoanalysis.* New York: Guilford Press.

Hanly, C. (1995). On facts and ideas in psychoanalysis. *International Journal of Psychoanalysis, 76,* 901–908.

Hanly, C., & Hanly, M. (2001). Critical realism: Distinguishing the psychological subjectivity of the analyst from epistemological subjectivism. *Journal of the American Psychoanalytic Association, 49*(2), 515–532.

Hirsch, E. (1976). *The aims of interpretation.* Chicago: University of Chicago Press.

Hirsch, E. (1983). *The politics of theories of interpretation* (W. Mitchell, Ed.). Chicago: University of Chicago.

Hirsch, I. (2003). Analysts' observing participation with theory. *Psychoanalytic Quarterly, 72,* 217–240.

Hirsch, I., & Iannuzzi, V. (2005). Interview with Edgar Levenson. *Contemporary Psychoanalysis, 41,* 593–644.

Hook, S. (Ed.). (1959). *Psychoanalysis, scientific method, and philosophy.* New York: New York University Press.

Jacobs, T. (1986). On countertransference enactments. *Journal of the American Psychoanalytic Association, 34,* 289–307.

Kermode, F. (1985). Freud and interpretation. *International Review of Psychoanalysis, 12,* 3–12.

Kogan, I. (2003). On being a dead, beloved child. *Psychoanalytic Quarterly, 72,* 727–766.

Kuhn, T. S. (1970). *The structure of scientific revolutions* (2nd ed.). Chicago: University of Chicago.

Kuhn, T. S. (1977). *The essential tension: Selected studies in scientific tradition and change.* Chicago: University of Chicago.

McLaughlin, J. (1991). Clinical and theoretical aspects of enactment. *Journal of the American Psychoanalytic Association, 39,* 595–614.

Michels, R. (1996). Gill, Gray, Mitchell, and Reed on psychoanalytic technique. *International Journal of Psychoanalysis, 77,* 615–623.

Modell, A. (1978). The nature of psychoanalytic knowledge. *Journal of the American Psychoanalytic Association, 26,* 641–658.

Ogden, T. (1994). Projective identification and the subjugating third. In *Subjects of analysis* (pp. 97–106). Northvale, NJ: Aronson.

Opatow, B. (1996). Meaning in the clinical moment. *Journal of the American Psychoanalytic Association, 44,* 639–648.

Panel. (2007, January). *The role of nonverbal interventions.* Panel conducted by J. Chused, D. Boesky, J. Davies, and A. Harrison at the winter meeting of the American Psychoanalytic Association.

Paniagua, C. (1985). A methodological approach to surface material. *International Review of Psychoanalysis, 12,* 311–325.

Poland, W. (1992). Transference: An original creation. *Psychoanalytic Quarterly, 61,* 185–205.

Popper, K. (1959). *The logic of scientific discovery.* New York: Basic Books.

Ramzy, I., & Shevrin, H. (1976). The nature of the inference process in psychoanalytic interpretation: A critical review of the literature. *International Journal of Psychoanalysis, 57,* 151–159.

Ricoeur, P. (1970). *Freud and philosophy: An essay on interpretation.* New Haven: Yale University Press.

Ricoeur, P. (1977). The question of proof in Freud's psychoanalytic writings. *Journal of the American Psychoanalytic Association, 25,* 835–871.

Rubovits-Seitz, P. F. (1998). *Depth psychological understanding: The methodological grounding of clinical interpretation.* Hillsdale, NJ: Analytic Press.

Schafer, R. (1976). *A new language for psychoanalysis.* New Haven, CT: Yale University Press.

Schafer, R. (1981). *Narrative actions in psychoanalysis.* Worcester, MA: Clark University Press.

Schafer, R. (1983). *The analytic attitude.* New York: Basic Books.

Snow, C. (1993). *The two cultures.* Cambridge, England: Cambridge University Press.

Spence, D. (1982). *Narrative truth and historical truth.* New York: Norton.

Spence, D. (1989). Narrative appeal vs. historical validity. *Contemporary Psychoanalysis, 25,* 517–523.

Spence, D. (1993). The hermeneutic turn: Soft science or loyal opposition? *Psychoanalytic Dialogues, 3*(1), 1–10.

Spence, D. (1994). *The rhetorical voice of psychoanalysis: Displacement of evidence by theory.* Cambridge, MA: Harvard University Press.

Spence, D. (1996). The "death of Freud" and the rebirth of free psychoanalytic inquiry. *Psychoanalytic Dialogues, 6*(4), 563–589.

Spruiell, V. (1983). Kuhn's "paradigm" and psychoanalysis. *Psychoanalytic Quarterly, 52,* 353–363.

Steele, R. (1979). Psychoanalysis and hermeneutics. *International Review of Psychoanalysis, 6,* 389–411.

Steiner, R. (1995). Hermeneutics or Hermes-mess? *International Journal of Psychoanalysis, 76,* 435–445.

Stolorow, R., & Atwood, G. (1997). Deconstructing the myth of the neutral analyst: An alternative from intersubjective systems theory. *Psychoanalytic Quarterly, 66,* 431–449.

Strenger, C. (1991). *Between hermeneutics and science.* Madison, CT: International Universities Press.

Thoma, H., & Kachele, H. (1975). Problems of metascience and methodology in clinical psychoanalytic research. *Annual of Psychoanalysis, 3,* 49–119.

Waelder, R. (1963). Psychic determinism and the possibility of predictions. *Psychoanalytic Quarterly, 32,* 15–42.

Wallerstein, R. (1976). Psychoanalysis as a science: Its present status and its future tasks. In M. M. Gill & P. S. Holzman (Eds.), *Psychology versus metapsychology: Psychoanalytic essays in memory of George S. Klein* (pp. 198–228). New York: International Universities Press.

Wallerstein, R. (1986). Psychoanalysis as a science: A response to the new challenges. *Psychoanalytic Quarterly, 55,* 414–451.

Wallerstein, R. (1988). Psychoanalysis, psychoanalytic science, and psychoanalytic research—1986. *Journal of the American Psychoanalytic Association, 36,* 3–30.

Wallerstein, R. (1990). Psychoanalysis: The common ground. *International Journal of Psycho-Analysis, 71,* 3–20.

Weinberg, S. (1998, October 8). The revolution that didn't happen. *New York Review of Books, 45*(15). Available at http://www.nybooks.com/articles/article-preview?article_id=735

Williams, B. (1998, November 19). The end of explanation: Review of *The last word,* by Thomas Nagel. *New York Review of Books.* Available at https://www.nybooks.com/articles/article-preview?article_id=678

Appendix A
Glossary

O F THE MANY THEORIES OF TRUTH, in this glossary I consider only the correspondence, the coherent, and the pragmatic theories of truth.

Coherence Theory of Truth

A popular alternative to the correspondence theory has been to identify truth with *verifiability*. This idea can take on various forms. One version involves the further assumption that verification is holistic—i.e., that a belief is verified when it is part of an entire system of beliefs that is consistent and "harmonious." This is known as the coherence theory of truth. (Audi, 1999, p. 930; italics added)

The view that either the nature of truth . . . is constituted by a relation of coherence between the belief . . . being assessed and other beliefs. . . . As a view of the nature of truth, the coherence theory represents an alternative to the correspondence theory of truth. Whereas the correspondence theory holds that a belief is true provided it corresponds to independent reality, the coherence theory holds that it is true provided it stands in a suitably strong relation of coherence to other beliefs, so that the believer's total system of beliefs forms a highly or perhaps perfectly coherent system. (Audi, 1999, p. 153)

Further definitional comments about theories of truth by Hanly (1990):

The *coherence theory of truth* adopts the view that the question "What objects does the world consist of?" only makes sense within a theory or description. . . .

Truth ... is some sort of (idealized) rational acceptability—some sort of ideal coherence of beliefs with each other and with our experiences as those experiences
are themselves represented in our belief system—and not correspondence with
mind-independent or discourse-independent "states of affairs" (Putnam, 1981,
pp. 47–9). Thus there may be more than one true description of the world. The
correspondence theory allows for only one. In effect the coherence theory aban-
dons objects as they actually are as the ground of truth for objects as they are
constructed or constituted by the belief and theory investments that govern their
observation and the way in which they are experienced by observers. The mind
must, as a matter of psychological and epistemological inevitability, subject the
objects which it seeks to know to the conditions under which it is able to know
them. The original form of this idea is traceable to Kant (1781) although Kant
was a scientific realist. Among its modern adherents have been Bradley (1897),
Merleau-Ponty (1945), Sartre (1943), Ricoeur (1970), Habermas (1971), and the
philosophers of science Kuhn (1970), Feyerabend (1965), and Putnam (1981).
The school of thought, in philosophy, to which the coherence theory belongs is
idealism. (p. 374)

The concept of critical realism or scientific objectivism includes the essential
idea that there is no pure knowledge, no complete knowledge, that often evidence is insufficient for knowledge of some aspect of nature, and that care must
be taken to understand what is sufficient knowledge in a given area, in this case
clinical psychoanalysis. (Hanly and Hanly, 2001, p. 515)

Correspondence Theory of Truth

The most widely held account of truth ... the correspondence theory, according
to which a belief ... is true provided there exists a fact corresponding to it. This
Aristotelian thesis is unexceptionable in itself. However, if it is to provide a complete theory of truth ... then it must be supplemented with accounts of what
facts are, and what it is for a belief to correspond to a fact; and these are the problems on which the correspondence theory of truth has foundered. (Audi, 1999,
p. 930)

Constructivism

Listed in Audi (1999) as *social constructivism*:

Any of a variety of views which claim that knowledge in some area is the prod-
uct of our social practices. . . . Mild versions hold that social factors shape interpretations of the world. Stronger versions maintain that the world ... is somehow constituted by theories, practices and institutions. Defenders often move

from mild to stronger versions by insisting that the world is accessible to us only through our interpretations, and that the idea of an independent reality is at best an irrelevant abstraction and at worst incoherent. . . . This idea has its roots in Kantian idealism, which claims that we cannot know things in themselves and that knowledge of the world is possible only by imposing pre-given categories of thought on otherwise inchoate experience. . . . Since there are no independent standards for evaluating conceptual schemes, social constructivism leads naturally to relativism. (p. 855)

Covering Law Model

The view of scientific explanations as a deductive argument which contains . . . at least one universal law among its premises. . . . The theory of scientific explanation was first developed by Aristotle. He suggested that science proceeds from mere knowing *that* to deeper knowing *why* by giving understanding of different things by the four types of causes. Answers to why-questions are given by scientific syllogisms, e.g., by deductive arguments with premises that are necessarily true and causes of their consequences. (p. 190)

Epistemology

"The study of the nature of knowledge and justification" (Audi, 1999, p. 273). There have been and there are various specific epistemologies, but this definition is commonly applied to all of them. The difference between truth and knowledge is a problem that has vexed philosophers for millennia. This was eloquently summarized by Nagel (as quoted in Williams, 1998) as follows:

This discussion will be concerned with an issue that runs through practically every area of inquiry and that has even invaded the general culture—the issue of where understanding and justification come to an end. Do they come to an end with objective principles whose validity is independent of our point of view, or do they come to an end within our point of view—individual or shared—so that ultimately, even the most apparently objective and universal principles derive their validity or authority from the perspective and practice of those who follow them?

Hermeneutic Circle

First developed by Schleiermacher. The circularity of interpretation concerns the relation of parts to the whole: the interpretation of each part is dependent on the interpretation of the whole. But interpretation is circular in a stronger sense: if every interpretation is itself based on interpretation, then the circle of interpretation, even if it is not vicious, cannot be escaped. (Audi, 1999, pp. 377–378)

Heuristics

A rule or solution adopted to reduce the complexity of computational tasks, thereby reducing demands on resources such as time, memory, and attention. If an algorithm is a procedure yielding a correct solution to a problem, then a heuristic procedure may not reach a solution even if there is one, or may provide an incorrect answer. The reliability of heuristics varies between domains; the resulting biases are predictable, and provide information about system design. Chess, for example, is a finite game with a finite number of possible positions, but there is no known algorithm for finding the optimal move. Computers and humans both employ heuristics in evaluating intermediate moves, relying on a few significant cues to game quality, such as safety of the king, material balance, and center control. The use of these criteria simplifies the problem, making it computationally tractable. They are heuristic guides, reliable but limited in success. There is no guarantee that the result will be the best move or even good. They are nonetheless satisfactory for competent chess. (p. 379)

Inductivism

The view that hypotheses can receive evidential support from their predictive success with respect to particular cases falling under them. (Audi, 1999, p. 700; see Ahumada references in Appendix B for discussions of inductive reasoning)

Justification

A concept of broad scope that has highly varied applications. It bridges epistemology and ethics. "We have to distinguish justification from truth since either of these might apply to a belief in the absence of the other" (Audi, 1999, p. 457). Logical discourse recognizes a variety of different forms of justification.

Methodology

Closely related to the theory of knowledge. It explores the methods by which science arrives at its posited truths concerning the world and critically explores alleged rationales for these methods. Issues concerning the sense in which thories are accepted in science, the nature of the confirmation relation betweeeen evidence and hypothesis, the degree to which scientific claims can be falsified by observational data, and the like are the concern of methodology. (Audi, 1999, p. 700)

Ontology

The ontology of a . . . theory consists in the objects the theory assumes there to *be*. In order to show that a theory assumes a given object. . . . We must show that the theory would be true only if that object existed. (Audi, 1999, p. 631)

Pragmatic Theory of Truth

Since the reality of objects cannot be known prior to experience, truth claims can be justified only as the fulfillment of conditions that are experimentally determined, i.e., the outcome of inquiry. As a philosophic movement pragmatism was first formulated by Peirce in the early 1870s. . . . It was announced as a distinctive position by William James (1898) and especially by John Dewey. (Audi, 1999, p. 730)

A third major account of truth (after the correspondence and coherence theories of truth) is James's pragmatic theory . . . [in which] true beliefs are a good basis for action. . . . True assumptions are said to be, by definition, those that provoke actions with desirable results. (Audi, 1999, p. 930)

References

Audi, R. (Ed.). (1999). *Cambridge dictionary of philosophy* (2nd ed.). Cambridge, England: Cambridge University Press.

Habermas, J. (1971). *Knowledge and human interests.* Boston: Beacon.

Hanly, C. (1990). The concept of truth in psychoanalysis. *International Journal of Psychoanalysis, 71,* 375–383.

Hanly, C., & Hanly, M. (2001). Critical realism: Distinguishing the psychological subjectivity of the analyst from epistemological subjectivism. *Journal of the American Psychoanalytic Association, 49*(2), 515–532.

Kuhn, T. S. (1970). *The structure of scientific revolutions* (2nd ed.). Chicago: University of Chicago.

Ricoeur, P. (1970). *Freud and philosophy: An essay on interpretation.* New Haven: Yale University Press.

Williams, B. (1998, November 19). The end of explanation: Review of *The last word,* by Thomas Nagel. *New York Review of Books, 45*(18). Available at http://www.nybooks.com/articles/article-preview?article_id=678

Appendix B

Selected Readings: Psychoanalysis, Science, and Epistemology

THE FOLLOWING READINGS ARE NOT DISCUSSED formally in the book. This list does not purport to be comprehensive but is meant as a selected although arbitrary introduction to a complex subject. The relevant literature is large, but these references have been personally helpful. For an introduction to the recent literature on this topic, I suggest consulting the 75th-anniversary issue of the *International Journal of Psychoanalysis* (1994, vol. 75, nos. 5–6): "The Conceptualization and Communication of Clinical Facts in Psychoanalysis" (especially, the section entitled "Validation in the Clinical Process"). Note that there are no references here to formal empirical research based on data derived from outside the clinical situation in psychoanalysis. For the purposes of this book, that constitutes a separate problem (e.g., see Fonagy 1999, 2000).

Ahumada, J. (1994a). Interpretation and creationism. *International Journal of Psycho-Analysis, 75,* 695–707.

Ahumada, J. (1994b). What is a clinical fact? Clinical psychoanalysis as inductive method. *International Journal of Psycho-Analysis, 75,* 949–962.

Ahumada, J. (1997a). Disclosures and refutations: Clinical psychoanalysis as a logic of enquiry. *International Journal of Psycho-Analysis, 78,* 1105–1118.

Ahumada, J. (1997b). Toward an epistemology of clinical psychoanalysis. *Journal of the American Psychoanalytic Association, 45,* 507–530.

Ahumada, J. (2001). The rebirth of the idols: The Freudian unconscious and the Nietzschean unconscious. *International Journal of Psychoanalysis, 82*(2), 219–234.

Bachrach, H. (1989). On specifying the scientific methodology of psychoanalysis. *Psychoanalytic Inquiry, 9,* 282–304.

Baudry, F. (1984). An essay on method in applied psychoanalysis. *Psychoanalytic Quarterly, 53,* 551–581.

Blass, R. (2001). The limitations of critical studies of the epistemology of Freud's dream theory and their clinical implications: A response to Spence and Grunbaum. *Psychoanalysis and Contemporary Thought, 24,* 115–151.

Boesky, D. (1990a). Criteria of evidence for an unconscious fantasy. In H. Blum, Y. Kramer, A. Richards, & A. Richards (Eds.), *Fantasy, myth, and reality: Essays in honor of Jacob Arlow* (pp. 111–132). Madison, CT: International Universities Press.

Boesky, D. (1990b). The psychoanalytic process and its components. *Psychoanalytic Quarterly, 59,* 550–584.

Boesky, D. (1998). Clinical evidence and multiple models: New responsibilities. *Journal of the American Psychoanalytic Association, 46,* 1013–1020.

Boesky, D. (2000). *Contextualizing criteria and the evaluation of psychoanalytic evidence.* Unpublished paper, Toronto Psychoanalytic Society.

Boesky, D. (2002). Why don't our institutes teach the methodology of clinical evidence? *Psychoanalytic Quarterly, 71,* 445–476.

Bucci, W. (1989). Reconstruction of Freud's tally argument: Program for research. *Psychoanalytic Inquiry, 9,* 247–279.

Bucci, W. (1994). Multiple code theory and psychoanalytic process: Research frame. *Annual of Psychoanalysis, 22,* 239–260.

Cavell, M. (1988a). Interpretation, psychoanalysis, and the philosophy of mind. *Journal of the American Psychoanalytic Association, 36,* 839–879.

Cavell, M. (1988b). Solipsism and community: Two concepts of mind in psychoanalysis. *Psychoanalysis and Contemporary Thought, 11,* 587–613.

Cavell, M. (1991). The subject of mind. *International Journal of Psychoanalysis, 72,* 141–153.

Cavell, M. (1993). *The psychoanalytic mind from Freud to philosophy.* Cambridge, MA: Harvard University Press.

Cooper, A. M. (1993). On empirical research. *Journal of the American Psychoanalytic Association, 41,* 381–392.

Dahl, H., Kachele, H., & Thoma, H. (Eds.). (1988). *Psychoanalytic process research strategies.* New York: Springer-Verlag.

Davidson, D. (1994). Truth. *International Journal of Psychoanalysis, 85,* 1225–1230.

Diesing, P. (1985). Von Eckhardt's "Freud's research methodology was unscientific." *Psychoanalysis and Contemporary Thought, 8,* 551–566.

Edelson, M. (1984). *Hypothesis and evidence in psychoanalysis.* Chicago: University of Chicago Press.

Edelson, M. (1986a). Can psychotherapy research answer this psychotherapist's questions? *Contemporary Psychoanalysis, 28,* 118–151.

Edelson, M. (1986b). The hermeneutic turn and single case study. *Psychoanalysis and Contemporary Thought, 8,* 567–614.

Esman, A. H. (1979). On evidence and inference, or the Babel of tongues. *Psychoanalytic Quarterly, 48,* 628–630.

Fisher, C. (1965). Recent research on sleep and dreaming: I. Empirical findings. *Journal of the American Psychoanalytic Association, 13,* 197–270.

Fonagy, P. (1999). Research in the IPA. *International Psychoanalysis, 8*(1), 9–11.

Fonagy, P. (2000). *An open door review of outcome studies in psychoanalysis.* London: International Psychoanalytic Association.

Friedman, L. (1985). Potentiality shrouded: How the newer theories work. *Psychoanalytic Quarterly, 54,* 379–414.

Friedman, L. (2000). Modern hermeneutics and psychoanalysis. *Psychoanalytic Quarterly, 69,* 225–264.

Garza-Guerrero, C. (2000). Idealization and mourning in love relationships. *Psychoanalytic Quarterly, 69,* 121–150.

Green, A. (2000). The intrapsychic and intersubjective in psychoanalysis. *Psychoanalytic Quarterly, 69,* 1–39.

Grunbaum, A. (1984). *The foundations of psychoanalysis: A philosophical critique!* Berkeley: University of California Press.

Hanly, C. (1990). The concept of truth in psychoanalysis. *International Journal of Psychoanalysis, 71,* 375–383.

Hanly, C. (1992a). Inductive reasoning in clinical psychoanalysis. *International Journal of Psycho-Analysis, 73,* 293–301.

Hanly, C. (1992b). *The problem of truth in applied psychoanalysis.* New York: Guilford Press.

Hanly, C., & Hanly, M. (2001). Critical realism. *Journal of the American Psychoanalytic Association, 49,* 515–532.

Hook, S. (Ed.). (1959). *Psychoanalysis, scientific method, and philosophy: A symposium.* New York: New York University Press.

Kachele, H., & Thoma, H. (1993). Psychoanalytic process research: Methods and achievements. *Journal of the American Psychoanalytic Association, 41,* 109–130.

Kantrowitz, J. L. (1993). Outcome research in psychoanalysis: review and reconsiderations. *Journal of the American Psychoanalytic Association, 41,* 313–328.

Kernberg, O. F. (1993). Empirical research in psychoanalysis. *Journal of the American Psychoanalytic Association, 41,* 369–380.

Klumpner, O., & Frank, A. (1992). On methods of reporting clinical material. *Journal of the American Psychoanalytic Association, 39,* 537–552.

Leary, K. (1994). Psychoanalytic "problems" and postmodern "solutions." *Psychoanalytic Quarterly, 63,* 433–465.

Luborsky, L. (2001). The meaning of empirically supported treatment research for psychoanalytic and other long-term therapies. *Psychoanalytic Dialogues, 11,* 583–604.

Luborsky, L., & Crits-Christoph, P. (1988). Measures of psychoanalytic concepts: The last decade of research from "The Penn Studies." *International Journal of Psycho-Analysis, 69,* 75–86.

Masling, J. (Ed.). (1983). *Empirical studies of psychoanalytical theories* (Vols. 1–3). New Jersey: Analytic Press.

Masling, J., & Cohen, I. S. (1987). Psychotherapy, clinical evidence, and the self-fulfilling prophecy. *Psychoanalytic Psychology, 4,* 65–80.

McLaughlin, J. (1991). Review of *Psychoanalytic process research strategies,* edited by H. Dahl, H. Kachele, & H. Thoma. *Psychoanalytic Quarterly, 60,* 108–114.

Meehi, P. (1955). *Clinical versus statistical prediction. A theoretical analysis and a review of the evidence.* Minneapolis: University of Minnesota Press.

Opatow, B. (1999). On the scientific standing of psychoanalysis. *Journal of the American Psychoanalytic Association, 47,* 1107–1124.

Peterfreund, F. (1990). On the distinction between clinical process and clinical content theories. *Psychoanalytic Psychology, 7,* 1–12.

Richfield, J. (1954). An analysis of the concept of insight. *Psychoanalytic Quarterly, 23,* 390–408.

Rubenstein, B. (1997). *Psychoanalysis and the philosophy of science: Collected papers of Benjamin Rubenstein, MD* (R. Holt, Ed.). Madison, CT: International Universities Press. (See, especially, chapters 6, 7, 10, and 13.)

Rubovitz-Seitz. P. (1992). Interpretive methodology: Some problems, limitations, and remedial strategies. *Journal of the American Psychoanalytic Association, 40,* 139–168.

Rubovitz-Seitz. P. (1998). *Depth-psychological understanding: The methodologic grounding of clinical interpretations.* London: Analytic Press.

Shapiro, T., & Emde, R. N. (Eds.). (1993). Research in psychoanalysis: Introduction, empirical approaches. *Journal of the American Psychoanalytic Association, 41,* 1–6.

Shevrin, H., Bond, J. A., Brakel, L. A. W., Hertel, R. K., & Williams, W. J. (1991). *Conscious and unconscious processes: Psychodynamic, cognitive, and neurophysiologic convergences.* New York: Guilford.

Snow, C. P. (1993). *The two cultures.* Cambridge, England: Cambridge University Press.

Spence, D. (1982). *Narrative truth and historic truth.* New York: Norton.

Steiner, R. (1995). Hermeneutics or Hermes-mess? *International Journal of Psycho-Analysis, 76,* 435–445.

Stern, D. (1991). A philosophy for the embedded analyst—Gadamer's hermeneutics and the social paradigm of psychoanalysis. *Contemporary Psychoanalysis, 27,* 51–80.

Tarski, A. (1956). The concept of truth in formalized languages. In *Logic, semantics, metamathematics* (pp. 152–278). Oxford, England: Clarendon.

Taylor, F. (1956). Review of *Clinical versus statistical prediction: A theoretical analysis and a review of the evidence,* by Paul E. Meehl. *International Journal of Psycho-Analysis, 37,* 490–491.

Teller, V., & Dahl, H. (1993). What psychoanalysis needs is more empirical research. *Journal of the American Psychoanalytic Association, 41,* 31–50.

Von Eckhardt, B. (1982). Why Freud's research methodology was unscientific. *Psychoanalysis and Contemporary Thought, 5,* 549–574.

Waldron, W. (1997). How can we study the efficacy of psychoanalysis? *Psychoanalytic Quarterly, 66,* 283–322.

Wallerstein, R. (1986). Psychoanalysis as a science: A response to the new challenges. *Psychoanalytic Quarterly, 55,* 414–451.

Wallerstein, R. (1988). Psychoanalysis, psychoanalytic science, and research. *Journal of the American Psychoanalytic Association, 36,* 3–30.

Wallerstein, R. (1998). The new American psychoanalysis: A commentary. *Journal of the American Psychoanalytic Association, 46,* 1021–1043.

Westin, D. (1999). The scientific status of unconscious processes. *Journal of the American Psychoanalytic Association, 47,* 1061–1106.

Wisdom, J. O. (1967). Testing an interpretation within a session. *International Journal of Psychoanalysis, 48,* 44–52.

Wolman, B. B. (1964). Evidence in psychoanalytic research. *Journal of the American Psychoanalytic Association, 12,* 717–733.

Index

About the Author

Dale Boesky is the past editor in chief of the *Psychoanalytic Quarterly*. He is a training and supervising analyst at the Michigan Psychoanalytic Institute.